Surviving

a
Law Enforcement
Career

A Guide for Cops
and
Those Who Love Them

Dr. Dennis L. Conroy

Christine Hess Orthmann

2014
Innovative Systems – Publishers, Inc.

Surviving a Law Enforcement Career: A Guide for Cops and Those Who Love Them
Dr. Dennis L. Conroy, Christine Hess Orthmann

Cover Photo: © Dennis Conroy

Innovative Systems – Publishers
13353 Cranford Circle
Rosemount, MN 55068
800.772.6592
www.innsyspub.com

ISBN-10: 0-940309-21-1
ISBN-13: 978-0-940309-21-0

Printed in the United States of America

DEDICATION

This book is written for all of the cops
who live this stuff every day
and the families who live it with them. . . .

Dedicated to those
whose lives are forever changed by this career,
including my son, Michael.

– D. L. C.

ACKNOWLEDGEMENTS

It took a small village to get this book into your hands, and the authors want to personally acknowledge several villagers whose roles were invaluable in making this book a reality.

First, Denny wishes to thank his wife, Ann, sincerely for her patience and understanding which made writing this book possible; Dr. Kären Hess, for her inspiration to begin this project; and Jennifer Wills for her diligent proofreading. Heartfelt thanks also go to Rob Fowler and Carrie Kralicek for their reviews of and contributions to the chapters on Surviving Legal Battles and Surviving Mental Illness, respectively.

Second, Christine extends her gratitude to Denny, for trusting her to help bring his brainchild to completion, and to her family, for always being supportive and understanding when "mom has to work." Which happened a lot.

Finally, we need to thank those early reviewers of the manuscript who threw their support behind us and endorsed the finished product, and a special thank you to our production and print guru, Todd Ashton, who keep this project moving forward even while enduring and recovering from emergency wisdom tooth extraction.

CONTENTS

Acknowledgements, iv
Foreword, xi

Chapter 1 Surviving the Decision to Enter Law Enforcement 1
    Choosing an Agency, 3
    The Hiring Process, 5
    What to Do While You Are Waiting to Be Hired, 8

Chapter 2 Surviving the Initiation 9
    The Initial Orientation and Training Program, 9
    Field Training, 12
        How Field Training Came To Be and Why It Is Important, 12
        Types and Structure of Field Training Programs, 13
        What Field Training Means for You in Terms of Surviving
            Initiation, 18
        Potential Pitfalls during Field Training, 20
    After Field Training, Are You "In" Yet?, 21
        Special Considerations for Female Recruits, 22
        Special Considerations for Minority Recruits, 23
        Special Considerations for Gay/Lesbian Recruits, 24
    A Final Word: Surviving Initiation as a "New Breed" of Recruit, 24

Chapter 3 Surviving the System 27
    Defining a Complex Role, 27
    The Public Perception, 30
    The Officer's Role within the Adversarial Criminal Justice
        System, 34
    Your Role within the Department, 37
    The Importance of Peers, 40
    Self-Perception, 41
    A Final Word, 45

Chapter 4 Surviving Marriage 47
    The Importance of Communication, 48
    Parenting Issues, 50
    Financial Issues, 52

Differing World Views, 52
Shared Interests and Activities, 54
Social Life and Others' Expectations and Perceptions, 55
Rumors and Gossip, 57
Fear or Lack of Intimacy, 57
Alcohol Use, 58
Support and Resources, 59
Resources for Police Spouses, 60
Guidelines for Communicating Thoughts and Feelings, 61
Change, 63

Chapter 5 Surviving a Divorce   65
Breaking the News, 66
Understanding and Dealing with Your Reactions, 67
Figuring Out What Went Wrong, 68
Getting Legal Counsel, 69
Finding a "Fair" Way to Split . . . Everything, 70
   Property and Pensions, 71
   Child Support and Child Care, 72
   Custody and Visitation, 73
   Holidays and Special Occasions, 75
Social Adjustments, 75
Work Adjustments (For Cops Married to Cops), 76
Establishing New Relationships, 76
Moving On, 77

Chapter 6 Surviving Life in a Police Family   79
Work Schedules to Meet the 24/7/365 Service Demand, 79
   Meal Time, 79
   Holidays and Special Occasions, 80
   Being On Call, 80
Special Assignments, 82
Undercover Assignments, 82
Dealing with Danger, 83
Guns in the Home, 85
Living under the Media Microscope, 85
The Need for Control: Living under a "Because I Said
   So" Regime, 87
Role Ambiguity: Being Able to Hang Up the Uniform at Home, 88
Managing Expectations, 89

Navigating the Change from Hero to Villain, 90
The Social Life of a Police Family, 91
Conclusion, 92

Chapter 7 Surviving Day-to-Day Stress   **93**
Stress: The Good, the Bad, and the Ugly, 93
Components of Stress, 95
Stress and Law Enforcement, 97
Stress and the Cop "Personality," 98
Stress and Expectations, 100
Stress and the Police Culture, 101
Stress and the Police Agency, 102
Stress and Assignments, 104
Getting Sued, 105
What You *Can* Do to Control or Manage Stress, 106
Quick Stress Management Tips, 109

Chapter 8 Surviving the Inevitable Trauma   **111**
Trauma Defined, 111
Types of Trauma, 112
Personal Trauma, 113
Response to Trauma, 114
    IIow Trauma Hits You on the Inside, 115
    Post-Traumatic Stress Response, 117
    Survivor Guilt and a Search for Control, 118
Before the Trauma: Plan Ahead, 119
After the Trauma, 121
    Immediately after the Trauma: Your Plan, 123
    Critical Incident Stress Debriefings, 126
    A Word about Critical Incident Policies, 127
    Legal Fallout, 127
    Knowing When to Seek Professional Help, 128
The Bottom Line: Don't Rush the Healing, 129
A Final Word, 130

Chapter 9 Surviving Burnout   **131**
Burnout Defined, 132
Factors Contributing to Burnout, 133
    Noble Aspirations, Initial Enthusiasm, and Unrealistic
        Expectations, 133
    Lack of Criteria for Measuring Accomplishment, 134

Unfair Pay, 135
Inadequate Institutional Support, 135
Inefficient Use of Resources, 136
High Public Visibility and Popular Misconceptions, 136
Types of Burnout, 137
The Effects of Burnout, 140
Knowing When You're Burned Out, 141
Getting Beyond Burnout, 142
Eliminating Burnout, 144

Chapter 10   Surviving Mental Illness   145
Mental Illness Defined, 146
Prevalence of Mental Illness, 147
The Stigma of Mental Illness, 148
Types of Mental Illness, 149
    Panic Attack, 150
    Depression, 150
    Schizophrenia, 152
    Post-traumatic Stress Disorder, 153
    Adjustment Disorder, 154
    Generalized Anxiety Disorder, 154
    Bipolar Disorder, 155
    Eating Disorders, 156
    ADD/ADHD, 157
Dual Diagnosis, 159
Therapy and Counselor Selection, 160
Psychotherapeutic Medications, 160
Conclusion, 164

Chapter 11   Surviving Addiction   165
Addiction Defined, 165
Addiction versus Dependence and Abuse, 166
Multiple Addictions, 167
Individual Differences in Addiction, 168
Chemical Addiction, 169
    Alcohol, 169
    Prescription Medications including Steroids, 170
    Street Drugs, 171
    Anabolic Steroids, 172
Gambling Addiction, 173
Sexual Addiction, 174
Getting Help for Addiction, 177

The Twelve Steps of Alcoholics Anonymous, 178
Closing Thoughts, 181

Chapter 12   Surviving Legal Battles   183
Before You are Ever Sued, 184
   Choosing a Legal Defense Plan, 184
   Knowing When You Need a Lawyer and Where to
     Get One, 185
Getting Served, 186
Putting Your Pre-Lawsuit Plan into Action, 186
Why Me?, 188
Admitting a Wrong, 188
Knowing Who to Confide In: Confidential versus Privileged, 189
Reports, 190
Legal Warnings and Rights, 191
Facing Both Criminal and Civil Consequences, 193
What's at Risk?, 194
Where Your Case Is Filed, 195
Trial versus Settlement, 195
Media Fallout, 196
Other Fallout: Punitive Transfers and Licensing Issues, 198
The Waiting Game, 199
Being a Witness against a Fellow Officer, 200
A Quick Final Word, 200
Example of a Legal Defense Plan, 201

Chapter 13   Surviving and Thriving in Retirement   203
Planning for Retirement *Before* You Get There, 204
   Who Am I? Finding a New Identity, 205
   What Will I Do With All That Free Time? Staying
     Relevant, 206
   Who Will I Hang Out With? Finding Your New Social
     Circle, 208
   Who Will Remember Me? Leaving a Legacy, 209
How Retirement Changes Things at Home, 210
Being Financially Prepared, 211
Being Physically and Emotionally Prepared, 212
Forced Retirement, 213
Changing Careers, 214
In Summary, 215

Index, 217

FOREWORD

Cop Doc Dennis Conroy has outdone himself with this raw classic. As one of the most tenured and experienced cops to ever pound a beat, he shoots from the hip and carries you from the beginning of a police career right through to the end, his written words flowing with keen insight.

Having shouldered both worlds—as a first responder and a healer—Dr. Conroy draws on his unique position to craft an incredible real-deal resource for anyone considering or already living in the police world, including those who care about their cop. First, the breadth and depth of this volume, covering the life cycle of a cop from Point A to Point Z, is like no other. It shows you what you're really in for, from the cradle of initiation to the retirement blues. For the 18-year-old gal or guy who is thinking, "Do I really want to be a cop?" *Dr. Denny converses with you* as an experienced and friendly guide. You will gain an awareness of aspects of the job that it takes a shrink with decades of experience to know and distill, which he expertly does for your consideration.

And that is just the beginning, because if you take that leap of faith to serve as a police officer, as Sergeant Dennis Conroy did in St. Paul, Minnesota, and as I did in New York City, this book is made even more relevant to you, regardless of your department's size—from the 5-person agency to the mega-agency with more than 30,000 officers. Even if you choose to not become a cop, this book is invaluable in helping you make that choice.

Another key feature of this book is his guidance on how to keep your own shield of integrity and commitment, and do "the job" by doing the "right thing," without taking out the complexity and individual power of choice and responsibility. It's as if the words fall off of his Sam Browne Belt when he says cops are not allowed to be human within the system. And then he shares with you what to do through your development in the life cycle as a maturing human being, while not neglecting the speed loaders of police experience that layer on cynicism, depression, and addiction.

Which brings me to the third key feature of this guide—it has the broadest application and is filled with reality and check points to care for yourself and your wellbeing. Put another way, it is *not* P.C. It is real deal and respects you as an officer and individual and the choices you make. There is a profound and respectful approach to who you are and what you stand for as a federal, state, city, or local township officer.

I wish I'd had a guide like this as a rookie in Brooklyn on the midnights to eight. I wish I had known Dr. Conroy's CYAs way back when. If, as a rookie, I had been given the choice between the newest playboy and this book, knowing what I know now, I'd have to choose this guide. As I read it, I felt as though I was on my own journey down memory lane.

I can only suggest to officer-patients and colleagues that this is the guide to get. An ounce of prevention is worth a pound of cure, and this guide offers words of wisdom to cover every topic in your world as a police officer: probation, marriage, divorce, trauma, department trials, getting sued, burnout, alcohol addiction, domestic issues, and more. This guide offers you a direction when you are in need. It will help you more than any guide ever written, even before you trip and fall, as all of us do, whether we work in the concrete jungle or the rural zoo of crime.

I will tell you that I'll be the first to buy at least two extra copies to keep with me. Why? Because then I'll have a copy to hand to the student in my office who is struggling to be a cop, and another one for the street-worn officer in crisis. Because this guide breaks all previous molds on the press that prints such guides. Get the guide, and cherish the guide as much as all who know Denny cherish him!

Cop Dr. Dan Rudofossi
Retired Sergeant and Licensed Psychologist (NY and CA)
Chief Psychologist – NY and NJ Detectives Crime Clinic
Author of *A Street Survival's Guide for Public Safety Officers: The Cop Doc's Strategies for Surviving Guide for Trauma, Loss and Terrorism.*

Chapter 1

SURVIVING THE DECISION
TO ENTER LAW ENFORCEMENT

Since you're reading this book, odds are you or someone close to you is either considering a law enforcement career or is already in one. If you are thinking about entering this field, ask yourself what you really know about it. And understand this: It's not like it looks on TV. The bad guys don't always get caught; you don't always find physical evidence that will solve the crime; and you certainly don't get DNA evidence back within an hour. Ask yourself what really attracts you to this career, and it had better be more than just a fleeting thought that you'll look good in a uniform. There needs to be a real commitment that will carry you through the tough times, and there *will* be tough times. Law enforcement is not a career for the faint hearted. It is a tough profession that takes a toll not only on those who practice it but also on those closest to them—spouses, partners, children, parents, and friends. Consider it carefully.

So, you've decided you want to go into law enforcement. What's next? As you tell your parents, friends, or spouse, what do you think their reactions might be? Factors that may affect their views of your decision and the potential effects on your relationships with them include their previous experiences with other police officers or with a particular agency, their perceptions of the danger involved, or their opinions about the type of agency you have chosen. Remember, this is *your* career choice; make sure you are doing what is best for *you*. Once you have made your decision to become a police officer, the work has only begun.

Getting hired by a law enforcement agency can be an intimidating process. You will be competing with a large number of applicants for every position and must do as well as you can in all aspects of the hiring process. Therefore, you need to prepare and make yourself as employable as possible. Certainly in some areas you will have little or no control over how well you do. For example, if you have an old knee injury, that knee is as it is; you cannot change it. But in some areas you can prepare and increase your chances of being hired. In preparing for the exams, *Careers in Criminal Justice and Related Fields*[1] is an excellent guide.

Make sure you are in top physical condition. Most jurisdictions require recruits to pass a physical agility exam, and the training remains physically challenging once you're hired. You may not be able to run a 4-minute mile, but you can make sure you are in the best shape possible. You don't want to "just squeak by." You want to excel. Many veteran police officers already have concerns about the "new breed of cop" being hired. Don't feed those concerns by being marginal in any area in which you can (and should) excel. You want to be noticed in positive ways. Your appearance is part of the first impression you create, both with the hiring agency and with the other police officers. Don't slack here.

When you get the application, take the time to fill it out as accurately as possible, because errors here can come back to haunt you later. When you have completed the application, make a copy of it, and keep it in a safe place. Application forms are often lengthy, and if you need this information later for another agency, it can save considerable time to reference the first form you fill out. Rest assured that most agencies will conduct a thorough background investigation prior to hiring you. If they find you have omitted, embellished, or fabricated information, it will be discovered, and you will be called on to explain or, worse, disqualified without an opportunity to explain. The more complete the better. Don't even think about intentionally omitting something you didn't do well. Everyone has some area he or she is not proud of, but honesty is most important here. However, get the paperwork done in plenty of time. Don't wait until the very last minute to get your background package submitted; something may go wrong, and it will be late. At the very least, last minute submissions may make it appear as though you are unreliable, disorganized, or don't really care about getting hired; at worst, they may not be accepted.

While the process of getting hired is similar across the country, there may be subtle differences depending on the agency you choose. In fact, one of your first decisions is where you want to work.

---

[1] Harr, J.S., & Hess, K.M. (2010). *Careers in criminal justice and related fields: From internship to promotion* (6th ed.). Belmont, CA: Wadsworth Cengage Learning.

CHOOSING AN AGENCY

Where do I want to work? This is one of the first questions you need
to answer. You may already have a specific department in mind,
know you want to live in a specific state, or aspire to work for a
federal agency. Be aware that different agencies have different
entrance requirements and may also require different levels of
residential flexibility or mobility. For example, if you work for a
state or federal agency, you may be required to move every few
years. If you want to advance within the federal agencies, it is often
essential to relocate for a promotion. This may be fine for a single
person, but what will your spouse and children, if any, think of this?
This decision needs to be made with input from your family. Police
marriages are often unsuccessful, but to make these decisions
without input from your family creates an avoidable risk.

The type of agency you choose may affect the type of police
work you do. If you work for an urban police department, you are
likely to spend more time working with a greater cross section of the
population than if you work in a rural agency. If you work for a state
highway patrol, you will find that traffic enforcement and accident
investigation are the focus of your work. The Drug Enforcement
Agency is another highly specialized agency, with the work
consisting primarily, and not surprisingly, of drug investigations.
While some people find this work exciting and challenging, others
find it exhausting and are unable to continue for extended periods.
Decide what is best for you. There is no "right" or "wrong" here,
only what will be the most appropriate and comfortable "fit" for you.

The size of the agency will also make a difference in the type of
career you can expect. Not many agencies with fewer than 10
officers can afford to allow officers to specialize. If your goal is to
work in a specialized area of law enforcement, you may choose a
larger agency. For example, if you would like to be a "homicide
detective" as opposed to a "detective," you will need to work in an
agency with enough homicides to justify a full-time investigator in
that area. If your goal is to be a generalist, you may be better off in a
smaller agency where officers handle whatever cases come up. You
may work traffic, investigate domestic abuse, and take a lost child
home all in the same day. Officers in smaller departments may find
more time to follow up on calls than officers in larger agencies,
where they are answering more calls for service per day. In a large

department, you may be kept busy going from one call to the next
and miss out on the opportunity to examine each in depth.

In selecting an agency, it is also important to look at that
agency's philosophies, both formal and informal. What does the
official written material state, and what does the agency show in its
relationships with the public? Where does the agency see itself on
the continuum of law enforcement versus public service? If the
agency you are selecting views itself as being high towards the law
enforcement end of the scale and you have a strong desire to "help
people," you may find you don't fit in well with that particular
agency. The philosophy of a police agency is usually written by the
police administration but lived, interpreted, and displayed by the
officers within the agency. Therefore, no matter how much a police
administration would like the officers to work in a service capacity,
it is difficult to force that if the officers see themselves as crime-
fighters.

Once you select your agency, you will need to know their hiring
requirements. Federal agencies may each have different hiring
requirements. Each state has different requirements for law
enforcement. Check your state requirements, and then look at the
agency you have selected. Some agencies require a bachelor's degree
in specific areas, while others may require a high school diploma,
GED, or a certificate from a specialized training program. Some
agencies require specific work experience prior to application, and
others require a particular type of training before you can apply.
Fairly common standards for admission to the hiring process include
that the applicant:

- Is at least 21 years of age
- Has a high school diploma or GED
- Is legally eligible for employment within the United States
- Has no felony convictions or Class A misdemeanor convictions
- Is not on probation for a criminal offense
- Has never been convicted or placed on probation of any type by
  any state or federal government for driving while intoxicated or
  driving under the influence of drugs in the past three years
- Has not been discharged from any military service under less
  than honorable conditions
- Some agencies may require a 4-year degree.

Some states require specialized training. For example, applicants in Minnesota must be "license eligible" to apply for work as a police officer. To become "license eligible," an individual must complete a specified course of training in both academic and practical skills, which takes approximately two years to accomplish and leads to an Associate of Arts (AA) Degree. The individual may then take the POST (Peace Officer Standards and Training) License Exam which, if successfully completed, makes them "license eligible" and able to apply for law enforcement positions within the state. Once hired, the individual is granted an active license to practice law enforcement in Minnesota.

THE HIRING PROCESS

In a typical hiring process, each applicant must successfully complete the following:
- Preliminary interview or written exam
- Physical agility test
- Background investigation
- Applicant interview board
- Psychological evaluation
- Medical evaluation

The initial interview is designed to screen out the least qualified applicants and establish a smaller group for the next hiring phase. A written exam is a common element at this stage of the hiring process. Police departments use a variety of written exams, which are designed not necessarily to test your specific knowledge of law enforcement but rather your general knowledge and potential to learn. These exams may also be designed to test such things as your honesty, experience, and problem-solving abilities. There doesn't seem to be one single type of standard initial interview.

Following the initial interview is a physical agility test, typically a pass/fail exam. Applicants are not usually rank ordered on their performance. Physical agility exams are supposed to be based upon bona fide occupational qualifications. In other words, they are supposed to reflect the physical requirements of the job. This exam can be difficult even for those in good physical condition and virtually impossible for those who are not. You must prepare for this exam at least several months in advance. You can't get into shape overnight. The older you are, the longer you should give yourself to prepare. Women may find some portions of the exam more difficult because of physiological differences between genders; for example, tests that focus on upper body strength are, on average, disadvantageous to females.

After the physical agility test comes a background investigation. This in-depth, time consuming investigation is based on the application form you filled out giving detailed information about yourself, and it often takes an investigator at least one week to thoroughly "background" each candidate. Do not lie or hide information on the application form because it will be uncovered during the background investigation, and you are likely to be dismissed based more on the lie or omission than on the facts themselves. Any omission, intentional or not, can be problematic and may even be grounds for dismissal, if the facts come to light after you are hired.

The background investigation may be divided into several phases. During the initial phase you may be fingerprinted and asked to fill out a form with demographic data, which will be used to check for criminal history and other superficial background information. Along with your fingerprints, the background investigators will want to know your age, date of birth, race, and sex. This information facilitates the criminal history check, although any data pertaining to gender, age, race, and medical conditions cannot be used as part of the hiring process. Today's agencies must be very careful to ensure their background checks and hiring processes show no bias toward an applicant's age, race, or gender. If this check determines you have a felony conviction in another state, you may be disqualified, but if the criminal history check comes up clear, the information will probably be sealed and not included in your general background file. Information pertaining to age, race, and gender cannot be used at all in the hiring process. Medical information can be considered only *after* a conditional offer of employment is extended, and then such information is used to help determine whether or not the applicant successfully passes the physical and psychological exams.

A second phase of the background check will provide a more in-depth investigation. During this phase, you may be asked to complete an extensive questionnaire regarding where you have lived, where you went to school, where you worked, and who you know.

You may be asked if you know any police officers on the department to which you are applying, and you may be asked for references. Also during this phase you are likely to be asked questions designed to reveal anything that may call into question your suitability for police service. You may be asked about driving offenses and civil actions. The forms may seem like a real pain, but be honest. Tell the truth, the whole truth, and nothing but the truth. This means don't lie, don't omit facts, and don't add to information in ways that are not true. Most agencies put a lot of time and energy into the background investigation, as this is the time for them to really find out what type of applicant you are. Remember, the agency is looking at a potential 30-year hire. They will look very carefully.

Following the background investigation is a more in-depth interview. This is often the point at which candidates are either rejected or given a conditional offer of employment. You can prepare for this important interview by doing some simple research that lets the interviewers know you are interested in the position, their agency, and the community you will serve. Before the interview, take some time to go to city hall or check online to get demographic and population projections for the city. Study this information until you are comfortable with it, and find a way to include some of it in your answers during the interview. This will demonstrate to the interviewers your active interested in their city and will help create a favorable impression during the interview, which will strengthen your chances of getting the "conditional job offer."

The third and final phase of the background investigation will not occur until after you have been given a conditional offer of employment because the Americans with Disabilities Act (ADA) requires such an offer prior to any medical or psychological evaluations. This phase will include questions about mental and physical health, including whether you have ever been to treatment for chemical dependency, whether you have ever received counseling for anything, and, if so, for what. You will be asked if you have ever had any surgery or if you have any physical disabilities that might interfere with your ability to do police work. The background investigator will most likely ask for copies of medical records. If you refuse to provide them or provide incomplete medical records, you may be disqualified from the hiring process.

An offer of employment usually results from successful completion of the medical and psychological evaluations as well as results of the background check. After successfully completing these phases, you are ready to be hired.

WHAT TO DO WHILE YOU ARE WAITING TO BE HIRED

You have passed all of the tests and are waiting to be hired. This is an important time, because you can still make mistakes or do stupid things that will cost you your job. While it is necessary to have an income to survive, it might be wise to avoid some jobs even though they are legal, such as places sworn officers are not allowed to work "off duty." For instance, in many jurisdictions officers are prohibited from working in licensed liquor establishments. Some agencies disallow employment at both on-sale and off-sale establishments, while others limit the restriction to only on-sale. The reasoning: Police officers are charged with enforcing laws relating to sale and distribution of alcoholic beverages, and it might easily be seen as a conflict of interest for a police officer to work in such an establishment. If you are working in such a place, be careful. If there are fights that you become a part of, or if you inadvertently sell alcohol to a minor, you may lose the job you are just getting.

A second concern is the nature of the work. If you are working as a bouncer, you have increased the likelihood that you will get into a fight, become involved with police officers in a negative encounter, and perhaps become involved in a civil suit. This doesn't contribute positively to your chance of getting hired, and, in fact, may make it more difficult for you to secure a job in law enforcement.

Another occupation which may be of questionable value for a person waiting to be hired by a police agency is that of taxi driver. Again, many agencies do not allow officers to drive taxis while off duty. If this is a violation for police officers already employed by the agency to which you've applied, it's not a good idea for someone in your position—waiting to be hired by that agency—either. Find a stable, clean job, such as working in retail or construction, to provide income while you wait for your chance to be a police officer. Such jobs might pay less, but you won't get into trouble, and you won't damage your chances for being hired. If you are denied employment by one police agency, you have also hurt your chance of employment with many others.

Chapter 2

SURVIVING THE INITIATION

You've been hired. Congratulations! But this is no time to sit back and relax because your first involvement with the new agency, right out of the gate, will, in many cases, make or break your career. Your reputation will be built during the first few weeks after you begin work, as you make your first contacts with officers. If you've already had considerable contact with the officers of this department, you have undoubtedly started to build that reputation, whether good or bad. You might be thought of as "that smart alec kid" no one wanted to be with or who never knew when to keep his mouth shut. You might also be seen as a "groupie," especially if you've dated a number of police officers before your entry into the department. Such prior personal associations will dramatically affect your professional reputation.

If prior personal associations are good, they may carry over into your professional life; if they are bad, they will most definitely carry over. If, for example, the officers on your new department do not see you as taking the job seriously, they may be extremely reluctant to put their lives in your hands. If they knew you as someone with a "temper," they may be hesitant to walk into a tense situation with you. If they see you as being "out of touch with the real world," they may be uncertain about working with you. All of this happens within the first two or three weeks on the department, so be ready. If you are isolated in a police academy, it takes longer to build a reputation, either good or bad.

THE INITIAL ORIENTATION AND TRAINING PROGRAM

After you've been hired, you usually will need to complete the police academy or another type of agency training program. This is your first real involvement with the police department and the other officers. You will be interacting with both peers (other new recruits) and the veteran officers who serve as your training staff, and the roles you play with each group will be different. The training staff will see you as a recruit and will be your teachers or mentors. Your peers will have different expectations; they will expect you to carry your own weight, even though you are new, and they will expect you to know and follow the informal rules of the organization. The informal rules are unwritten, and you will only learn them by listening closely and observing your fellow officers. How you begin with these groups will help shape your reputation and the role you will play within the police department for the rest of your career.

A brief word about when and where to be *competitive.* In the academy there is a fine line between confidence and arrogance, competence and "hot dogging." It is to your benefit to be competitive here, with your academy peers, and to work toward the top of the class. Do this with quiet performance. Don't brag, just do. This is your first chance to show the police department and the other officers what your work ethic really is. However, as you move forward into a regular assignment, you will need to listen and watch the veteran officers as they indicate how you are to behave. Your early days after the academy, among the department "regulars," are neither the time nor place to be competitive with your peers. The beginning of your career is no time to challenge the veteran officers.

Up until now you have only taken tests to get into the academy. This does not tell anyone anything about how you work to learn, only what you already know. Many police academies will present awards to the top academic, the top shooter, and the most physically fit. Work toward getting one or all of these awards, but as you do, recognize that it is also important to help your peers who may be struggling to pass the exams. You can excel and still be a team player. Do not sacrifice being a team player over individual excellence, or vice versa. A good police officer needs to be both. Your training will give the staff and other officers a chance to observe your character traits. Shine on this one.

While most agencies provide some type of internal training program for new hires, these programs vary from a 2-week orientation to an 18- or 20-week police academy. During a shorter orientation, the department expects you to already know everything you need to know about police work, and this training serves only to teach you the specifics of that agency. For example, they will teach you how to use their report forms and computers, where you report for roll call, where to get uniforms, how to fill out the necessary paper work for personnel and payroll, shift assignments, where to get squad car keys, etc. They are also likely to include a training session on organizational philosophy and the "do's and don'ts" of this particular agency.

The longer training programs, or police academies, are usually found in larger police departments and state and federal agencies. They will not begin with the assumption that you come to them fully trained in police work, lacking only the agency particulars. Instead, they will take the approach that you possess some of the basics but may not be ready to function as a police officer. They will cover the areas taught in a shorter orientation but will likely go into much more depth. They may teach a number of different subjects, including criminal law, search and seizure, arrest practices, dealing with emotionally disturbed persons, defensive tactics, physical training, interviewing, firearms, and traffic investigation.

You are likely to be instructed not only on the department's philosophy but also the mission and goals of other community agencies and organizations, as taught by people from those agencies and organizations. This will allow you some insight into the depth of the relationship between the police and the community. You may get a class on domestic violence taught by a representative of a women's shelter, or you may get a class in human relations presented by a leader within the local minority community. Although the longer academies do allow more time to cover a wider variety of subjects, the reality is they are rarely able to accommodate every special interest group within the community. MADD wants to make sure that recruits understand their mission and will work on their behalf. Sexual offense services want the recruits to understand what they do on behalf of victims. Homeless shelters will want to make sure the recruits understand their purpose and that officers will work as the shelter would like. All of these special interest groups take time during training, and even with a lengthy academy, there are some groups who are either left out entirely or feel they are not given adequate time with the recruits.

FIELD TRAINING

After completing the police academy, you are likely to go into some type of field training program in which you will be paired with a veteran officer who will teach you and evaluate you daily. If you do as you are instructed, and it seems you genuinely want to learn police work, your field training officer (FTO) will do everything he or she can to help you succeed in your field training.

How Field Training Came to Be and Why It Is Important

The first modern day field training program began in San Jose, California. In 1969 a very likable, enthusiastic, but naive young recruit was hired by the San Jose Police Department. He looked like he would make a great cop. He was trained in the academy, graduated, and was placed with a veteran officer for field training. From the beginning almost everyone involved with this new officer formed the same opinion—he didn't have the "right stuff." This new officer had problems in several areas, the most notable being his weak driving skills. He was also said to be lacking in judgment, neglected to adhere to officer safety, and consistently demonstrated a substandard quality of work. He was rated on three separate occasions, but never explicitly failed his evaluations. His reports simply indicated he was "in need of improvement."

This new officer's poor scores were balanced by high marks in appearance, work quantity, and cost consciousness. He looked good and sounded good, but there was a shortage where the rubber met the road, and he just couldn't put it all together in practice to do the job. In this case documentation (or lack thereof) was insufficient to terminate, and so he was kept on. In hindsight, the trainers admit that it really came down to the fact that no one had the guts to tell this kid he wasn't going to make it. As with most people, the trainers wanted to be liked and didn't want to be the bearer of ill tidings. However, this lack of formalized field training; absence of routine, continuous evaluation; and widespread unwillingness by others in the department to deliver harsh but necessary constructive criticism was unfair to all involved. The recruit didn't realize he wasn't cutting it; the agency was at legal risk by keeping a recruit they should have dismissed; the other officers' safety was at risk because they couldn't rely on this recruit for the backup they needed, and, in the end, the public was placed at risk and an innocent civilian died. Because in the early spring of 1970 this officer was involved in a two-car accident in which he was gravely injured and the passenger in the other car was killed. Suddenly someone had the guts to fire this officer. This was only one of many such cases across the country, and it emphasized the critical need for a field training program with some form of evaluation after completing the formal police academy or classroom training.

As the field training concept developed and spread across the country, many programs began incorporating a number of standardized tasks with daily written evaluations. Key performances were identified along with behavioral descriptions of each key performance, and new officers began to be evaluated systematically and held to consistent performance standards in areas deemed essential to success as a police officer. However, not every agency adopted such a formalized field training program, and presently, considerable variety exists in the types and structures of such programs in police departments across the country.

Types and Structure of Field Training Programs

The most basic type of field training is an unstructured program where the new officer is placed with a veteran officer to "learn the ropes." During this informal field training there may be no formal evaluations, just an acknowledgment to your supervisor when you are ready to be on your own. Although this system has some strengths, the weaknesses severely outweigh them. For example, there is no provision for formal feedback or formal critique. Consequently, you may have no idea where you stand at any given point in time, and you might find out too late that you haven't been doing what you should've been doing. Additionally, there are no guidelines to ensure that you are proficient in specific areas of police work. If, for instance, you do not encounter a particular type of call or situation during the entire training period, you will receive no evaluation or training in that area and, as a result, neither you nor your supervisors will likely be aware that such training is lacking.

Such informal, unstructured field training may leave agencies open to suffering the same unfortunate series of events experienced

by the San Jose Police Department in the spring of 1970. In an effort
to avoid repeating their past mistake of allowing an unsuitable recruit
to proceed into the ranks of regular officers, the San Jose PD
developed a standardized field training program and divided it into
progressive training phases with rotation of recruits to different
FTOs to ensure comprehensive evaluation. The FTO completed a
daily evaluation of the recruit, and the FTO supervisor completed an
evaluation at the end of the phase or earlier, if there was some type
of difficulty in the recruit's performance.

Many agencies began with the San Jose model of field training
and adapted it to fit the particular needs of their department, taking
what was applicable and useful and combining it with components
from their own agency. The field training phases are likely to
progress somewhat like this:

- *Phase I* – During this phase you are little more than a ride-a-long
  in uniform. You are not expected to do more than perform the
  most basic tasks. One attribute evaluated most heavily during
  this phase is your attitude. Specific areas include attention to roll
  call, appearance, report writing, use of the radio during non-
  stress situations, and ability to check out the squad car before
  beginning patrol.

- *Phase II* – During this phase you are expected to perform more
  of the patrol officer's tasks, including taking more responsibility
  in handling calls. Some tasks evaluated during this phase may
  include investigating certain types of crime, low-risk traffic
  stops, etc. Performance begins to be evaluated in this phase.

- *Phase III* – During this phase the books say you will be working
  with your FTO as an equal partner. Don't believe it. You may be
  sharing the work load more evenly, but you are *not* equal
  partners. It is still the FTO's responsibility to evaluate your
  performance daily. Real partners don't do that. While you are
  expected to carry an increasing part of the work load, you are not
  expected to function as a fully autonomous "police officer." You
  are still a trainee, and it remains your role to learn from the FTO.
  During this phase the required performances may include felony
  stops or more complex investigations.

- *Phase IV* – During this phase you are supposed to be in charge of the car. The roles are reversed from Phase I, where you were little more than a ride-a-long in uniform. During this phase your FTO is supposed to ride along and let you do the bulk of the work. However, FTOs are often selected from the hardest working and most aggressive of police officers, and it is not in their nature to simply sit back and let someone else do all of the work. The "hands off" approach that is necessary during this transitional phase can be challenging for FTOs and can become a problem when an FTO has trouble turning over the reins and letting you carry out the required tasks while they evaluate your performance.

  Another difficulty that often occurs during this phase is that in the community, citizens are still likely to gravitate to the Field Training Officer because that officer's greater experience is often evident in their nonverbal communication. Through no fault of their own, they carry themselves with more authority and just look more comfortable during police-citizen contacts. Even though it is your role at this stage of field training to take the lead when responding to a call, and your FTO is supposed to play a supporting role and evaluate your ability to handle the situation, the FTO will project more confidence—the inevitable result of working the job for so many years—which will make people want to speak with that officer first.

- *Phase V* – During this phase the FTO is often in "plain clothes" and is supposed to be in the car strictly as an evaluator. Ideally there should be no training during this phase. However, as a practical matter, even the daily evaluation should serve as a training opportunity. It should be a constructive evaluation and should show you better ways to perform tasks and accomplish police objectives. The problems of Phase IV are reduced because the FTO is in "plain clothes." However, they are not eliminated from the picture entirely. For example, on a robbery call, your body language may tell a victim that your FTO is the officer in charge, which will lead the victim to want to speak with the non-uniformed officer first. Do not be offended, and try to work with this. Politely ask the victim to talk with you. Your FTO should support this. You need to gather your own information because in this phase you are likely to find yourself writing most of the reports.

Your evaluation will probably be ongoing and occur on a daily basis, a weekly basis, and at phase end, with each evaluation focusing on different aspects of your training. The daily evaluation will focus on tasks—commonly categorized as *core functions* and *knowledge competencies*—and how you accomplish them. Core functions of policing are broad categories of activities that include low-risk traffic intervention, officer-initiated investigations, order maintenance calls, traffic and accident investigations, high-risk intervention, and preliminary investigation. Knowledge competencies are more specific areas of skill that officers integrate into the core functions, such as radio communication, reporting writing, safe weapons handling, towing protocols, searching persons, etc. Evaluation of a recruit's ability to perform core functions and knowledge competencies is guided by department policy, state statutes, city ordinances, traffic code, and the FTO's own understanding of the best practices in law enforcement.

Each task (core function and knowledge competency) will be evaluated independently, and you will likely be rated as "not acceptable," "satisfactory," or even (hopefully) "superior." For instance, you will be evaluated on your driving, with the FTO looking at such things as your ability to follow traffic laws, drive safely, and make appropriate stops and starts in the squad. Obviously a crash that's your fault is going to be unacceptable, but so will near misses. If you scare the daylights out of your FTO with your driving, you will struggle to pass this element of field training. Other tasks you will be evaluated on may include the use of the radio, knowledge of the appropriate codes, and proper use of lights and siren. Suffice to say that everything you do during the field training period of your career will be evaluated, either formally on a report form or informally by veteran officers.

Some agencies evaluate the recruit on not only performance but on character as well. Research conducted under a grant from the Department of Justice, Office of Community Oriented Policing Services (COPS), identified fifteen character traits that community members viewed as being essential to police officers, particularly as our society becomes increasingly diverse: enthusiasm, creativity, self-motivation, understanding, self-confidence, independence, courage, tenacity, respectfulness, compassion/tolerance, honesty, loyalty, responsibility, ability to interact well with others, and possessing good judgment. In character-based evaluation, the FTO observes the recruit's demonstration of these traits through their daily behaviors and actions, with this type of evaluation occurring in the same teaching, training, and evaluating settings as the performance evaluation. The necessity of integrating character- and performance-based assessment was summarized succinctly in the researchers' conclusion: "To be successful in the field training program it is essential the recruit officer pass *both* the performance portion of the evaluation and the character portion. Failure in either area will constitute failure in the program."[1]

While the FTO program is designed to provide a gradual increase in responsibilities, it doesn't always work that way. In most cities you cannot select the day or week, or even the phase of training, during which you will be involved in a homicide investigation. When (or if) it happens while you are working, you are likely to be evaluated on your performance in that area, even if you are still in Phase I.

One problem in many field training programs is the absence of a clear indication of what the department or agency is looking for in its new officers. Will the field training program be used to create younger versions of the old officers, or will the department be looking for a "new breed" of police officers and encourage individuality? With this uncertainty, it is difficult to establish any type of consistency in the field training, as each FTO may see it as his or her task to create in the new officers a younger version of themselves. When an FTO program does not define specific

[1] Conroy, D. & Bostrom, M. (2006). *Recruitment, hiring, and retention of community policing officers: Character-based selection and assessment.* Washington, DC: United States Department of Justice, Office of Community Oriented Policing Services, pp.43-44. Grant # 2003-HS-WXK043.

behaviors as "acceptable" or "unacceptable," FTOs will tend to align
their expectations and evaluations with their own characteristics,
evaluating more favorably those recruit behaviors that more closely
resemble the FTO's own behaviors. For example, what might be an
acceptable traffic stop during an evening shift with a young,
aggressive FTO might be perceived as completely over the top by a
slower-moving, older day-shift FTO. Each police officer does police
work in their own way, and you might well be expected to know how
that is and then model your work after their unique style.

What Field Training Means For You in Terms of Surviving Initiation

The goal of the field training program is to help new officers make
the transition from the academy setting to the real world. However, it
is very different to attempt to disarm a "suspect" in a simulated
training exercise than it is out in the real world. Officers know they
will go home when the training session is over. And while the tactics
may be the same, trainers have to follow guidelines, which usually
stipulate that the recruit is not to be injured. Obviously, no such
guidelines exist in day-to-day police work. Although it is field
training, the danger out there in the field is real.

There may be other conflicts between the academic setting and
the real world. For instance, it may technically be a crime to assault a
police officer in some minor fashion, but the reality is that such a
crime may not be charged and prosecuted by the agency prosecutor
nor considered a "real crime" by judges. Thus another task of the
field training program is to help new officers learn to resolve these
conflicts. That means an opportunity to integrate theory and practice,
to learn the difference between what "should" work and what "does"
work.

Another skill your FTO will evaluate, either formally or
informally, is your ability to understand situations from a unique
police perspective. A case in point: as one FTO and his recruit were
driving by an all-night gas station at about 2200 hours, the attendant
was nowhere in sight. When the FTO asked the new officer what he
thought, the new officer said, "I think he must be in the bathroom."
The FTO said, "Or he's lying on the floor, shot during a robbery, and
bleeding to death." This suspiciousness is essential to a police

officer. This mindset and questioning way of seeing the world is evaluated in new officers. If you prove too trusting or naive, you may not be accepted into the police world because you will not be perceived as "safe."

The field training program also gives the police department the opportunity to evaluate new officers' writing skills. Aside from the basic skills pertaining to proper use of grammar, punctuation, and sentence structure, a police officer must be able to translate observations into a written record that makes sense. It is important to write the facts but not to spend the entire shift writing a report to cover one lost dog.

Perhaps the greatest task of a field training program is to socialize the new police officer. During this phase you will learn a number of informal details that will make or break your career as a cop. You will learn who to talk to and who not to talk to. You will learn where the emphasis for enforcement is placed and, of equal importance, where it is not. The informal power structure within a department is often more powerful than the formal structure, and your peers will often have more power than your chief. For example, some agencies place an informal emphasis on traffic enforcement through peer competition while others find that traffic enforcement is *only* a tool to be used to make felony arrests. This informal direction may be in conflict with stated departmental standards. Thus, during field training you will learn your place within the departmental structure. You will learn that you are not a "real" police officer yet and you won't be until you prove yourself. Each department will have different informal standards for this, and these standards will be conveyed sometime during the field training program.

In many cases new officers have had limited experience with the department that has hired them. If you have done an internship with that department, you are more likely to have some impression of the department and the work they do. However, it is likely to be a skewed view, as interns are seldom given a realistic view of police work and are typically shown only the good sides of the department. Interns are often used in some sort of clerical function and sent as "ride-a-longs" with selected officers. They are still not a member of the department, and the officers will not include them as though they were. Do not attempt to insert yourself into the department as an equal or a peer until you have had time to prove yourself.

An ideal field training program is a systematic, objective method for training and evaluating police recruits. It is the most realistic training you will receive and it answers the oldest question in police recruitment: can they do the job? Many recruits have said things like, "I may not be big, but I can do the job," or, "I may not be smart, but I can do the job," or, "I may not be tall, but I can do the job." Each individual who progresses this far in the testing process is given their chance to prove they can safely and effectively perform as a police officer.

Potential Pitfalls during Field Training

A negative attitude is one of the most common pitfalls during field training. Some attitudes that cause problems for recruits are reflected in statements like, "We didn't do it like that at the last police department I worked for," or, "My other FTO didn't have me do it that way," or, "Why are you picking on me?"

Avoid challenging your FTO; he or she is specifically trained to work with you and help you learn to work as a police officer. When given training feedback, thank your FTO for the positive comments and acknowledge your mistakes. Some of the greatest problems in field training are caused by a recruit's failure to acknowledge his or her own mistakes. Mistakes are expected; everyone makes them. Accept responsibility for your mistakes (don't blame someone else), and once you've admitted to them, do your best to learn from them. Try not to make the same mistake twice. The most grievous mistakes a recruit can make are those that put the FTO or other police officers at risk. Remember that police officers are trained and practiced at spotting trouble. You may not be, and you must listen to their advice to avoid creating more risk. It is surely going to irritate your FTO to find a situation aggravated because of having to divert attention from bad guys to get you out of a jam.

Be patient; the time will come when you will be a "real" police officer. You will work alone, you will be in your own squad car, and even though you won't get daily evaluations, you will still find yourself "second guessed" on a significant number of occasions. The chief will wonder why you handled a call a particular way, witnesses will wonder why you did what you did, and citizens will complain because you didn't do as they wished. In fact, a certain amount of citizen complaint is unavoidable if you are doing good police work. It is commonly generated through misunderstanding because citizens often think we could do something if we chose to, even though in many situations we are bound by laws or departmental policy and cannot do as they would like. Don't worry about it. Most good cops generate some complaints because no one can please all of the people all of the time. There will always be someone who is unhappy with what you have done.

How many police officers do you know when you start working with a police department? Having acquaintances may not be as helpful as it sounds. While trying to fit in as a rookie, you may find a role conflict with associations from the past. You can no longer relate to the veteran officers as you did when you were a police reservist, a bartender, or even a civilian employee. They see you now in a different light, and you are in a different role. You are trying to become a member of their exclusive club. Before there was no concern about you becoming an insider, and you saw what they wanted you to see. Now the situation is different because you are asking for membership. Yet you will bring with you some of the old reputation. If you were honest, loyal, trustworthy, etc., hopefully some of that will come with you. If you were dishonest and untrustworthy, that will certainly come with you, and it will be something you will need to overcome.

AFTER FIELD TRAINING, ARE YOU "IN" YET?

When you complete the police academy or field training, remember that you are not yet necessarily thought of as a police officer. You may still have to pass some tests. For example, do you seem to understand and follow the unwritten rules of the department? One officer who had just been hired and had completed his training stopped a motorist for having one headlight out. As the officer gave the motorist a citation for the equipment violation, the motorist pointed out to the officer the he also had a headlight out. The officer issued himself a citation for the equipment violation. Is there any wonder that the rest of the department thought of this officer as a little "strange"? He didn't fit in, and shortly thereafter he left the department and is no longer in law enforcement.

Most officers who leave police work do so because they don't fit. It has nothing to do with whether they like the job; it is that they don't mesh well with and are not accepted by the other officers. Learn the informal rules of the department you work for. You can best learn them by *listening*. Even though you may feel as though you have something to contribute to every conversation and want to be accepted, listen and learn before you speak up. One of the greatest mistakes you can make at this point in your career will be to talk about other officers, even to other officers. If you are standing in a group of officers and they start talking about another officer, *keep your mouth shut.* Even though you may have had experience with this officer and may completely agree with what is being said, resist the temptation to speak out or you will be the one who suffers, because many veteran police officers will not see that you have been there long enough to have an opinion, much less to pass judgment on a veteran officer.

Special Considerations for Female Recruits

If you are a woman entering law enforcement, you may find yourself facing additional difficulties in surviving the initiation. If you are the first woman officer on this department, you may face major hurdles, including the need to shatter stereotypes. There could well be a belief from some male officers that a woman is not able to "do the job." You will be tested and will find that you walk a fine line. The stereotypical ideal for new police officer is a white male, 6 foot+ with broad shoulders and narrow hips. His physical conditioning is beyond question. You will need to show the veteran officers, the administration, and the community that you can "do the job." You will need to show them there is more to being a good police officer than sheer physical strength. Furthermore, not only will the other officers not know how to relate to you, the public may be in doubt as well. You may be seen as a smaller male or not seen at all.

Female recruits may find instances of harassment and downright cruelty. As you deal with these issues, make sure you are not looking only at short-term solutions. You may find that reporting a veteran officer for an off-hand, offensive comment gets him a reprimand, but what has it done to your reputation? Remember, more people leave police work because they don't fit in with their particular department than leave because they do not like the work.

Your relationships with veteran officers will be different than those of a male police recruit. You may find that some of the officers are inviting you on dates (both the married and the single officers). Until you have settled in and found your niche within the police department, it is generally not a good idea to date other officers within your department. Not only will it complicate your new relationship but it will make it more difficult for you to establish yourself as a police officer. Dating cops is not a shortcut to acceptance. It is most often a recipe for disaster. If your romance goes sour, so may your career. Being seen as a "party girl" is another formula for trouble—it gets you no real relationship and no respect.

As time goes on you are likely to find you will be judged on the basis of what you have done. You will be judged on your own merit and will find acceptance for the unique individual you are and for your own particular style of police work. But it does take time.

Special Considerations for Minority Recruits

Racial issues can be of concern to minority applicants. You may find you need to deal with stereotypes. First, there may be an assumption that you have been hired through an affirmative action program *and* the standards have been lowered on your behalf. Certainly no one wants to work with an officer who is not able to "do the job."

Another issue may be the assumption that if you are of a particular minority group, you will want to work in neighborhoods with similar racial demographics and will be more effective in those neighborhoods. This is a myth, but it is one you may need to explain as you indicate your preference to be treated as a "police officer" and not as a "minority police officer."

The racial issue may bring about other fears among other police officers. If, for example, you are an African American police officer, there may be concerns about where your true loyalties lie. If another police officer should be in danger in a neighborhood comprised mainly of African American residents, would you be there to back him or her up?

Special Considerations for Gay/Lesbian Recruits

If you are a gay/lesbian officer, you may find a unique set of difficulties in being accepted by police officers. Again, you may be singled out for unwanted attention based on inaccurate stereotypes and anticipated improprieties based on myth. While this may not be politically correct, it is, unfortunately, the reality in many police agencies. It may seem as though you need to put your personal life on hold while you are working towards acceptance into the police world. The advice of several gay police officers is to avoid being conspicuously gay during your probation period and consider limiting your dating, especially within the jurisdiction where you work. If you are in a long-term relationship, be sure you establish yourself within your department before you try to introduce your partner within departmental circles. You want to become known as "a good cop (who happens to be gay)" rather than "a gay cop." Any deviation from the norm can be dangerous at this point in your career, and the larger the deviation, the greater the danger that it will adversely impact on your career.

A FINAL WORD: SURVIVING INITIATION AS A "NEW BREED" OF RECRUIT

Although progress has been made in recruiting more women and minorities into the ranks of policing, especially in larger metropolitan agencies, the policing field is still perceived, in many areas of the country, to be one dominated by white males. In fact, a census of local police departments found that in 2007 (the most recent data available as this book goes to print), the percentage of full-time sworn officers who were male ranged from a low of 82.1 percent in agencies serving populations of 500,000 to 999,999 to a high of 94.4 percent in the smallest agencies—those serving populations under 2,500.[2] Similar trends were found regarding the racial and ethnic composition of local police departments. In 2007, the percentage of full-time sworn personnel who identified themselves as "white" ranged from 56.0 percent in agencies serving

---

[2] Reaves, B.A. (2010). *Local police departments, 2007.* Washington, DC: U.S. Department of Justice, Bureau of Justice Statistics. (NCJ 231174)

populations of 1,000,000 or more to 88.3 percent in departments serving populations under 2,500, with a fairly consistent increase in the percentage of white officers found as jurisdiction size diminished (Reaves, 2007). Although there are always exceptions, and these percentages represent only an *average* value among departments serving populations of various sizes, these data indicate a general trend that more women and minority officers are found in agencies serving larger populations, and smaller agencies serving smaller jurisdictions tend to maintain more of the "traditional" officer profile, with white males comprising the greatest percentage of uniformed police officers.

What this means for you, if you are any type of a new minority police officer, is that it will be important to have patience and allow the veteran officers to evaluate you, not based upon your minority status but upon your work performance. Don't be impatient, but don't allow yourself to be treated unfairly either. Do everything you can to insist you be treated as an individual and that your performance be evaluated on an individual basis as a police officer.

Chapter 3

SURVIVING THE SYSTEM

sys·tem *noun* \ˈsis-təm\

a regularly interacting or interdependent group of items forming a
unified whole

—Mirriam-Webster Online Dictionary, 2013

As a police officer, you will be one "item" within a law enforcement
"group" that operates within the criminal justice system—a massive
"unified whole." Being part of this system brings many pressures and
challenges. One key to surviving a law enforcement career is to
understand how you are perceived by others in "the system" and the
roles you are expected to play—by the public, prosecutors, the
courts, corrections, law enforcement in general and your department
specifically, your peers, and, most importantly, yourself.

DEFINING A COMPLEX ROLE

You will get conflicting messages about what your job is. The
community will be one of the groups that define police work, and
they will define it as *they* see it. If you work in a large agency, your
job may be defined differently by each of several different sub-
communities within the larger community. In some communities
your job may be very law-enforcement oriented. In others it may be
very service oriented. In some jurisdictions you will be a part of the
community, and in others the community may want you to be
invisible and remain apart from it.

   Not only will different communities define your role differently,
the same community may define your role differently at different
times, posing some difficult double standards. They may want crime
fighters when there is a rash of burglaries or traffic enforcement after
a child is struck by a speeding car, but they will not want to be

27

stopped if they are driving through alleys in a suspicious manner nor given tickets when they are speeding through their own neighborhoods. Furthermore, your job is defined by state and local laws. In some cases you will be required by law to make an arrest, and in other cases you'll be prohibited.

Your role is also shaped by those who work with you inside the criminal justice system, including prosecutors and judges. Prosecutors—lawyers who represent the state in criminal matters— hold the power to decide which of your cases will move forward, which ones will get dropped, and which ones you need to do more work on. Sometimes when you make an arrest as required by law, you may be viewed by prosecutors as simply giving them busy work. They often see the police as only a small cog in a huge machine that metes out justice to law breakers, and officers are viewed as little more than the thugs who deal with other thugs in the community. Within this hierarchy police officers are seen as separate from the court system and the least important part of the criminal justice system, certainly well below the status of prosecutors and judges. Yet, when you think about it, without police officers both prosecutors and judges might find themselves out of work.

Police officers and correctional officers are similar in that, as groups, they are both "outsiders" to the courtroom; however, there can be friction here as well. Police officers often view correctional officers as somehow less important in the system. It is common within sheriff's offices for deputies to start their careers first as correctional officers and then, after sufficient time and when there is an opening, be promoted to deputy. This informal hierarchy system is supported in some ways by the pay each group receives. Correctional officers are most frequently the lowest paid of the group, followed by deputies or police officers. Prosecutors commonly make more than police officers, but for prosecutors who may make less early in their careers, they often have the opportunity to go into private practice with a prestigious law firm later, where the potential earnings are far greater. Finally, judges usually are at the top of the heap, with higher salaries than any other work group within the criminal justice system. This hierarchy is not expressed in formal terms or written down anywhere but, rather, is communicated in subtle, nonverbal ways. For example, when a police officer meets with a prosecutor, it is generally at the prosecutor's convenience and what works with his or her schedule, not according to what the police officer's schedule allows. Similarly, when a prosecutor meets with a judge, it will be at the judge's convenience, not the prosecutor's.

The department you work for, and the philosophy of its top management, will define your role as well. If your chief sees the department's function as nothing more than maintaining the status quo, your role might be to follow the well-worn path established by officers who preceded you. If your chief sees the department as partnering with the greater community in an active role to make the area better and safer for its residents, your role may be entirely different. You may find conflicts here if the community is asking for a service model and your department adheres to an enforcement model, because your supervisors will assess your performance quantitatively based on the number of arrests and traffic tickets written, while the community will be judging your performance more on qualitative measures such as how compassionate or respectful you treated them during a call for service.

Your job is further defined by your peers. If peer influence says that a "good cop" is one who performs a police function in a specific way, that is a powerful job descriptor. You may well find that none of these groups agree on what the job of policing really is, or what aspects are most important.

Finally, your job is defined by your internal value system. This is the most important job descriptor and one you live with every minute of every day. As long as you know you are doing the job the way you believe it needs to be done, you can live with yourself. This will, however, be an ongoing battle throughout your career. Your personal values will be challenged on a daily basis, and each time you will need to ask, "Is it worth it?" Does the decision involve a moral issue for you that will make any subsequent consequences worth taking a stand at this point? For instance, if you are working in a police department that has adopted a strict "law enforcement" model and the issue is something like giving out traffic tickets each time you stop someone for speeding in a school zone, that is one thing. While you might not believe that everyone speeding in a school zone deserves a ticket, it is also not a hill worth dying on. If, on the other hand, you are being pressured by peers into doing something illegal or unethical, you may decide that it *is* a line you are unwilling to cross and refuse to be a part of that activity.

Understand that there will still be times when you are forced to do things you don't like, but remember, you don't have an option, and you don't have to like it. In fact, if you find you are starting to like evictions, child abuse calls, or death notifications, there is something wrong and you need to seek help. The point here is: don't compromise your personal values to do the job as someone else thinks it needs to be done. If you think someone deserves a second chance, give it to them if you can.

THE PUBLIC PERCEPTION

Police officers find themselves a living stereotype, embodying a number of typecast attributes fairly clichéd in this culture. This image is often encouraged by police officers themselves. For example, "No one messes with a police officer and gets away with it." This comment represents a stereotypical attitude about the cohesiveness of police officers, which may be entirely inaccurate. It is not uncommon for people to "get away with it" because a judge or jury doesn't do their job.

Police officers are coming under closer scrutiny every day, and people do "mess with" police officers. In years past if a citizen happened by while a police officer was doing something and the officer told the citizen to "get moving," there was no argument; the citizen simply left. Now, there is a greater chance that a citizen who is told, more or less, to "butt out" will feel an urge to push back, at least verbally. This may lead the officer to escalate their command for the citizen to "move along," which may cause the citizen to push back even more, leading to an argument and perhaps even a fight and arrest. Police officers seem to be increasingly involved with those who will claim, "I know my rights," even when they don't. An arrest made under these circumstances may appear to be an arrest for "contempt of cop." Such arrests have come under increased scrutiny in recent years and may reflect poorly on those who make them. While these arrests are frequently justified emotionally, they may be weak on legal standing.

The advance of video technology has also changed policing. Police officers performing their daily functions are often recorded by people using cameras or cell phones. While the quality of these recordings may leave much to be desired, even grainy images are capable of reporting police actions. Police are also routinely recorded by cameras and wireless microphones mounted in squad cars. The increased use of recordings has been a double-edged sword for police, as in some cases it has helped convict the criminal, and in others, the officer.

While it is true that police are public servants whose salaries come from the taxpayers, many times the people who use the phrase "I pay your salary" are those on welfare or some other public assistance. Nonetheless, because citizens pay our salaries, they often want input into what they are paying for, an expectation most officers find very frustrating. Taxpayers may feel entitled to tell the police how to do their jobs, even though the majority of the community has no idea what policing really entails. And while giving the citizens a voice may seem like a good idea in theory, it can pose difficulties in practice. As the diversity of a community's population increases, so, too, does the variety of interests and concerns of the individuals within the community. If each special interest group gets a piece of us and sends us off in one direction or another, even though each cause may be worthwhile, the various agendas often disconnect with one another and may even contradict each other. Imagine this conflict: a mandate from the tenants' union states that no one may be evicted except upon a 30-day notice delivered in person by a police officer, and property owners insist that tenants by given only 30 days written notice. What happens when you can't find the tenants?

Another special interest group is Mothers Against Drunk Drivers (MADD), whose mission is to stop drunk driving, support the victims of this violent crime, and prevent underage drinking. The courts, however, have ruled that the police cannot conduct random stops of vehicles (i.e., stopping without reasonable suspicion is a violation of Fourth Amendment rights), which has made enforcing drunk driving laws more difficult. Efficient enforcement of drunk driving laws has come into conflict with constitutional rights. Who gets caught in the middle? The police officer. Consider something even more basic: a parking complaint. If a person calls and wants to complain about a car parked in front of his house or that someone is "taking his parking spot," you may be unable to do anything because the car may be parked legally.

The system often puts police officers in an adversarial role. The most obvious of the adversarial roles is external. Police are in a position to make people do things they don't want to do or to stop them from doing things they do want to do. The police officer exists to enforce laws, laws that people may disagree with, may find inconvenient, or may simply believe should not apply to them. Recall the double standard: Citizens want speeding laws enforced to ensure traffic safety, unless they are the ones who are stopped for speeding. Then they think that a warning is sufficient and may argue that the officer should be focused on fighting more serious crime and catching more dangerous criminals. Seldom, if ever, does a police officer hear, "Thank you, officer," from an individual just cited for speeding, yet that same driver will think, "Good, the police stopped that maniac," when they see someone else pulled over.

Police are put into an adversarial role with young children by parents who may see a uniformed officer and tell the child, "There's a police officer, and if you don't behave, he'll take you away." This is certainly no way for children to establish a positive relationship with law enforcement. This same parent would never dream of saying something similar about an attorney or a judge. Police officers are not only used as a threat by some parents to frighten children, but some parents have gone so far as to ask police officers to impose parental consequences. It's not uncommon to hear such things as, "I can't do anything with him. Why don't you just arrest him?" when the child has not committed a crime but has, perhaps, simply been rude to his parents. Such requests have come from parents with children as young as six or seven years old. They want the police to assume a parental role and are critical of the officer who refuses to do so.

Even more adversarial are the times when an officer is required to enforce a law that may be unjust. Certainly, sometimes actions are "right" or "wrong," but how is it viewed when a man is arrested for stealing a loaf of bread to feed his family because he has been unable to find work? The officer is placed between these two citizens—on one side is the shop owner, who is legally justified in demanding that the "thief" be arrested, and on the other side is the father pleading that, in his desperation, he saw no other way to feed his family. Such situations generate not only an external adversarial role, but internal as well. The police officer is, in these types of situations, caught "between a rock and a hard place," required to act because he or she has sworn to uphold the "law of the land," even though there is obviously no justice.

It is not uncommon for someone who is shopping and carrying an armload of stuff to put a small item in their pocket because they can't carry it. At checkout, they pay for all of the items except the small one in their pocket, which they have inadvertently forgotten about, and then they are arrested for shoplifting when they leave the store. An example of this scenario involved a man who was shopping in a large hardware store. He bought several hundred dollars worth of tools and other merchandise but had put a 79-cent pencil in his pocket because his hands were full. He forgot to pay for it at checkout, and when he left the store he was arrested for stealing the pencil. The "no exception policy" cost this man dearly. Often such arrests are insisted upon by a retailer with a "no exception" policy.

A common misperception is that police officers have the discretion to end an encounter at the scene of the crime. There are cases where police may be required to make an arrest even though no one on the scene wants anyone else arrested, for example, in a domestic assault. In such cases, officers are often required by departmental policy or even by state statute to make a mandatory arrest if there is any evidence of an assault, even though the victim does not want their abuser to be arrested. While an arrest may be an appropriate action in most cases, it is not always the answer. This is yet another example where police discretion is eroding and complex decisions are addressed with a simple policy. There is no "one size fits all" in police work. Such simplistic solutions cannot possibly consider all variables and may actually do more harm than good.

Police officers are also expected to be social workers and mediators. Fewer and fewer of the duties of police officers are related to law enforcement or apprehending criminals. Legislative and procedural mandates have forced police officers to respond to more and more calls for assistance that would have previously been handled between the parties involved. Police officers are called because one neighbor disagrees with another or has called the other "names"; police are called because someone has parked a car "in front" of the complainant's home, even though it is not restricted parking; and the police are called because children no longer show parents the respect the parents believe they deserve but may not have earned.

Police officers are supposed to maintain law and order from a logical perspective in a world driven by emotion and chaos. Police officers are often a focal point highlighting the disparity between fair and legal. A family being evicted from their apartment because the breadwinner was unfairly terminated from their job, they lack the legal resources to fight the employer, and they have been unable to pay rent as a result, may see the police as an enforcement arm and not as fair and impartial enforcers of the law, and certainly not someone there to help them. This can be troublesome for police officers as well and may lead to frustration, a decay of personal values, and a sense of hopelessness or powerlessness to make change where it is important.

While standards for police officers must be high because no other group in our society is given such power by the public, there must be a balance between that public trust and a capacity for human error. As a police officer you will have legal authority to use deadly force and take another life. There is an expectation—by the public, the prosecutors, courts, your peers, and even yourself—that all of your decisions, made in a split second and often under extremely stressful and rapidly unfolding circumstances, will be perfect, well thought out, and logical. However, these are unrealistic, inhuman standards imposed upon police officers from the outside (communities, courts, special interest groups) and from the inside (the officer second-guessing their own actions), which often leave police officers feeling that they are not allowed to be human.

THE OFFICER'S ROLE WITHIN THE ADVERSARIAL CRIMINAL JUSTICE SYSTEM

The police have a unique role within the criminal justice system. And while the specifics of law enforcement may have changed over the years, the basic role of police officers within the criminal justice system has not. It is still the individual officer who deals with the public, on the public's own turf, whenever they call, and for whatever reason. In a criminal matter, the police officer arrests suspects and gathers the evidence, which is presented in court by a prosecuting attorney, argued by a defense attorney, admitted or excluded by a judge, and evaluated by a jury. Each party plays a specific role within this system of checks and balances. However, police officers alone function outside the boundaries of the courtroom, entering this arena only to report what was done outside of it, while the actual work of the other parties takes place in the courthouse. The courtroom is also where the officer's work is tested, disputed, evaluated, and sometimes dismissed, and where the officer's judgment and actions, honesty, and integrity are questioned and challenged, often in minute detail. Consequently it may feel to the police officer as though court is a lonely, even hostile, place and that the other members of the system—those whose domain is the courtroom—are the officer's adversaries.

It is the police officer who, every day, makes split-second decisions in an emotionally charged and often dangerous atmosphere; on the turf of victims and perpetrators; facing the threat of assault, exposure to communicable diseases, or even death. It is also the police officer who must go home at the end of each shift and try to deal with the cruelty and senselessness of crime and violence and the pain and suffering it causes. Meanwhile, behind the safety of courtroom walls, distanced from violent events by both space and time, the others in "the system" begin to scrutinize the officer's actions.

Attorneys will spend weeks, months, or, in some cases, years arguing about a police officer's decision to search, arrest, or use deadly force on an individual. Judges and juries will hear sanitized versions of what happened, from a sanitized defendant. Attorneys for both sides will bring in "experts," such as psychiatrists or psychologists, to testify yet who will often contradict each other and who will describe emotional trauma or mental illness in such clinical terms that they may present little or no connection to the reality of the events. These experts may argue that the defendant is not responsible for his actions and should not be punished, but many times, they argue these things without having seen the victims and the pain and suffering caused by the perpetrator. The propriety of an officer's actions will be evaluated with the benefit of 20/20 hindsight, with all of the facts at hand, and will very commonly exclude the pressure and intensity of emotion that prevailed at the moment in which the officer's decision was made. Even anger, fear, and sadness are discussed in court within a logical structure according to constitutional principles generated by our founding fathers, with their impact on the situation diminished or eliminated by passing time.

"The system" is often referred to as "a revolving door of justice," with perpetrators often back out on the street before the ink of their booking fingerprints is dry. It is frustrating to deal with those offenders who "beat the system," and every police officer will have, over the course of their career, countless experiences with those who seem to do so. However, in most cases, these offenders' luck holds out for only so long. For example, one individual I know brutally beat a police officer. Several years later this same individual was killed in a motorcycle accident. That lifestyle seems to catch up with those who live it, eventually. Yet it causes extreme frustration for the police officer in the short-term.

Others seem to "beat the system" and cause further problems for those you are trying to protect. Be careful. If you begin to see yourself as some sort of savior, you are doomed to failure and self-destruction. The system is not designed for "saviors" or "rescuers." There will always be those you arrest who are later freed and cause further pain and injury: the abusive husband who is released and continues to beat his wife or his children, the pedophile who strikes again with other children, the habitual drunk driver who crashes into and kills a teenager on her way home from her job. Yet, it is imperative that you are doing your part, making the arrests when you can, bringing this person into "the system," and hoping justice works. Do not take responsibility for what happens after you have made the arrest. Your job is to make a good arrest, write a solid report, and testify in court in a professional manner. Beyond that you have no control and no responsibility.

Plea bargaining may make you feel as though justice has been cheated. Again, if you have done your part, accept that you have done well and realize you cannot control what others do. It seems that plea bargains have become a standard method of avoiding a "waste of taxpayer's money through trial" and of tempering justice with "thrift." If you continue to throw your self-image into this process, you will find few rewards and an eroding self-esteem.

YOUR ROLE WITHIN THE DEPARTMENT

Police officers are required to work all hours. If you are a new officer you are likely to work the worst of those. You may find yourself working a midnight or afternoon shift, working all or most holidays, and may not see a decent vacation pick for several years. This will certainly have an impact. If you are working nights with rotating days off, you must realize that it isn't just a change in work days or hours, it is a completely different lifestyle. Some people adapt better than others to working nights and sleeping days. As your career progresses, you may find that your ability to adapt decreases with age and that you are sleeping less or not as well. It's important to realize that if you're not sleeping, you won't be healthy and you likely won't be a great cop, parent, sister, brother, or any other role in your life. Make sure to adjust your lifestyle, not just your schedule. Far too often the first thing to go is our sleep time, but other activities get sacrificed soon after because you're too exhausted to complete them. Treat your sleep like the precious commodity that it is. Don't give up sleep time for anything that is not really, *really* important. Lack of sleep can sabotage your plans for success and ruin the rest of your life by impacting job performance, marriages, and all other relationships.

Civil service has been both a blessing and a curse to police officers. It has been a blessing because it removes the stigma of political favoritism from many police departments. The curse, however, is that sometimes this system protects those who do not deserve protection. For example, in one case, an admitted child molester was protected by the civil service process because, in the decision of the arbitrator, "it didn't happen at work" and, therefore, it couldn't affect his job and he couldn't be fired for what he did. Yet, the other officers were forced to live with the stigma that a member of their agency was a child molester. So while civil service has given us protection, it has also saddled us with some who should not be police officers. Civil service also protects those officers who choose to "do nothing." These are the officers who do not really work. They may answer assigned calls marginally but are not fired because they have "done nothing wrong." The civil service system seems to encourage mediocrity in performance or a lack of effort and involvement on the part of police officers.

As with any occupation inter-agency rivalries exist. Businesses compete for a market, an image, or personnel. It is no different in police work. Police departments compete for turf by offering to "contract" for police services in adjacent areas, giving the department expanded jurisdiction, more personnel, greater flexibility, and generally a stronger influence in the larger community. This inter-agency rivalry is not just for turf but for personnel as well. Each agency wants to hire the best and the brightest.

Departments are always in conflict about "image." A self-description of any agency will say it is "the best." Federal agencies commonly sell themselves on having more "prestige" because their officers don't wear uniforms. The agency that seems to sell itself most strongly and devote the most energy to image is the Federal Bureau of Investigation (FBI). The FBI claims to be the most prestigious law enforcement agency in the country. Yet to a police officer who enjoys being in the trenches, working for the FBI may not even be considered "real police work."

The Los Angeles Police Department (LAPD) has actively promoted itself through television and printed media as one of the most advanced departments in the country. In fact, the first television series that showed uniformed police officers in a professional setting was *Adam-12*, which ran from 1968 to 1975 and focused on two LAPD patrol officers. Yet, when you get right down to it, all agencies are similar in that they all have their ups and downs. The image of the LAPD has taken a few hits over the years, but the scandals were most often caused by the misdeeds of a select few. The vast majority of the cops who work in any given department are not the ones who tarnish the department's image. Sure, some agencies are better than others, but none are without problems.

Gossip can make a police department a difficult place to work and has destroyed many individual police careers. Gossip races through police departments like wildfire. Gossip doesn't have to be true—it just has to sound good, and the more interesting it sounds, the faster and further it spreads. Gossip is as destructive to the person spreading it as to the person it is spread about. It is often spread under the guise of "information," and police officers want all the information they can get about everyone. Knowing things about people is not only an officer's job, it is often a hobby as well. While that may work well when criminals are involved, it is often detrimental to the police department's internal workings for too many to know all, whether true or untrue. Impressions are formed and relationships may be forged based on gossip. Officers' reputations have been destroyed because gossip, once out there, cannot be reeled back in, and many people are willing to believe that if someone said it, it must be true, at least in part. People often spread gossip because it makes them feel important. Don't get sucked into that. Keep your mouth shut. Don't talk about other officers.

As a police officer, you will find you have little control of your work environment. People call, and we respond. The vast majority of police work is "reactive" as opposed to "proactive." There are trends to modernize police work and for police departments to become more proactive; however, the basic response to crime is still reactive. Therefore, you can't plan much of your day if you're working in a squad. Investigators and administrators have more success in this area but are still limited by the overall need for police to always be ready to respond to crisis. Since most officers start out working in a squad, get used to such disruptions. You will have your dinner interrupted by calls. Your reports and even the time you take to go to the bathroom will be interrupted. You may plan to meet another squad for coffee and not make it because you are answering a call for service. Even when you tell a friend or spouse you will be home at a certain time, you can't guarantee it because you may get a late call or arrest and have no control over how long it takes to finish.

Not only is there little or no control over the calls that come in, most tasks cannot be left half finished. Imagine you are arresting an individual and, as you are transporting them to the station, you realize your shift is ending. Can you just leave that individual in your squad until tomorrow or whenever you come back to work? Not hardly. This will mean overtime and a push back (or cancelling) of any plans you had once you got off work. Of course some police officers have learned to *never* make an arrest near the end of their shift. In fact, some police officers have learned many different ways to avoid making an arrest … or writing a report . . . or answering their radio after a certain point during the shift. They have learned to do as little as humanly possible all shift long. You don't want to be one of these officers. There is often little or no satisfaction in such work, and you will not earn the respect of your peers. You want to be well thought of in your department and by your peers.

THE IMPORTANCE OF PEERS

One of the strongest influences on any police officer is "peer pressure." An officer cannot operate in a vacuum. Just as you need the other parts of the system to convict criminals, you need other police officers to survive, physically, socially, and emotionally. In police work, peer approval affects more than self-image. In many cases your very survival will depend on peer acceptance. In some cases officers have been injured or killed because of a lack of peer support and acceptance.

It is imperative that you find acceptance by your peers without compromising personal values. To gain this acceptance, you may have to walk a fine line between doing as others wish and maintaining your own integrity. If you go too far in either direction, you will lose not only your peer support, but also, perhaps, your integrity and self-respect. As a new officer you may feel pressured to go out after work for a few beers with the guys when you would rather go home to your family. You will not earn the long-term respect of other cops by going drinking with them. You will earn that only by the work you do. Go home to your family, if that's your preference.

After time on the job, you may feel closer to some of your peers than you do to your spouse, your children, or your brothers and sisters. You will spend more time with your partner than with anyone else in your life. No one may seem as important to you as your partner. This bond is often forged by sharing life-or-death experiences and moments of great physical and emotional intensity. Your partner is the person you will count on to keep you out of trouble, physically, emotionally, and legally. Your partner will share the dangerous calls with you. They will help in fights, protect your back when searching buildings, or deal with the other half of a domestic dispute. They will go through the same emotional problems you do, witness the same physical and emotional trauma, and need to talk about it. With luck and a good partner, you will be close enough so you can talk about the death and emotional pain you deal with, which is necessary to prevent the emotional buildup that leads to depression, alcoholism, or even suicide. Your partner is also going to be there to protect you legally. When you get to court and you say, "She did it," and she says, "No I didn't," you partner may cast the deciding ballot. Even more importantly, when you get to court and the bad guy says, "That police officer took my money," or, "That officer struck me with his nightstick 32 times," your partner can verify that you did not.

The stresses of police work can take their toll in many ways. Don't expect your actions to be above the law, that you can "get away with it." Where once other officers would "look the other way" if a cop was found breaking the law, it has become increasingly common for police officers to be arrested for domestic assault, drunken driving, and other offenses. It is a myth that police officers won't arrest one another. Now, in many jurisdictions, there are no options. If a police officer is found violating a law, whether it is a traffic law or a criminal offense, he or she is arrested. In fact, many officers are more likely to give a citizen a break than give a break to another officer, for fear of being accused of favoritism.

Every police department has its prima donnas, officers who are the chief's chosen favorites or who have somebody to "take care of them." They may never work a midnight shift, may never have an unpleasant assignment, and may get commendations for doing practically nothing. There is nothing you can do about these people. But it may help to look at their peer relationships, the lack of respect they get among "real cops," and ask yourself if you really want to be like that. It's sometimes tempting, especially when you are writing an accident report in the snow at 0300 hours in subfreezing weather. But is it worth it? Remember your self-respect and self-esteem. How will you feel about yourself if you sell out? What will you see when you look in the mirror?

SELF-PERCEPTION

Whenever you deal with the public, you must relinquish some degree of control. You *cannot* control everything and everyone. There are too many variables in play. You need to decide what is most important and pay attention to that, sometimes ignoring other things completely. Even when you give something your complete attention, often you don't get the results you hoped for. Some of today's police shows have storylines about cops who take the system into their own hands to make things work, portraying such cops as some type of saviors. Know that this kind of police work is fictional and succeeds only on television or in the movies. If you try such Hollywood hot dogging in real life, you may find you've put everything that matters at risk—your career, your reputation, your family, and even your freedom. Shortcuts can be tremendously hazardous. You took an oath of office to uphold the U.S. Constitution, yet shortcuts are typically unconstitutional. You risk lawsuits, punitive damages (more about this later), dismissal from your profession, and even criminal charges.

When a case goes "bad" it seems the police officer is one of the first to be blamed, whether it's because the officer is the first representative of the system to be involved in each case or that the police are just the most visible. Perhaps it's because it is the "work product" of the police officer that is being discussed, argued, or evaluated. Blame may fall on the police officer because the officer has the least wealth or fewest political connections. For whatever reason, the police officer is most frequently faulted for a "failure to convict" or "not guilty" verdict. The public often doesn't consider that there may have been an incompetent prosecutor, a biased judge, or a clueless jury.

You may blame yourself. If you have taken short cuts, chastise yourself. If you have made procedural errors, learn from them. If you have done the best job you could, congratulate yourself, realize you cannot control the attorneys, judges, or juries, and move on. Your job is to make a professional arrest, write a thorough report and provide professional testimony in court. It is not your job to guarantee a conviction or to punish the guilty (no matter how much you may want to or feel you need to). Most experienced officers realize that if a criminal gets away with something, that offender is not going to learn from their mistakes and you'll probably get another chance to arrest them at some future date. Leopards don't change their spots, and most criminals don't change either.

Police officers are seen by offenders as initiators or activators of the system because if illegal activity escapes the officers' notice, the criminal is likely to "get away with it." There will be no arrest or trial. Consequently, the arrest process presents the most danger for the professional criminal. In fact, most serious criminals are more afraid of the arrest process than any other part of the criminal justice system, because it is at this point, when officers are attempting to take a suspect into custody, that the offender is at the greatest risk of being shot and killed, and there is no court of appeals after that. Criminals also understand that, having survived the arrest process, they are entitled to defend themselves in court and that the state has to prove the defendant's guilt beyond a reasonable doubt. The offender can hire an attorney (or have court-appointed counsel if they can't afford a lawyer), stretch out a trial and the appeals for several years, and perhaps even win their case, based not on right or wrong but on logical argument, a technical issue, or even an emotional appeal to a jury. Therefore, again, if an offender can elude the police, they have greatly reduced the dangers of their criminal enterprise. While many states do not have capital punishment, police in all states carry guns and are authorized to use deadly force.

Police officers frequently see themselves as targets. While officers have been accused of being paranoid, it is a fact that the police are the most visible arm of a government that some may see as oppressive or hostile. The police officer, not the system, is the barrier that stops some individuals from achieving unlawful ends. Seldom do prosecutors or judges become targets in the same ways police officers do. Prosecutors and judges are much less visible and are perceived as having more power than the police. After all, the prosecutor can plea bargain a case to almost nothing, and a judge can impose a meaningless sentence or even throw the case out of court. When police officers are threatened, they may well be told that such threats "come with the territory." But when a judge or an attorney is threatened, there is a call for more courtroom security, a heightened search for the perpetrator, and stiffer sentences when convicted. Such threats to judges or attorneys bring an official outrage, while threats to cops are just something to be expected.

Being a target means that the officer may be a target for abusive remarks, lawsuits, threats, and even bullets. It is easier for a gangster to work in a community where there is no respect for police officers. If you don't have the respect of your community, your effectiveness is seriously diminished. Therefore, criminals will do what they can to make you and the other officers ineffective, first through words spoken in the community such as personal character attacks and other slanderous comments. Second, criminals will try to tie your hands with a lawsuit so you become ineffective. Finally, criminals will attempt to render you ineffective through death. The means used to achieve these results are not so important as the end results themselves. The criminal wants you to be as ineffective as possible.

In his poem *IF*, Kipling advises not to deal in lies.[1] Yet it seems that lies are the lot of the police officer. You will be lied to almost every day during your career as a police officer. When the police officer asks that rhetorical question, "Do you know how fast you were going?" and the driver responds, "Why no, officer," it almost seems as though the lie is a formality. It is refreshing for police officers to stop someone and ask, "Do you know how fast you were going?" and to have the driver respond with something like, "At least 70." Suspects will often lie about where they were or what they were doing in an attempt to evade arrest and/or punishment for what they have done.

Officers are lied to and used by victims or "would-be" victims who have an ulterior motive for calling the police. For example, it is not uncommon for couples going through a divorce to play dirty and act vengeful toward each other. A soon-to-be-ex-wife may call the police to say her husband is beating her or is dealing drugs, even if he's not, in the hopes that his arrest can be used to her benefit in an upcoming custody battle. A citizen who tends to abuse the system and wants the police to get to her home quickly may lie to dispatch and say that there's a gun or a knife involved in the dispute. These situations are difficult for police because we need to respond quickly and as though the lies were truth until we can sort through them later. If a victim falsely claims he was robbed, we need to investigate the robbery until we can prove it was false. We cannot simply dismiss it out of hand.

Police officers are frequently caught in the middle of other people's lies, those "he said, she said" conflicts where both parties simply cannot be telling the truth. Police officers are also accused of lying, both overtly and covertly. In an internal affairs investigation where a suspect (complainant) accuses the officer of using excessive force and the officer denies it, the officer may be openly accused of lying. More subtle accusations are equally abundant. When testifying in a traffic trial, an officer may report that he saw the suspect fail to

---

[1] http://www.kipling.org.uk/poems_if.htm

stop for a stop sign, and the driver testifies that he stopped. If the judge finds the driver "Not guilty," the police officer may feel as though the court does not believe he is telling the truth. Or when being cross-examined in a courtroom and the defense attorney asks an officer to repeat, again and again in different ways, the truth she originally stated, it may feel to the officer as though she is being accused of lying.

Sometimes officers do lie in order to get a conviction, justifying it by saying that the defendant is also lying. Do not lie; the end cannot justify the means. Lying under oath won't make things better, and the risk is just too great. If you are caught perjuring yourself in court, your credibility will be destroyed and your career severely impacted.

And finally, sometimes police officers are expected to lie in the course of their duties. When an undercover vice or narcotics officer is asked by a suspect, "Are you a cop?" the officer will lie and say that he is not. These lies are simply a part of the assignment. Everybody working undercover lies from their name on down. Just make sure that you keep the lies a work tool that you can admit without any shame or guilt.

For most officers, being lied to becomes part of the job, but it can lead to cynicism and difficulty believing in anything or anyone, including the values you hold most dear and those people you love the most.

A FINAL WORD

A final word about self-perception and surviving the system: This is the career you have chosen. It has the potential to help you to feel good about what you do or the potential to destroy you. Many good men and women have been eaten alive by this system. They enter with enthusiasm and are eager to make a difference, but they leave at the end of their career angry, bitter, and cynical, and with a trail of divorces and emotional pain. Decide from the beginning how you are going to end this career and continually work toward that goal.

Chapter 4

SURVIVING MARRIAGE

Tim and Debbie were high-school sweethearts, together since their sophomore year. As soon as Tim completed his service in the U.S. Marine Corps (where he was decorated several times for bravery), they married. Tim decided he wanted to be a police officer. And although Debbie wasn't real excited about the idea, she agreed it would be all right if that's what Tim really wanted to do. So he went to school while she worked to support them. Between the money he got from the government for his education and the money she earned from her sewing business, they did all right. After graduating, Tim applied to several police departments and was hired by one. At this point both partners began to wonder how this new venture would affect their relationship. Very much in love and not wanting to let anything get in the way of their marriage, they worked to overcome the obstacles—odd shifts, part-time jobs, and temptations.

As Tim's career progressed, he saw a lot of things he wasn't able to understand or make sense of. When he got home after those shifts, he would talk to Debbie and reaffirm, just by spending time with her, that there was still love and goodness in the world. They took time together and worked to maintain a strong relationship. Meanwhile, Tim became active in police functions, associating with other cops in social settings. Through that, however, Tim and Debbie continued to spend time together. They traveled together, played softball together, and attended church together. In short, the law enforcement career did not get in the way of their marriage. Tim didn't tell Debbie all the gory details of the things he saw; she was just there to support him—and he let her. They were able to make their marriage last. Both were committed to the union and to each other. While they shared the law enforcement career, it was not more important than their marriage to either one of them. Their marriage was a success story, unlike the many police marriages that end in divorce. This chapter will identify pitfalls and offer suggestions on how to keep a marriage alive and well throughout a law enforcement career.

THE IMPORTANCE OF COMMUNICATION

Statistics for cops staying married are not good. Rough estimates are that 75% of police first marriages will fail and 85% of second marriages will fail. As officers get married more often, it seems that the chances of a successful long-term relationship diminish. After each failed relationship people tend to become less willing to risk an emotional commitment. Divorce seems easier each time.

However, police marriages can be wonderful and long-term. Each differs significantly, but one thing lasting marriages have in common is that the couple *communicates* with each other. Communication is so important that no marriage can survive without it. With no communication there can be no intimacy; and with no intimacy, no love; and with no love, no marriage. The relationship becomes symbiotic, two people living together like roommates if they have some trust in each other, or like enemies if they don't.

Yet, how often do you practice communication skills with your partner at home? If you are like most cops, not at all. You may simply assume that if you are married, you can communicate. But that's not how it works. Even in the best marriage, it takes work to communicate and to make the relationship grow and last. There are no shortcuts and no substitutions for solid communication.

Communication skills can be learned just like anything else and, like any other skill, must to be practiced to maintain proficiency. If you become a good pistol shot, you still need to practice to maintain that proficiency. It also takes *desire* to become a good pistol shot. Communication is no different. You must *want* to communicate. Too often we become disillusioned with the world and throw away a marriage that might have been saved if we had only worked on it. Many cops struggling through their second divorce have said, "I wish I had worked harder on my first marriage."

You need to pay attention to the relationship. Police officers often report they think their marriage might be in trouble. When I ask why, they might respond, "Because my wife (or husband) told me to leave." While tragic, it's not that uncommon. Police officers miss the common cues in all but crisis communication, unaware of problems until it is too late. One officer with over 20 years of marriage, going through his first divorce, said, "She told me I have become emotionally unavailable. I don't even know what that means."

Police couples need to determine *how* they can talk about police work. It isn't going away, and it will be a major part of both their lives. It is important for officers to know how much to tell a spouse. How much does their spouse want to know? How much is the officer comfortable sharing? It may be that the spouse doesn't want to know anything about police work, but does want to know how it is affecting the officer. The focus may be on the person he or she loves, not the blood, gore, pain, and disappointment the officer may have dealt with at work that day.

Sometimes this communication can be manipulative. An officer who says, "Be nice to me because I might die today" is being manipulative. The officer is using the inherent danger of the job to unfair advantage in the relationship and almost threatening the spouse—"If something happens to me tonight and I die, it will be your fault and you won't see me again." Such manipulation can destroy a marriage because it is dishonest. It hits an area the spouse has no control over yet may already fear. It doesn't deal with the issues, whatever they are, and cannot be productive in solving any problems. It only puts one person in control and the other in a subservient position. It is not intimacy; it is a power play.

When police officers experience emotional pain or are exposed to enough tragedy, they often are very careful not to "contaminate" loved ones. They mistakenly believe that if they hide their pain their loved ones will not know they are hurting and will not feel the hurt as well. So when their spouse asks, "What's the matter?" they respond with a resounding, "NOTHING." It doesn't take a rocket scientist to see that isn't true. The real translation is, "I don't want to talk about it." Or maybe, "I *can't* talk about it because that makes it more real and may affect those things I treasure most." But this may be when communication, not silence, is needed most, where closeness is more helpful than distance.

Cop-to-cop marriages can be even more difficult to maintain, and statistics indicate that 90% of marriages between two police officers end in divorce, a higher failure rate than that for marriages between an officer and someone who is not in law enforcement. While most officers believe that being married to another officer makes for an ideal relationship because "they have been there and they understand," this is only a partial blessing. Sure they have been there and they "understand," but they are also dealing with their own issues of the job and may face equally difficult challenges in talking about it. You may find that when one of you has a "bad day," the other has had one as well. Neither of you might be able to provide the support the other needs. Police officers are not noted for their ability to provide emotional support, just to get the job done. This can lead to more arguments than normal and an increased distancing because of this lack of support or perceived lack of support. So while the understanding of the job might be there, the ability to provide support in that world can be decidedly lacking. If you and your spouse are cops, you may have to work even harder to overcome the difficulties of a police marriage and make an extra effort to communicate with each other about important issues in the marriage.

PARENTING ISSUES

Parenting issues can get in the way of a marriage. Any marriage. Police officers tend to be somewhat conservative, and if the non-police parent is less conservative or downright liberal in their parenting style, conflict can evolve. There may be arguments over discipline, privileges, and just simple tolerance or intolerance of adolescent behavior. When the children are very young, the problems are fairly straightforward, such as how many toys to buy? Day care? Reasonable bedtime? However, as children become adolescents, a great difference in parenting styles may emerge. On duty, a cop deals with delinquent adolescents, smart mouths, and disrespectful attitudes, contacts that constantly reinforce in the officer's mind that "my kid won't grow up like that." It becomes increasingly difficult for the officer to separate factors at home from those at work, and in far too many cases, the officer ends up treating his kids like suspects, making them prove their innocence on a regular basis.

Cops can be very protective of their spouses and family members. Officers also know their community in-depth, as few others know it, and often choose to not share this knowledge with their family. And while they don't share this knowledge, they certainly let that knowledge affect their decisions about activities in the marriage and family life. Cops may not go certain places with their family, allow their spouses to do certain things, or allow their children to hang around in certain areas because of things they know. Yet this feels controlling and often arbitrary to the spouses or family members because it is not based on any understanding they have of their world. For example, an officer may tell their teenage child that they can't go shopping in a certain area because of the kids who hang out there, a decision the teen and the other parent may see as unreasonable because "all of his friends get to go there."

This protective attitude can also be seen when cops look at their daughters' boyfriends – in depth, from a very intimidating posture. It is probably true that most cops really are "ok" with their daughters' boyfriends being afraid of them. While the officer is very willing to protect in this way, they may be very unwilling to give their spouse and child enough of a glimpse into the reasons for their actions and attitudes, leaving the rest of the family to see the officer's decisions as "arbitrary." This creates a dynamic tension within the officer, who is torn between wanting to protect their child from the ugly and dangerous world they see and, at the same time, not letting the child know that the ugly and dangerous world even exists. Hence, it often seems to the child as though the officer parent is trying to protect them from an imaginary boogie man. The officer knows, however, that evil is far from imaginary and very dangerous.

Parenting your partner's children by a previous marriage—your stepchildren—can be very difficult. Many issues come into play. One key issue is the relationship with the biological parent who is not your partner. A child's struggles in a relationship with the noncustodial biological parent will impact the relationship you have with that child and your relationship with your spouse. There are often two sets of rules for the child, one set in each house, and they are likely to be very different. Often the noncustodial spouse is very permissive, without worry about the impact on the child's long-term behaviors. When the child comes home, the behaviors may not change to fit the different set of rules. The relationship your spouse has with their "ex" will impact your marriage. It has already created the "buttons" you need to avoid pushing and a foundation for the marital relationship. Furthermore, sharing the costs of raising children can cause additional conflict between spouses and ex-spouses, especially if communication is poor. A good rule of thumb here is to stay out of the relationship between your spouse and their ex if at all possible. Your role is to support your spouse, nothing else.

FINANCIAL ISSUES

Sometimes money becomes an issue in a police marriage. Police
officers frequently handle money problems by working extra jobs
such as security duty at weddings or stores, or directing traffic for
some event. This can become a deadly trap when it seems the answer
to any problem is more money. False assumptions might be, "If there
is more money, we need not communicate," or, "We won't have
these communication problems if I can only earn enough money."
     Because of the two (or more) jobs, the officer is absent a lot,
which contributes to marriage problems. Suddenly the couple finds
they are counting on the money the officer makes working part-time
jobs to support the lifestyle they have adopted. Now the need for
money has gotten in the way of communication because there is
either no time to talk or the officer has no energy left to talk. If the
off-duty work dries up, this places an additional burden on the
couple by forcing them to change their lifestyle or let go of things
they value. When this happens, fingers are pointed—one blames the
other for not working enough, and the other blames the one for
spending too much.
     Arguments about money may also be a way to avoid talking
about sensitive issues that are too hard to discuss directly—issues
such as respect, trust, love, vulnerability, and commitment. Cops
may have difficulty talking about feelings as they really are, so they
talk about them in terms of money, using phrases like, "I work all the
time so you can have all the things you want." The cop may not
realize that the "things" their partner really wants are love, respect,
trust, and an emotional involvement. Or maybe the cop does realize
it but those "things" are more than the cop is willing or able to give.

DIFFERING WORLD VIEWS

As the officer spouse works more and more, the couple has less and
less time together. Less time together means less time to
communicate and less time for intimacy. Each partner ends up
having their own interests, their own friends and separate activities.
Time together is important in any marriage, but is even more
important in police marriages. The worlds of officers and their
spouses may become very dissimilar, and they may each see the
world from very different perspectives. One may see the world as a

safe, nurturing, and beautiful place while the other sees it as a place of hurt, sadness, and loss. If the couple does not spend time together, these disparate world views can destroy the marriage. It takes time and effort to work through these differences and build a strong, positive relationship.

As world views come to differ more and more, mutual respect may be lost. Each sees the other as misdirected at best and as out of touch and untouchable at worst. With loss of respect come a loss of love and a loss of commitment to the relationship. Love without respect is not possible. Both partners stop working at the marriage because they see no pressing need to be in a relationship with someone they don't respect. This becomes a vicious cycle where loss of respect brings diminished effort to maintain the marriage, which brings an increased loss of respect, and so on (See Figure 1). When this happens, it is very difficult to make the marriage work. Neither party has enough invested in the relationship to devote the energy to save it. Typically both partners have already moved on emotionally and are living together only because of the pension, the house, or the children, or they have no time or energy to get a divorce.

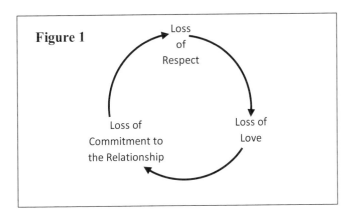

Figure 1

Loss
of
Respect

Loss of
Love

Loss of
Commitment to
the Relationship

When police officers work one shift and their spouses another, they may not see each other much from day to day. If they have only a few minutes each day, on a hit-or-miss basis, to talk to each other, what meaningful communication can really occur? There doesn't seem to be enough time, even if both partners are so inclined, to discuss serious marital issues. Lack of time is a ready excuse to avoid talking about subjects many police officers already dislike talking about, such as emotional issues. And since these are difficult to talk about anyway, any excuse to avoid these conversations is welcome. It may also be that the cop doesn't want to talk about what is bothering them, and the lack of time just provides another reason not to. Another concern couples have when time together is limited is to avoid arguing. So often, when there's only a few minutes available to spend together, neither party wants to start an argument, and so a lot of problems don't get talked about. If arguments are all there is in a marriage, it won't last anyway.

SHARED INTERESTS AND ACTIVITIES

The chasm between the officer and spouse that began with different ways of seeing the world is expanded by different ways of relating to and interacting with the world. One way that things change for police officers and their spouses is through a gradual loss of shared interests. As the police career takes more and more time in an officer's life, the marriage relationship risks distancing. Officers become more involved in the police world while the spouses stay involved in the civilian world. For example, new officers may be interested in crime rates, informants, and cop shows, and experienced officers become focused on pensions and retirement. Meanwhile, their spouses may become increasingly active in a church, school, or civic group, which the officers may see no purpose in or as a waste of time. Yet to the spouses, these activities are very meaningful and purposeful, a reflection of their own spirituality or place in the world—in fact, part of their identity.

A conflict in spirituality may also occur. Spouses may see the world as a good place to live and that, despite the presence of pain and suffering, there is also goodness and kindness. Officers, on the other hand, may see only pain and suffering, becoming hardened through daily, monthly, and yearly exposure to the worst sides of people. The balance that exists in the spouses' world, or even the opposite imbalance, may not be present in the police officers' world. Cops often get to a point where they no longer see a world of good and evil but simply a world with varying degrees of evil. Those who once believed in God (or a god) may feel abandoned, or flat-out deceived. Officers may easily become angry with God for allowing the pain and suffering they see daily to continue. The question they ask is, "If there really is a loving God, how can He let this stuff happen to those kids, old people, and the helpless?" These spiritual differences may lead to conflict between spouses about everything from where to go on an evening out to whether to have children. This difficulty in believing in God (or a god) can also cause the officer to lose contact with people who are not either victims or perpetrators, again, making the officer's world one of extremes where there are no classes of people other than predators and prey. These definitions become more than just terms used to define events in someone's life; they tend to define the people in the officer's world.

Even when officers and their spouses share an interest in something, it can be difficult to plan joint activities together if their work schedules conflict. Many law enforcement agencies work rotating shifts of one form or another. An officer may work a month of days, followed by a month of afternoons, with a month of midnight shifts after that. This pattern could repeat endlessly. Other rotations might be a month of 12-hour day shifts followed by a month of 12-hour night shifts. In addition to the time rotation, officers frequently rotate days off. So you might be off Monday, Tuesday, and Wednesday of one week; off Tuesday, Wednesday, and Thursday of the next week; and so on. Such rotating schedules make it difficult for officers to have consistent interaction with the civilian world. Consider this: For most organized activities, consistent participation is essential. How can you bowl in a league that bowls on Thursdays if you only have one-half or one-third of the Thursdays off? Or play softball for a team that has evening games when you're working from 4 p.m. to midnight?

SOCIAL LIFE AND OTHERS' EXPECTATIONS AND PERCEPTIONS

Police couples may face difficulties in their social lives. The hours, the job itself, and the fear people have of the police can cause problems. Many people don't want to socialize with police officers because they're concerned about what officers may know about them and what the officers may have shared with their own spouses. People may also be uncomfortable because officers do, in fact, know something about them they wish the officers didn't. For example, if an officer has been sent to their house to handle a domestic argument or is aware that one partner is having an affair, it may be difficult for the couples to socialize. If the officer has arrested someone, it may interfere with their ability to socialize together.

One officer discovered a couple, naked in a car in the park one night. The officer knew the man, he knew the woman, and he knew the man's wife as well as the woman's husband. The officer and his wife had socialized with both couples. A few weeks after the car-in-the-park incident, the officer and his wife were at a party and one of the couples came in, saw that the officer was there, and left about 15 minutes later. When the officer's wife commented that the couple had left rather quickly and wondered aloud why, the officer shrugged it off with, "I don't know." But he knew. They left because he made one-half of that couple uncomfortable by his presence. This officer didn't tell his wife about the incident in the park because both of the women involved (the woman in the car and the man's wife) were friends of the officer's wife, and the officer didn't want to put her in a position where she needed to decide whether or not to tell the one friend that her husband was having an affair with the other friend.

Social activities with non-police couples also drop off because officers may not be "allowed" to get away from their job by others. When they walk into a social gathering and hear comments about cops being there—"Shhh, the cops are here," or the conversation that starts out with, "So, you're a cop…," or complaints about traffic tickets other officers may have issued, or the way another officer treated someone—it gets to the point where officers no longer find the social relationships worthwhile. The benefits from the social activities do not exceed the conflict generated because even in social settings, while off-duty, officers still frequently find themselves in an adversarial relationship with some idiot who doesn't understand what "off-duty" means. This means that police couples are often forced to socialize with each other. The work schedules may fit, the interests may be the same, and the job doesn't get in the way. But, this also means that the officers don't get away from work, and their spouses are still on the outside—perhaps jealous of the energy the officers devote to the department and the community.

Another way police careers get in the way of a marriage is that others expect you to always be a police officer, 24/7. One officer reports that, once, when he was enjoying a day off, simply trying to be a husband and father, a neighbor called and asked if he would come over to her house and discipline her children because "that was his job." Imagine being the "neighborhood disciplinarian." Take it one step further and imagine being married to the "neighborhood disciplinarian," or being the child of the "neighborhood disciplinarian." This creates additional distance between police couples and neighbors, as well as distance within the family.

RUMORS AND GOSSIP

Rumors and gossip have ruined a number of police marriages. Police officers are notorious gossips. No one is better at gossiping, and no one is a better target for gossip, than other officers. Couples need a strong enough relationship to be able to ask their partners when they hear something that bothers them, or to know their partners well enough to not believe it. Allowing such rumors to undermine the trust between partners may lead officers to shun intimate relationships altogether. When a spouse hears rumors about an officer having an affair and she feels distance in her marriage, she may begin to wonder if her husband *is* having an affair. There are certainly lots of temptations out there for police officers. If you're a married cop and considering an affair, DON'T. It can destroy your marriage, and affairs *always* end badly.

FEAR OR LACK OF INTIMACY

Often police officers give up looking for any true meaning or value in relationships. Afraid of intimacy, they substitute sex, cars, alcohol, or work. In the words of one police officer, "I'm always looking for a brief, meaningless relationship." But fear of intimacy is often accompanied by the pain of loneliness. True intimacy can be described as a combination of trust and vulnerability. It means letting someone get so close to you that they can hurt you worse than anyone else in the world, and then trusting them not to. Police officers are not good at intimacy. Officers spend 8 or 10 or even 12 hours each day actively working to distrust those they come into contact with in order to stay safe, protecting themselves on-duty by minimizing their vulnerability. But it's a big leap from actively distrusting and being as invulnerable as possible on-duty to actively being vulnerable and trusting off-duty. There is no on/off switch for this safety mechanism.

John Wayne, Clint Eastwood, and others have made great television and movie heroes, but in their roles they didn't make much of a husband. In most of their movies, they are either an estranged husband or gone a lot. There isn't a lot of intimacy modeled by their characters. In fact, in some movies we find they are off "catching bad guys" when their family needs them. The officer may be a neighborhood hero but "idols are best when they're made of stone and saviors a nuisance to live with at home."[1] A marriage to a stereotypical "cop" is difficult if not impossible. There needs to be a real human being underneath the badge.

ALCOHOL USE

In response to frequent exposure to trauma, police officers may use alcohol as a self-prescribed relaxant or even a medication to control the impact of their job. If officers use alcohol as a medication to control the impact of their job, the marriage and family relationships often become secondary. If family seems to threaten the officer's alcohol use, the marriage may be the first to go. It is important for officers to find a way to respond appropriately to trauma and find outlets to talk about feelings within the relationship. This can strengthen a marriage. Officers and spouses can become resources to each other, but only if they are willing to take risks. Officers must risk trusting someone and reaching out with pain instead of turning it inward with alcohol, and spouses must risk being pushed away. Such communication might bring the problems to a head, but they were there anyway and won't go away by themselves. Such problems are like an elephant in the middle of the room that everyone sees but no one is talking about. It's better to take the risk of talking about things than to pretend they are not there and just let them get worse and worse. Unspoken problems rarely solve themselves.

---

[1] *Winds of the Old Days*. Words and music by Joan Baez.

SUPPORT AND RESOURCES

Many times police and spouses feel ignored by police departments, even though there are quite a few programs available to help officers deal with trauma. Many states have regional or local Critical Incident Stress Management (CISM) teams to conduct debriefings for officers after trauma. Yet, trauma affects the entire family as often as it affects the officers. Spouses need programs to help them understand what has happened, what it means to their lives and to that of the officer, and how, as a couple, they can move beyond the incident.

It is also important that police officers and spouses learn to support each other during troubling times. If the officer or spouse has had a tough day, each needs to know how to meet the other's emotional needs. Sometimes the officer or spouse will really need to talk or to vent. In this case it is essential for the other one to be there and to actively listen to what their spouse is saying. Other times, the officer may simply need some quiet time to get their head straight and to reconnect with the really important things in their lives. This can amount to nothing more than a few minutes to shift from "cop" thinking to "husband" or "dad" thinking.

Couples can only meet each other's needs when they understand those needs. No one is a mind reader in a marriage. Couples need to discuss their needs and the ways the other person can meet those needs when not in crisis. When you're up to your elbows in alligators, it's hard to remember you set out to drain the swamp. During a crisis is no time to develop a crisis response plan. Couples need to learn to talk about troubles *before* they become disasters.

In its infinite wisdom, Congress has deprived law enforcement spouses of resources available to most other couples. They have passed a gun control law, the Lautenberg Amendment to the Omnibus Consolidated Appropriations Act of 1997, which effectively ends the career of any police officer convicted of a misdemeanor domestic assault. The provisions of this law do not impose such penalties for felonious assault convictions, nor are they limited to current assaults. According to this amendment, even officers convicted years ago can lose their ability to carry a firearm. Although certainly not condoning these assaults, take a look at what the law does. Any person convicted of a domestic assault cannot own a firearm, which essentially means they cannot be a police officer. So, if a domestic assault occurs in a police family, the spouse calls for help, and the officer is arrested and convicted, the family has lost the police portion of their income. This legislation does not cure the problem of domestic violence in police families; it simply makes reporting the assault more punitive.

If a police spouse calls for a squad because of a violent argument, how safe is that? She may well be calling the officer's friends to discuss the problems in their marriage, which is an embarrassing situation for all involved and may make matters worse instead of better. If there is real physical danger, the police need to be involved, but be sure to consider the long-term impact before calling, and don't call on a whim.

It is unrealistic to expect police couples not to fight. Therefore, it is essential that the officer and spouse communicate and identify resources to help them through tough times. Since police spouses have fewer resources, it is imperative that those be used well.

RESOURCES FOR POLICE SPOUSES

Traditionally many police organizations had "police wives groups," or a "law enforcement auxiliary," organizations designed to support the officer in his law enforcement career. Remember that women's entry into law enforcement has been fairly recent by historical standards. It was only in the late 1960s and early 1970s that women began to assume uniformed patrol duties. Prior to that, departments may have had "police women" on staff, but their roles were often limited to working in the Juvenile Unit or perhaps in a Sex Crimes Unit. They were not considered "real" police officers who patrolled beats and investigated crimes as equal partners with male cops. Frequently women had different requirements to be hired and were paid on a different scale than uniformed male officers. So there was no need for a "police husbands" group because there were very few, if any, "police husbands."

Frequently officers did not want their wives to participate in the official police wives organization because it was seen as little more than a place for women to gossip. Whether true or not, that was often the perception of the male officers, and they discouraged their wives from participating. There was also the risk of wives interacting with ex-wives at these functions.

More recently support groups such as *Wives behind the Badge*[2], *PoliceWives*[3], and the *Law Enforcement Family Support Network (LEFSN)*[4] have been created, organizations that provide a more comprehensive range of support services than the stand-alone departmental police wives groups. There are still relatively few support groups for male spouses of police officers, not because of need but because of numbers—the male police spouse population is significantly smaller than the female police spouse population simply because the number of female officers is significantly less than the number of male officers. Additionally, husbands seem more reluctant than wives to join a support organization.

GUIDELINES FOR COMMUNICATING THOUGHTS AND FEELINGS

It is often difficult for police couples to talk about feelings. Officers may have such intense feelings that they are afraid to let them out. Some have said they are afraid that if they start to cry, they may never be able to stop. It is also important to officers that they appear strong for their partners. This is perhaps more true for male officers because of the combined, stereotyped "protective" roles of *male* and *police officer*. For whatever reason, it can be particularly difficult for male officers to be seen as vulnerable by their spouses. The myth of the "always strong, never in doubt" police officer is self-perpetuating; once it starts, both partners buy into it. The officer needs to be strong, and the spouse needs the officer to be strong.

There are special considerations for women cops and marriage. The stereotypical police officer is very unfeminine. It may become difficult for women officers to find a relationship based on who they are. As one officer said,

> Oh, I would go to a dinner or something, where there were couples, and the women would all go in the kitchen to talk about babies and new curtains for their kitchens, and they sure as hell didn't want me there. But the guys didn't want

---

[2] www.wivesbehindthebadge.org
[3] www.policewives.org
[4] www.lawenforcementfamilysupport.org

me either, 'cause they were going to sit in the living room
and talk about football. So I didn't fit in anywhere, and I
spent a lot of time at dinner parties roaming around. It was
really wild. I really didn't fit any place.

When I was single, talk about hard-to-get dates. My
God, who wants to date a cop, a woman cop, except another
cop? I did not want to date other cops, but it was very
difficult. I went out with a few non-police officers, and it
seemed like they either had an intensely morbid interest in
what I did—"How many people have you shot?" "Are you
carrying your gun now?"—things like that, or they wanted to
negate the value of my profession because they found it
threatening, and so it was, "So what, you're a cop." "Can we
talk about something else?" And there was no balance there.
I couldn't find someone who could deal with the middle
ground, which is that I have an interesting profession, it's
fun to talk about, but that's not all I am.

A majority of communication about feelings is nonverbal;
feelings are best communicated in every way *except* words, which
are the domain of the legal system and "logical" communication.
Nonverbal communication includes the speed of the communication,
tone of voice, posture, facial expressions, gestures, and even time set
aside for communication. Think of the ways you can show love for
your partner. How about holding hands, or just sitting quietly
together? Both of these contribute to the feeling of being loved or
"cared about," feelings so essential to a strong, healthy marriage.

It's unrealistic to think couples will always agree about
everything. This may be even more true for police officers and their
spouses. It is essential that police couples know how to fight fairly.
Establish some "fight rules," and stick to them. Some examples are:

- Stick to the issue; don't make the argument about personalities.
- Don't involve others by asking them to take sides.
- Fight fairly—don't focus on sensitive areas.
- Make sure the issue is worth the argument.
- Allow the other person to process the issues in their own way.
- Try to see your partner's point of view.
- Finish the fight as soon as possible. Try to settle things before
  they reach crisis proportions.
- Don't shout; speak to each other respectfully.

- Listen to your partner—make sure you understand the issue.
- Be understanding of how the other person processes these difficulties.

CHANGE

As any marriage matures, changes occur. It's important to continuously look at how you show your love for each other. Ask yourself, "How does my partner know I love her?" If your answer is something like, "I'm still here, aren't I?" then you need to examine the messages you are sending your partner. This certainly isn't a message of love.

Steps To Keep a Marriage Lively

- Make sure you have time to talk, every day if possible.

- When you talk to each other, be honest but not hurtful. Try to be constructive even in your complaints.

- Communicate your feelings through touch or other nonverbal means whenever possible.

- Treat your partner with respect no matter what you are feeling at the moment.

- Don't go to bed with hard feelings. Work things out the same day you have problems.

- Fight according to the rules and stick to the issue, not personalities or shortcomings.

- Remember that you love each other—no matter what.

Chapter 5

SURVIVING A DIVORCE

So Chapter 4 didn't help. Go back and read it again before moving on. A lot of cops, in the midst of their second divorce, have told me, "I wish I had worked harder on my first marriage." But if you have given it your best shot and it still didn't work, you must move forward. This *will be* a difficult time. If it's not difficult, you didn't put enough into the marriage and perhaps shouldn't have gotten married to begin with. The more connected you were, the more this will hurt.

So, the marriage didn't work, and it can't be fixed. Well, now what? It's not the end of the world; life goes on. The only question is, "What kind of life do you want?" Do you want to get bitter, old before your time, even suicidal? If not, how you deal with the divorce is even more important than how you dealt with the marriage. What did you learn so you don't make the same mistake(s) again? Cops frequently don't learn from their mistakes and end up going through a series of marriages and divorces. Some cops get married and divorced as often as 5 or 6 times, or more.

Kevin met Mary, and she was the woman of his dreams. He was working as a cop. She was a waitress with a good figure and a wonderful smile, and she thought he looked good in uniform. They dated a few months and decided to get married. Shortly after they were married, they got pregnant and decided Mary would stay home with the baby. As she did, their income dropped, but their spending didn't. Kevin started to work more and more hours at part-time jobs to make up for the lost income. When he got home he was tired and just wanted to rest; he had no energy left for anything else. Meanwhile, Mary had been home with the baby all day and wanted to go out and have a good time. They began to argue—he needed downtime at home, she needed to get out of the house. They couldn't find a way for both of them to get what they wanted. Eventually, after many nights of fighting, Mary began going out anyway with her girlfriends, leaving her exhausted husband to care for their small child. Kevin and Mary spent less and less time together until, finally, they realized they had nothing in common except the baby, wondered why they had ever gotten married, and decided to separate. They had become roommates with a child, nothing more. Now comes the important part: how each survives the divorce and maintains a positive relationship with their child.

BREAKING THE NEWS

So who gets to tell the kids? This unpleasant task often falls to the parent who is moving out of the house. The best way to break this news to the kids is to be honest and take their feelings into account. They probably love both of you and don't want to hurt either of you, or to see either of you hurt each other. They are likely to be upset by this development, and you can either help them through it or you can make it worse, depending on how you tell them. Remember that you are the adult (even if your children are adults) and the parent here. If the children are pre-adolescent, they may still lack the cognitive ability to understand abstract thought, meaning they won't understand the concepts of love, anger, hurt, or sadness from a cognitive perspective. Certainly, they can *feel* these emotions, but there is a disconnect from an intellectual standpoint. Therefore, don't get them enmeshed in the abstract of what happened; they won't understand. Keep it simple for the younger children. If the children are teenagers, they may want to hear all of the abstract issues in as much detail as possible. However, only answer their questions. Don't volunteer too much information by telling them things they are not asking about. Also, make sure you are not using them to help you through this divorce. You need to help them, not the other way around. Remember, whatever you say about the other parent, you may be saying to the child about the child. Half of who they are came from that other person.

How are you going to tell your friends that you are going to get a divorce? These may be "your friends," your "spouse's friends," or even "couple friends." It's not a good idea to just start bashing your soon-to-be ex. Instead, begin by simply telling them that things are not working out between the two of you. Don't give them blow-by-blow descriptions of your disagreements. Keep it simple and leave them out of it.

Telling your family is no different. Be very cautious in what you tell your family. Many cops have told their families horrible things about their soon-to-be ex spouses only to find that they have resolved their differences with their partner and want to move forward rebuilding the marriage. But there are now major issues with each other's families because of what was revealed before the reconciliation, and the families now use that information to define that relationship. Don't bad-mouth your soon-to-be ex to make yourself look better in the separation or the divorce because it may very well come back to haunt you later. When you throw mud, you are going to get yourself dirty as well.

UNDERSTANDING AND DEALING WITH YOUR REACTIONS

Before you can really begin to move forward you need to deal with all the new thoughts and feelings going through your mind. They may be overwhelming. You might feel fear, anger, love, sadness, confusion, and frustration all at the same time. You might think you can't move forward and that you have nothing left. Why not? Your entire world has changed. This is even truer if the divorce ends a long-term marriage because you are likely to have connected with your spouse in so many more little ways that you didn't even realize. Now those connections are gone. So, accept that whatever you are feeling is appropriate. Feelings are always appropriate even though some behaviors may not be.

Accept the feelings and control your behaviors. It may not be pleasant, and it may not be what you want to feel, but you need to go through the emotional gauntlet and work through these feelings to move on with your life. Don't just leap into another marriage or a series of short-term affairs to fill the void that comes with being "suddenly single." Realize you are going through something difficult and take time to heal before moving into another relationship. Talk about these feelings, but don't just indiscriminately dump them on whoever will listen. Find someone you can trust, and be honest with them. Don't lie and say, "Everything's fine," when you are still crying every night or are so angry that you've broken almost every breakable thing in your house. Be honest with that friend and, even more important, be honest with yourself. Denying the hurt and anger doesn't change the reality that they are happening, nor does it make these feelings go away. Denial only presses them deeper inside and makes it more difficult for you to really heal.

If you find that you are really in an emotional rut about this and cannot seem to move forward, seek professional help. There are a number of good counselors who can help you move forward. Don't just look in the yellow pages for "marriage counseling." Get recommendations from one or more of your coworkers who have sought counseling and found a therapist who was helpful. Then, realizing that "one size does not fit all," make an appointment to meet with this person, see if your personalities mesh, and determine if this is someone you can talk to. If it's not a good fit, move on to another one. Not every counselor is appropriate for every person. If you don't feel comfortable with a counselor, it is not likely you will trust them enough to get the help you want and are paying for.

FIGURING OUT WHAT WENT WRONG

It is important to look honestly at why this marriage didn't work. Chances are, both of you share the blame for this divorce. Seldom is only one person at fault. Realize that you both made mistakes, you both gave up, you both didn't work at the relationship enough. If you were truly wronged and were not to blame in any way, be glad it has ended. It probably would not have gotten any better. Most likely, however, as you look back on what happened, you'll realize this was a gradual process. The marriage didn't end overnight.

Some of the questions you need to ask yourself pertain to your behavior, attitudes, and priorities. Did you work too much? Was there too little time together? Did you put too little emotional energy into the marriage? Did you stop working to communicate as a couple? You not only need to ask yourself these difficult questions, but you need to answer them honestly.

If you were married to another cop, did you come into the union with false expectations about communication and understanding? As discussed in the Marriage chapter, many officers mistakenly believe that being married to another officer makes things easier because you both understand the stresses of the job and believe that these shared experiences will make communicating with your spouse that much simpler. The reality is, cops often struggle with communicating their feelings to anyone and are not always the most forthcoming with emotional support. Thus, two cops who go into a marriage assuming that just because they have the same job means they won't have to work as hard at communicating or supporting each other emotionally are setting themselves up for failure.

As much as you may want to, you can't put all the blame on your partner; it's usually a combination of things that causes a divorce. No matter how long you repress the feelings or lie to yourself about what they mean, they won't change or go away. They will ferment like a sour wine and, at some point, explode, destroying everything and everyone around them. They may destroy you and those you love most, including your children.

It's not uncommon for police officers to come for counseling and report that their marriage is in trouble. When I ask them, "Why do you think that?" they will often reply with something like, "Because my wife told me to leave." The reality is that this marriage has been ending for months on an emotional level but is only now reaching the point where a physical change has to occur, where "something has to give," or, in cases like this, someone has to go.

Perhaps one of you had an affair and that's what ended the marriage. However, neither of you got to the point where you had the affair overnight. The emotional distancing has begun long before the physical affair. I've counseled hundreds of couples and have never seen anyone who is in a happy marriage have an affair. While you might still have been living together, the emotional side of the marriage ended before the affair began.

GETTING LEGAL COUNSEL

At some point you need to select an attorney. Rarely can a divorcing couple use the same attorney. If you and your soon-to-be ex's interests are incompatible, as is often the case in a divorce, it is impossible for one lawyer to represent both of your interests fairly. So, select your own attorney.

As you begin the search, know that there are a number of different places to look. Don't just go to the yellow pages and look up "attorney, divorce," close your eyes, and pick one. If you have friends who are divorced, ask them how satisfied they were with their attorneys. That's a starting place. Look at what you want your attorney to do. If you want this attorney to take every nickel he can from your ex, you will select one type of attorney. If you want someone to protect your interests and work toward an equitable settlement, you may select another. Look for an attorney who isn't trying to send four of his own kids through college on the money he makes by handling your divorce. Find an attorney who listens to what you want and will offer sound legal advice. Don't hire an attorney who "tells" you how things are going to be. Remember through all this, you are the consumer and are paying for the lawyer's services. To paraphrase a line you hear frequently, "You pay his or her salary."

FINDING A "FAIR" WAY TO SPLIT . . . EVERYTHING

As you go through the court system, remember that it is seldom fair. Cops learn that early in their careers. But when we go through a divorce, we *expect* fairness. We get angry when we think we're not being treated fairly. Yet we can't even agree on what fairness is. Each person thinks the other one has all of the advantages. You think you may be paying too much; your ex thinks you're paying too little. You don't think you see the kids enough; your ex thinks you see them far too often. You don't like the way your ex is parenting; she believes you're not a good influence on the children. You want to sell the house; your ex wants to stay there. Nothing seems fair.

So . . . . Do you fight it out in court, hurting this person you once loved (and still may) more than you ever thought possible, or do you try to settle out of court? What's really best for you? How much of your desire to go to court or "show her" is revenge? And if there are children involved, will your actions hurt them too? How are you watching out for their interests in all of this?

Can you keep the children out of the middle? They are both of yours and probably love you both dearly. Don't force them to choose between you and your ex or you will all lose. They lose a parent; you lose your children. Also, don't use the kids to keep you up to date on your ex's activities. As long as the relationship between you is over, each person has every right to develop new relationships. When you ask your children to spy for you, it puts them in an awkward position because it carries with it the assumption that your ex is doing something wrong and casts doubt on their parenting skills. Is this what you really want? To generate insecurities in your children?

Children will often take responsibility for their mom and dad not getting along and blame themselves for their parents' divorce. This gives them an "illusion of control," believing that if they were to blame for some of this, they can prevent it from ever happening again by acting differently. Yet, the children are rarely to blame, and it is very destructive to let them feel they are in any way at fault for the breakup. Parents may use children as *tools* to get at the other parent, yet it is vital to work through the divorce with your children without blaming your spouse. When you blame your ex, the only one who really suffers is the children. They need to continue a relationship with your ex. Your marriage might be over, but you will still have a relationship with your children, and you will have a relationship with your ex through them for a long time.

Property and Pensions

When you start to divide community property, make it as fair as you can. Don't take things just to spite your ex. If you know the ex really wants a piece of furniture and, while you would like it, it really isn't that important to you, let the ex have it. It will mean more to them than it does to you, and perhaps they will return the favor.

Financial settlements can be difficult. Don't be short-sighted in all of this. If there is any way for you to salvage your pension, do it. You might be in your 30's now, with more career years ahead of you than behind you, but retirement will get here faster than you realize, and then what? If you have split your pension, you may find that you don't have enough left to retire on. This can leave officers who have put in a full career angry and bitter, going to work every day only because they can't afford to retire. In their bitterness, some officers delay retirement because they refuse to give any money to their ex-spouse. While this does neither of them any good, there is so much anger that it clouds the officer's judgment. Keeping your pension may mean that you have to sacrifice all of the joint equity in the home or all of your deferred compensation. But in the long run it is generally worth it. Don't hesitate to put yourself in difficult or uncomfortable times right now if it will save your retirement.

A final caution about picking up extra work: Cops sometimes try to hide the pain of the initial separation by getting immersed in part-

time work. While this helps avoid the hurt by keeping you too busy
or too tired to think about the split, it also kicks your income out of
sight. This is the figure used in calculating settlements from the
divorce. You may end up working these jobs forever just to make
child support or spousal maintenance payments because your
"police" salary isn't enough. Don't get sucked into that trap. Work to
make it on your police salary alone, at least until after the final
divorce settlement. Don't work the "cash" jobs. If the divorce isn't
going smoothly, your ex can cause a lot of headaches by reporting
you to the IRS. In all likelihood, they will come after you, adding
complications you don't need to an already complicated life.

Child Support and Child Care

You will probably end up paying some child support and perhaps
spousal maintenance as well. This amount will either be agreed on
by the two of you through your attorneys or determined by a judge as
part of the divorce settlement. Child support is often much more than
you thought it would be and may well leave you with little or no
money to begin a new life. This is not going to last forever. It will
depend on the children's ages when you divorced and your income in
relation to your ex's income. Typically a formula is set by the courts
for child support, depending on the above figures and the number of
children. Talk with your attorney before you get to court and try to
reach a settlement. If the court sets the child support amount, you can
do nothing about it except appeal and pay. Don't let it take an
emotional toll as well as a financial toll. The more anger you let this
generate, the greater your monthly payment really is.

These financial decisions are not the most significant area of
"child support." How you continue to love your children, show them
you love them, and provide the emotional support that can come only
from a parent will be essential to their growth, development, and
future relationships. Make sure that, no matter what the financial
arrangements are, you continue to provide the necessary emotional
support for your children. Find ways to stay actively involved in
their lives. Coach their sports teams; go to their choir concerts; spend
time *doing* things with them.

Another complication if you are both cops is that you may find
yourselves looking for "nightcare" (instead of daycare) providers

between the hours of 11 p.m. and 8 a.m. Such child care providers are difficult to find and expensive. Now complicate this situation further by throwing in rotating days off and you may need these child care providers on weekends and holidays. Good luck trying to find such a provider between 11 p.m. on Christmas Eve and 8 a.m. Christmas morning.

Custody and Visitation

Figuring out who should be the custodial parent is always an issue. Let's face it. Some people are born to be parents; some are not. Of the many considerations, most important is who can be the best parent for the children *at this time.* A number of circumstances affect this, including personality. You, or your ex, may not have the patience to deal with young children, the capacity to work with adolescents, or the ability to make an emotional connection with teenage daughters or sons. You may not be best at providing consistency in the parent-child relationship, and you may not have the time to be a full-time parent.

You need to ask yourself why you want custody. Be honest here. If you are looking for custody just to make things difficult for your ex, you are seeking custody for the wrong reasons. If you are trying to get custody because you want to minimize your child support, you are seeking custody for the wrong reasons. If you want custody for any reason other than because it's what is best for your children, you are seeking custody for the wrong reasons. The only "right" reason is the welfare of your children.

Some courts will take the child's wishes into consideration when making a custody determination, especially if the child is a teenager. Let the child decide without pressuring them or making them feel that by choosing one parent to have custody means that he or she is choosing not to have the other one as a parent. This should not be an either/or decision for the child, and making it into one is a losing proposition for both you and your child. Much of the time kids want to spend time with both parents. They may choose one parent as the custodial parent because of issues having to do with friends, schools, or even sports. Their decision may have nothing at all to do with you.

If you are going in to see a mental health professional for a custody evaluation, don't take it to mean you're crazy or a "bad" parent. It's simply one tool the courts use in determining custody for your children. This doesn't need to be scary, and you don't need to be defensive. What you do need to do is go in as assigned, ask the evaluator what will be involved in the assessment, and ask when the results will be completed and who will get them. Be open and honest and relate as well as you can to your children, because the purpose of this evaluation is to determine what is best for them. It will not help you get custody by saying a lot of negative things about your ex. The evaluator is looking at how *you* relate to your children, not how you think your ex relates to them. Be upbeat and positive, if possible. Sometimes one parent will lie about the other in hopes of looking better themselves. Don't get sucked into either lying about your ex or responding to their lies about you. Simply tell the truth in as positive a manner as possible. And remember, if you alienate the evaluator, it is likely to have an adverse impact on the outcome of the evaluation.

Visitation is always a problem. You may love your kids dearly, but to make visitation work, you need to make time on someone else's schedule. Frequently visitation schedules will be dictated either by a court or your relationship with your ex. If you do not have custody, you may need to make yourself available at difficult or inconvenient times. It takes effort to be a parent, but remember it is important to your children to have a relationship with the non-custodial parent, and it is important to you to have a relationship with your children. You can add things to their lives that no one else can.

If you are the custodial parent, make sure you provide ample opportunities for the children to visit their non-custodial parent. It will make your life easier and the children happier. It may be an inconvenience because it will seem as though every time you have something planned, the other parent wants visitation. Work to establish and maintain a regular visitation schedule, even if it is difficult and you feel you are scheduling your life around that of your ex. Make sure you provide this most important type of "child support" and an opportunity for your ex to provide it as well.

Visitation can be complicated by shift work. If either the custodial or noncustodial parent works afternoons, nights, or rotating shifts, a straight visitation schedule is often impractical because of changing work hours or changing days off. It might be that one week you are off on Tuesday, Wednesday, and Thursday and the next week you are off on Thursday, Friday, and Saturday. If you have a locked-in visitation schedule for every other weekend, it won't work.

Holidays and Special Occasions

Holidays may pose a special problem. If you were a "family," you will see your children only some of the holidays. If you went to your in-laws for all the holidays, where will you go now? Can you still go there and be with your ex? That's a question you need to work through and answer. Typically the children will go with one parent for one holiday and with the other for the next. On multiple holidays like Christmas Eve and Christmas, the children are likely to spend one day with each parent unless special arrangements are made. That certainly rules out any holiday trips with the children unless you have a positive working relationship with your ex, again emphasizing the importance of an amiable divorce.

As your kids get older, if you and your ex remain on hostile terms, the divorce may continue to make holidays and special events difficult. Don't force the kids to choose which parent they invite to special events like graduation parties, weddings, and even the baptism of your grandchildren.

SOCIAL ADJUSTMENTS

You may find your social relationships are abruptly and dramatically changed. You may have built most of your social relationships with other couples. So, now you aren't half of a couple and may feel like a fifth wheel when couples get together to socialize. You may find that your "friends" are less likely to want to socialize because they don't want you spending a lot of time with their spouses. This is going to be even more true if their marriage is shaky.

It may be necessary to develop new social relationships, new patterns of relationships, and find new places to develop these friendships. This may be exceptionally difficult if you have been married for a long time. If you have been married only a short time, you may still have friends you socialized with before you were married and it will be much easier. However, you will still find that even those relationships will have changed.

If your relationship was a same-sex relationship, the difficulties can be even more significant because the outside social support network is likely to be smaller and more of a closed group. It may mean that you cannot keep the end of your relationship from interfering with a large number of your social relationships. It will be essential for you to focus your energy on a few close friends and trust them to help you through this difficult situation. You may find that the best sources of support are some of the people you work with even though they may not be involved in same-sex relationships.

WORK ADJUSTMENTS (FOR COPS MARRIED TO COPS)

If you weren't married to a cop, it is most likely your fellow officers will take your side and simply write off your ex. But when cops are married to cops, there is a tendency to take the divorce or separation issues to work, which often makes other officers in the department feel as though they have to choose sides. This gets in the way of responding to calls, working in a collegial atmosphere, and just getting the job done. If they don't feel as though they need to choose sides, often other officers will simply distance from both of you, not wanting to get in the middle of your domestic squabbles. When this happens, both of you lose the social support you might find helpful in getting through this in as healthy a manner as possible.

ESTABLISHING NEW RELATIONSHIPS

Suddenly single can be terrifying. Your whole world has been turned upside down, and nothing will be the same. Don't try to restructure it in a day. It wasn't built that way to begin with, and you can't rebuild it that way now. Take your time. Hopefully you are building for the rest of your life—go slowly.

As you are working at finding a home, adjusting to living alone, making sure you visit your kids or allowing your ex time to visit them, and getting your financial situation stabilized, you will have enough on your plate. You don't need the complications of trying to build another long-term committed relationship. Relationships, especially new relationships, take energy. If you have all of these other things going on in your life, you may not have the energy necessary to devote to a new relationship. If you're already in a relationship, ***go slowly***. Don't scrap everything in your life because you've been divorced, but don't act manic in trying to fill it up again. Take time to re-establish a stable sense of who you are and how you will relate to your ex, your children, your family, and your friends.

Friends or acquaintances from work may try to "fix you up" with someone they know who is single. Remember, there is a reason this person is single. While a new relationship may seem rewarding, convenient, or financially necessary, don't rush in until you know what you want in a relationship and can determine whether it is possible to get it in this relationship. If you want someone to be at home with and the other person is looking for someone to go out and party with, the relationship is not likely to last. Both parties need to be looking for the same or similar things from the relationship.

MOVING ON

General agreement is that it takes two years to really get over a divorce. Even though you may have known on an intellectual level that it was coming, accepting the reality of the situation on an emotional level takes some time to get through. And while everyone heals in their own way and there is no specific time table for working through the stages of loss, two years is a general rule of thumb.

After you have finally accepted that this divorce has happened to you and that no reconciliation is possible, you begin to move forward. You might start by looking at a dating service like "It's Just Lunch," where you can meet someone for a midday meal and if the relationship continues, great; if not, it was just lunch. You might try an internet dating service such as EHarmony or Match.com, in which you submit a profile of yourself and what you're looking for in a partner and a computer program generates possible matches. If you truly want this kind of service to work, be honest in your profile and realize that not everyone else will be as honest as you were. Don't be afraid to meet people, but if it doesn't seem to be working, end the relationship. It's better to be honest from the beginning and to acknowledge it won't work, end it as gently as you can, and move on. Hurt feelings at this point heal much more quickly than if you wait and let the relationship go on for a while before ending it. If you find the relationship going well, remember to go slowly. Keep in mind that many "rebound" marriages fail after a few months.

When all is said and done, the impact of your divorce will be measured by how well you move forward from it. Can you say, without anger or bitterness, "I'm ok with what I did"? It is helpful if you've been able to establish a constructive parenting relationship with your ex, where you both work to ensure that the other parent gets the opportunity to have a positive impact on the children's life. And finally, you need to ask yourself if you can look forward to happiness and fulfillment in your life. You might get married again, or you might not. What's important is that you can be satisfied with whatever path you choose and that you have things to look forward to—new friends, new hobbies, and perhaps a new relationship.

Chapter 6

SURVIVING LIFE IN A POLICE FAMILY

What's "normal"? I think everyone asks themselves that at some point. When we live in a police family there are lots of things we simply take for granted as "normal" or wonder, "Isn't this the way it works for everyone?" But it's not. This chapter, perhaps more than any other in this book, is written for the spouse, partner, or child of a police officer and discusses some of the challenges you will likely face because you live in a police family.

WORK SCHEDULES TO MEET THE 24/7/365 SERVICE DEMAND

Most adults work day shift, Monday thru Friday, with weekends and holidays off. Police departments, however, operate 24/7/365. There are no days when the "office is closed," and no times when everyone gets the day off. Even on holidays, someone has to work. Think for a moment what it might be like if we could say that all police business had to be conducted during "regular" office hours and that no calls for service would be accepted between 5 p.m. and 8 a.m. It would be unimaginable. Simply can't happen, wouldn't work. It's not even something we could consider. But working those night shifts or rotating shifts with rotating days off has an impact on family life.

Meal Time

Supper for breakfast? It means that someone in your family is on a night shift. How many families have tacos for breakfast? Or what if your evening dinner is at 4 p.m. because your cop parent or spouse starts work at 1800 hours for a power shift? Meals are often disrupted by police work, and shift hours can make it difficult to conform to those meal times we might consider standard. However, in many families, meal time is when you connect with each other, share the events of the day, and discuss future plans. This regularly scheduled time and the connecting that takes place during shared meals is an important part of being a family.

Holidays and Special Occasions

Holidays are another important part of family life. And if daily meal schedules are often disrupted by police work, holiday meals are certainly no different. In my house we never missed a family Christmas dinner, even though I worked afternoon or night shifts with rotating days off, which meant I was frequently working on Christmas and many of the other holidays. Still, we never missed a Christmas dinner—it just meant that our family Christmas dinner happened sometime between Thanksgiving and Martin Luther King, Jr.'s birthday. We adjusted the celebration to fit a schedule we could make work. It's important to have these family times together.

It might be that the kids open their Christmas presents a day early or a day late because of mom's or dad's work schedule, but it's important that the cop parent be a part of this event. Think about how we connect family memories to holidays. How many times have you said something like, "Do you remember when you got...for Christmas?" Or maybe you're talking about what you got for your 8th birthday (if you can remember that far back). These are family events, and it's important they are celebrated by the *entire* family. If that means they are rescheduled, then that's what ought to happen. It's important that the "cop parent" not be the "absent parent," because when this happens, the whole family loses. The kids lose because they are only sharing the holiday with one parent when they might have been sharing it with two. The noncop parent loses because they don't get to share the joy with their cop spouse, and the cop parent loses because these are events that will never happen again. We can't go back 20 years and say, "I can be here now so let's do it over again." Once these opportunities are gone, they are gone forever.

Being on Call

Another thing that gets in the way of family time is when the officer is "on call" and subject to being recalled to duty at any time. I know of one officer who was called out from family dinners four nights in a row. The on-call status can come about for any number of reasons. It might be that the officer is a member of a SWAT or other tactical unit that is only called in when needed. Or the officer might be part of a task force that works varied hours and when something is happening, all members of the task force are called in. Or it might be that this is a small department and there are times when all officers are needed. When an officer is on call, for whatever reason, it is disruptive to family life.

It's hard to commit to family activities knowing you might be called away at any moment. It's also difficult for family members to commit to family activities that they know, from experience, may either be cut short or might never happen at all because the officer has been called in to work. On some level these abrupt departures may cause the other family members to wonder what is most important for the officer—the job or the family. This uncertainty and disappointment can lead to further lack of commitment by family members and increasing emotional distance between them. Even if an officer is "on call," there need to be times when that's not so, times when the family comes first and the job can wait. Remember, there will always be drug dealers, barricaded suspects, and all of that, but you only have one family and your kids are growing up. Once they are gone, you can't go back. Take advantage of and appreciate what you have now—don't let yourself get called in to work on an unrestricted basis.

Another downside to being "on-call" is the restriction it puts on your activities, alone or with your family. It might be simply that you can't have a beer or a glass of wine with dinner because you might get called back to work. But it might also mean you can't take your kids to the water park or a movie because you need to be available to be called in if necessary. Departments sell "on-call" as easy money; you don't necessarily need to do anything, and you are still getting paid. But take a look also at what you are being paid to *not* do. You are being paid to *not* have that beer with dinner, to *not* put your family ahead of your work, to *not* venture beyond a specific geographical area because you have to be able to report to the station within a certain length of time if you are called in. So remember, when you are "on-call," you are being paid to do nothing—nothing work related or family related.

SPECIAL ASSIGNMENTS

Special assignments impact family life from a number of perspectives. First, the hours are frequently irregular and varied. It might be that an officer is set for a narcotics buy at 6 p.m. but that the deal doesn't happen until 3 a.m. It's a common understanding that drug deals never go on time. Preparing for a search warrant might mean that the officer is up late into the evening doing surveillance and then back bright and early the next morning to do a trash search to help establish probable cause for the warrant. This might be followed up by a 2 a.m. warrant execution the next day.

UNDERCOVER ASSIGNMENTS

Undercover assignments can also cause problems within a family because the officer needs to look whatever part they are playing and they need to be convincing in that role. Their life may depend on it. There are very few undercover assignments in which an officer needs to portray an "upstanding" member of society, such as a banker or attorney. Most of the undercover work has to do with vice, narcotics, and gangs, and all require the officer to vary their appearance to blend in with those they are planning to arrest or get information from. So this clean-cut police officer may suddenly grow a scruffy beard, let his hair grow long, and wear clothes he would normally avoid. This works for work. But suddenly when he is out with his family, things are different. When I worked undercover and looked the part, I could see people at church looking at my family and feeling sorry for them because they were with such an apparent low life. When I went to the grocery store where I had shopped all of my adult life, suddenly I needed to produce three forms of identification to cash a check.

When the undercover persona and the family come into contact, there are often problems. On one occasion I had been buying cocaine from a guy who watched adult films on a regular basis with his 6-year-old daughter. We needed one more buy before we arrested him. I was at a matinee movie with my wife and he saw me with her. I had to walk away from her, leaving her alone in the theater, to go talk with him so he didn't come to my wife and me. She understood, but it was awkward. I didn't want him to know my wife. I didn't even want him to know I had a wife. And, I certainly didn't want her to know him. Sometimes these roles blend unavoidably and it's important to discuss what to do when things like this happen.

Alcohol use is another risk associated with undercover work. When the officer is hanging around in bars and drinking alcohol in performance of duty, there is always the risk that this behavior will go too far and that the officer will become too accustomed to alcohol. The prolonged exposure and expectation to drink can lead to addiction.

Along those same lines, there are few things more exciting than making an undercover drug buy. Everything is high adrenalin, big risk, big reward. Yet when things go wrong, as they frequently do, it's all on the officer to make it work, to preserve their cover and get the evidence. Adrenalin can be addictive, and cops have frequently been called adrenalin junkies. I knew of a cop in one narcotics unit who got those adrenaline rushes whenever he made undercover buys. But, as happens with many substances, he developed a tolerance and needed more of the addictive substance to get the same effect. So this officer began setting up his buys in places where people knew him and knew he was a cop. He increased the risk of the buy. After a while he needed to raise the stakes again. This time he stopped taking a weapon with him when he made the buy, which he justified with his "concern" that, if frisked, his cover would be blown. So he was, at that point, making undercover drug buys, in places where people knew he was a cop, without a weapon. Finally, he did all of the preceding *and* stopped taking backup with him on these buys. He didn't let his fellow officers even know that he was going out to make a buy. It was at that point that the other officers asked him to transfer out of the unit. He was too much of a risk for himself and for them. Addictions impact families, as discussed in the addictions chapter. But this was not only about the addiction; it was also about the risks the officer was taking to satisfy those addictions.

DEALING WITH DANGER

Danger is a reality in police work, yet for some police families it is more real than for others. Some families have had direct, personal experience with this danger because their officer or one close to them was injured on duty; some live in areas where there may be more media coverage of dangerous events involving police; and some might simply be more aware of the dangers police face or spend more energy on preparing for the possibility of injury. The more police families understand about the real dangers in police work, the safer they can be. For example, while it is possible for an officer to be seriously injured by bad guys, it's also likely that the officer might be injured in a squad car accident or a training accident, that the officer will experience emotional difficulties or addictions, or that the family will be impacted by a divorce. These are also dangers that threaten the health and safety of the family. It's not just the bad guy with the gun.

It's important to be honest about the dangers of police work, both real and imagined. On television we see a very distorted image of police danger. We see police officers involved frequently in shootings, sometimes even multiple shootings, in the same episode. Yet in real police work, the vast majority of officers will go their entire career without ever firing their weapon other than for training purposes. In almost every television police story there are high-speed chases, foot pursuits, fights, and even officers killed. These things don't happen on a daily basis in real police work. A real cop might get involved in high-speed chases on several occasions during their career but most certainly not on a nightly basis. Not every arrest involves a fight or a foot pursuit. In fact, there are lots of cops who do not look as though they would excel in either of those events.

On television and in the movies, police officers are killed on a fairly regular basis, although it is rarely one of the stars of the show. Yet in real life there are not a lot of police killings. In 2011, 72 law enforcement officers were feloniously killed in the line of duty in the United States and another 53 officers died as the result of accidents that occurred in the line of duty.[1] Over the past five years, the average annual number of officers feloniously killed in the line of duty was 55. While this number is too large—even 1 duty-related fatality would be too large—it is not accurately represented by the number of police deaths depicted on television or in the movies. With fictional police deaths on television or in the movies, there is no way the media can accurately portray the immensity of the event and the impact on the family. In real life, when an officer dies in the line of duty, it's not just that officer's family who is impacted. Police

[1] Federal Bureau of Investigation. (2012). *Law enforcement officers killed and assaulted, 2011*. Retrieved from http://www.fbi.gov/about-us/cjis/ucr/leoka/2011

families for miles around are impacted. When the funeral is televised, every police family viewing it must think, at least for a moment, what it would be like if that happened to them.

GUNS IN THE HOME

There were always guns in my house as my kids were growing up. Guns were just a normal, natural part of the home environment. Each day when I went to work, my kids saw me in my uniform, with my sidearm. It wasn't something unusual or strange to them. They also knew that it was important that I shot it well. Each month when I qualified at the target range, my wife insisted I show her my target. It was important to her that I was good shot. As soon as my kids were old enough to understand what guns really were, they were taught how to safely handle a weapon, how to shoot, and how to clean the guns afterward. It was important to me that they knew about firearms so that there were no accidental discharges because of their ignorance. Guns are such a part of our everyday existence that one cop's child reports that the officer's service weapon was routinely kept right above the breakfast cereal.

While it's important for family members to understand what guns are, how they work, and what the safety features are, it's also essential that guns and ammunition be stored in a safe place, out of the reach of children (and some adults). The law demands it, and I cannot emphasize this point enough. Keep your guns out of the hands of your kids and other kids who might be at your house. You may not realize it but your gun might be something you child brags about and wants to show off to a friend. Few things can be more dangerous to families than kids with a loaded gun. A lot of cops keep guns at home in a small safe that might be bolted to the floor or a wall or kept out of sight in a closet or under the bed. In any of these cases the weapon is stored safely if it is inaccessible to children.

LIVING UNDER THE MEDIA MICROSCOPE

We live in a world of stereotypes. People are categorized, pigeonholed, and judged. No one knows that better than cops. After the Rodney King incident in California, cops all over the country, in a variety of situations, heard comments like, "You gonna beat me like they beat Rodney?" When one cop becomes the focus of media attention—whether good or bad—it affects every cop and every cop's family. When a cop saves a life, it makes lots of little kids want to be cops, and it is an opportunity for families to bask in that glory. However, most of stories about cops that get media coverage involve officers who are in trouble for one reason or another. It might be that there are very public allegations of abuse or misconduct. When things like this happen, it definitely affects every cop and every cop's family, especially if it is your department and your cop. Remember that allegations, once made, can become very public and take on a life of their own, no matter how untrue they are. There is almost nothing that makes better news than cops and, better still, bad cops. So if there is any story about police misconduct, it gets air time or newsprint. This becomes even more of a problem because so many people believe that if something is written in the newspaper or aired on television it must be true. The public then responds to the story or article as though it were fact and base future actions on this perception. This situation becomes even worse if it involves your cop. If your husband or wife, or father or mother, is publicly accused of misconduct, everyone you know is aware of it. Such allegations can destroy outside family friendships and even families themselves. It doesn't matter whether the allegations are true or false; once they are out there, you can't pull them back.

These days, things hit the Internet and are there forever because, unless you put it there yourself, it is nearly impossible to take it off. So when something like this occurs, it is essential that the family pull together and talk about what happened to set this story in motion in the first place and what is happening now. It's important to share frustrations and to deal with this adversity as a family. Too often it gets swept under the rug and becomes something that no one talks about. Yet it might be that the kids are having problems with their friends at school because one of them may have said something negative about the police parent getting the bad press. The cop's child is now forced to either abandon the parent or ditch the friend—a difficult place to be. It might be that the spouse hears negative comments from friends which causes disruptions in those important relationships. Whatever is happening, where an officer is judged by the actions of others, it makes things difficult in the family.

When one officer in an agency is accused of misconduct, too frequently, all officers in that agency are judged by the same standard and are considered to be part of the misconduct. Remember, where a cop is big news, a bad cop is bigger news, and a corrupt department is about the biggest news of all. If you live in a small town and work on a small department this effect is magnified because everyone in the community knows you. If one officer with NYPD is accused of misconduct, however, it may have little impact on most of the other officers because of the enormous size of the department. The NYPD is so large that most officers don't know even a small fraction of the cops working for that agency. But if your department size is 20 officers, everyone in town will know. News travels fast in small towns, but that doesn't necessarily mean it is more accurate. It just means it gets around quickly, and all of your friends and neighbors are likely to know before long. Imagine the officer who coaches little league baseball and who is very publicly accused of using excessive force in making an arrest. Might some of the parents whose kids are on his team decide that they really don't want their son or daughter being coached by someone with that kind of a "temper"? And what does that mean for the officer's own son or daughter who was friends with the kids pulled from the team?

If you are a cop parent and something like this happens, it is essential that you talk with your spouse and children because this will impact their lives. Your spouse needs to know what is going on, and your children need to hear the truth in a manner that is age appropriate. Kids need different amounts of information depending on their age. Teens will need to know much more than younger children but not necessarily as much as a spouse. Younger children will only need to know that the family is safe and that they are loved. Pre-adolescent children do not have the capacity to understand abstract concepts, and giving them all of the details is likely to confuse the issue. Answer their questions and assure them that you love them and the rest of the family.

THE NEED FOR CONTROL: LIVING UNDER A "BECAUSE I SAID SO" REGIME

Many say that cops have "control issues." For police officers, in many situations, a lack of control can result in physical injury or death. It is vitally important for police officers to be in control of their work situations, but this need for control often extends beyond their work environment to those individuals who surround them in their private lives. So in police families it's not uncommon to find that there are rigid rules with punishments for violations of those rules. These rules are described in black-and-white terms with little room for ambivalence. Things are either right or wrong, with no middle ground and no excuses for rule violation.

The need for control comes out in a need for information— constant, current information. The police parent might set a rule that when the child is not at home they must notify the parent where they are, who they are with, what they are doing, and when they are coming home. Such a rule might also include the requirement that if the child changes locations the parent is notified about that also. That child must be trackable at all times.

Another aspect of control is seen in the police parent's concern about their child's friendships. They want to know who their kids are hanging around with and are often judgmental of these peers. And while most parents want to know that their children are associating with "good" kids, police parents possess unique knowledge, information, and insight about their community's residents that most other parents don't have. You might hear comments from the police parent like, "I know that type," or, "I know his family. His brothers are always in trouble, and I don't want you hanging around with him." This "inside" information impacts how cops parent their kids. It might be that the child is forbidden from going certain places because of the danger the police parent imagines are there or because of actual police calls to the area. Many times, the police parent simply issues a rule without sharing the information or the source of the information that led to the rule. If the police parent doesn't explain the rationale supporting these decisions, they may seem arbitrary and unreasonable to the child. Yet the officer may not be able to share the information without revealing sources or putting current investigations at risk.

ROLE AMBIGUITY: BEING ABLE TO HANG UP THE UNIFORM AT HOME

Sometimes it's hard to know when the cop is a cop and when they are mom or dad, or the spouse or partner you've vowed to grow old with. You might find these lines blurred frequently. When rules are broken and punishments administered, is this the parent or the cop who is relating to the child? Are the consequences administered with love, or are they the voice of justice? Sometimes it's hard to know. The cop doesn't know, and the kid certainly doesn't know. I have frequently heard from police kids that they felt as though they constantly needed to prove their innocence and that they were always interrogated like suspects by their police parents. It's easy to say that cops are untrusting and are natural interrogators, but these are fuzzy lines and might very well be an unconscious blending of personality and profession by the cop parent. Still, it is unfair and can be emotionally damaging to treat your children as if they are guilty until proven innocent.

It's difficult to live with a cop spouse who can't hang up the uniform before they walk into the house. I know of one officer's wife who complained that she used to enjoy the Sunday afternoon drives with her husband but now all he wants to do is drive through the neighborhood with her and look for stolen cars. This doesn't make for good family time. When the police officer brings the "cop attitude" home and seems to be negative about most things, it's not conducive to a positive family life. Too many spouses complain when their young children learn (and too often use) words from the police vocabulary such as "scumbag."

MANAGING EXPECTATIONS

What might it be like to be the governor's child, or the president's child? These kids are put in a fishbowl, just like cops' kids. People have expectations of cops' kids. They expect cops' kids to never get into trouble and to be great students, athletes, and leaders among their peers. They expect that cops' kids will know all of the rules and will follow all of the rules all of the time because, "after all, isn't your dad (or mom) a police officer?" They don't expect cops' kids to cause trouble or be rude. Yet all kids need the freedom to rebel within safe parameters. Still, there is a stigma or an unreasonable expectation that cops' kids will be different from other kids because of their parents' choice of career.

Police officers themselves often have higher expectations of their children and take small infractions of the rules as indicators that bigger infractions are on the way. Consequently, the cop parent tends to deal with the small infraction as though it were a larger violation or is going to inevitably give way to larger infractions. For example, many kids try shoplifting at least once in their lives. It might not be uncommon for a police parent to over react when confronted with their child's shoplifting and to deal with the child as though, without swift and certain punishment, the next step will be breaking into houses. Cops tend to see the worst in people and this includes the worst things that might happen to their own kids as a result of minor infractions.

NAVIGATING THE CHANGE FROM HERO TO VILLAIN

Parents are their children's first heroes. A mom bandages up a skinned knee and tracks down the doll left behind at a restaurant; a dad purges the monsters from a dark closet and fixes the favorite toy that the mean neighbor kid broke. Most young children who grow up in healthy, loving homes regard their parents with awe. And when that parent happens to wear the uniform of a cop, the awe seems to spread to other young friends of those children.

As kids grow, their impressions about police officers change. When they are young, say pre-teen, many kids want to grow up to be police officers, fire fighters, or other public servants. The ideal at that age is for kids to learn that if they are in trouble they should look for and trust a police officer to provide help. As they move into their teen years and develop the capacity for abstract thought, kids begin to think about the entire world in different ways. They begin to think about concepts such as "good" and "evil," social service, and how to solve the problems of the world. While they are playing with these new ways of thinking, they are also thinking about police officers in different ways. They might be thinking of cops as "the man" or the one who is going to prevent them from doing what they want to do. In their teen eyes, police might move from the helper to the hinderer. Combine this perspective with the normal adolescent rebellion and there is a real potential for conflict within a police family.

Then let's add the idea that police officers are often more controlling than other individuals. As noted, cops are used to being in charge at work and often feel like they have to remain in control at home as well. This can lead to overly restrictive parenting which, when combined with a view of cops as the enemy and normal adolescent rebellion, can make the teen years especially difficult for kids growing up in cop families. In fact, when you think about it, it might seem amazing that kids in police families get through this time in their lives at all.

I don't mean to paint a picture of doom and gloom for police families with teenage children. These kids may be very proud of their police parent and admire police in general but can't openly show such support without fear of alienating their peers. I've seen lots of police families raise kids they are proud of. In fact, it is common for cops' kids to grow up to be cops themselves. Frequently they work for the same department, maintaining a family legacy within that agency.

THE SOCIAL LIFE OF A POLICE FAMILY

Cops often find that the majority of their friendships are with other cops. The extension of this is that cops' families will find that their friendships are often with other cops' families. Cops share lots of things that impact friendships. They have common interests, shared views of the world, similar incomes, and often the same mixed up days off. So you might find that your family is going camping with another police family on Monday, Tuesday, and Wednesday because those are the days the cops aren't working. Or it might be that you all have similar troubles finding babysitters on Tuesday night, which is the cops' day off that week, so you can go out for the evening. Another feature of socializing with other cops' families is that your crazy patterns don't seem so crazy. It's not unusual among your friends to have supper for breakfast or to use words like "vehicle" rather than car. Your world and their world seem to mesh on a lot of different levels.

When the police parent arrests a person who has a social relationship with someone in the family, like a friend of a child or spouse, it becomes very personal for all involved. Imagine the high school student who says to the cop's kid, "Your dad (or mom) arrested me Friday and it was just crap. I didn't do anything wrong." Or the golf buddy who says to the cop's husband, "Your bitch wife arrested me last weekend for giving my jerk neighbor what he had coming. Geezus, he didn't even need stitches." Now the spouse or child has, in most cases, lost a friend. Seldom does the friendship take the path where the friend will admit they were doing something wrong and that the police officer was simply doing their job.

CONCLUSION

Cops can make great parents and can have great families but it takes effort and attention to details. Police work is not conducive to family life, and the police stereotype doesn't usually include a spouse and children. As indicated, there are a lot of things that interfere with the officer and family life. If you find that your energy is not going to your family, look at where you are spending your time and resources and find a way to change things. One officer, when asked what the most important thing in his life was, replied, "My family, of course." Yet, when I dug deeper about what he did when he wasn't working, he told me that on Monday and Wednesday nights after his regular shift he works at the bank for extra income. On Tuesday and Thursday nights he plays softball in two different police leagues. Friday is poker night with the guys, and on the weekends he is usually hunting or fishing with his friends. So it doesn't seem as though this officer was accurate when he said that his family was the most important thing in his life. Look at where his energy was going—to his friends and his work. He didn't need the extra money from the Monday and Wednesday shifts at the bank except to fund his softball nights and fishing or hunting trips. Make sure that what you say is important is what you treat as important. Your actions must match your words.

When you retire from the police department no one is going to remember you, at least not for long. They will begin to forget you the moment the door shuts behind you for the last time. In 10 years maybe half of the department will remember you, and after 20 years very few will even recall your name. Yet your family will remember you far beyond that. If you want to make a real difference in this world, pay attention to your family and leave your legacy through them.

Chapter 7

SURVIVING DAY-TO-DAY STRESS

"If you can't handle it, quit." This statement by a police officer was more of a truism than he realized at the time.

Day-to-day stress is a debilitating factor in law enforcement. If you can't deal with the stressors you face every day, they will destroy you. Job-related stress can be deadly and can destroy a life in many different ways. Some cops end up divorced, alcoholic, angry, bitter, cynical, and old before their time. The stress just got to them. If you don't learn how to effectively manage the day-to-day stress, as the officer said, "quit." You will be better off in the long run.

Stress is an engineering term that was originally used to identify how much tension, strain, or pressure something could take before it would break. So as we have humanized the term, it has come to describe how much tension, strain, or pressure a person can take before they break. Stress can be defined in many different ways, some of which are humorous and make for amusing cartoons and catchy slogans and bumper stickers. But the bottom line reality is that *stress can kill.*

STRESS: THE GOOD, THE BAD, AND THE UGLY

Not all stress kills. There is positive stress and negative stress. Positive stress comes from things that excite us or things we look forward to, such as winning an award, graduating from school, getting married, or taking a long-overdue vacation. These are positive events in our lives, but they still fire up our systems. Think about the night before your last major vacation, and remember how you felt. Your system was revved up, and you were excited about the trip. During that time your focus was on the positives, and you tended to forget the negatives. The excitement replaced the worry. The positive stress eliminated the negative stress.

Negative stress comes from things that threaten our safety or happiness. We tend to think of physically dangerous things as negatively stressful, and they certainly can be. But they can just as easily be positively stressful. Many things cops do are physically dangerous but they look forward to them, such as making undercover drug buys. The adrenaline rush that comes from engaging in a dangerous activity is something many cops acknowledge as a main reason they like their work. Something very stressful but exciting is a positive stressor, and danger, in itself, is the determinant. There must be a negative aspect to the danger to make it a negative stressor. It might be something like a fight during an arrest that is physically dangerous and negatively stressful. The danger is certainly present, but there are also a number of negative aspects such as the potential for injury, additional paperwork, and other administrative problems that must be dealt with after the arrest is made. These negative aspects can be entirely non-physical.

Imagine it is 0900, you are sitting in a training session, and you get a message that you are to report to the chief's office at 1300 hours and bring all of your equipment. Your brain is going to be spinning out of control for the rest of the morning. It doesn't matter that you haven't done anything wrong; if you don't know why you are being summoned, it will wear on you for the rest of the morning. Seldom will cops jump to the immediate conclusion that they are about to be surprised with a promotion; they most often worry about negatives. This is also stress. Even just sitting in a courtroom waiting all day to testify is stressful because you can't control the outcome and can't make it happen sooner. Your day is spent waiting.

Often it is not the event itself as much as it is our perception of the event that causes stress. For example, several officers can be exposed to the same event, and one or two may find it to be stressful, whereas the others find no stress there whatsoever. It is their perception. A young officer may find it incredibly stressful when a defendant is found "not guilty" by a judge or jury. An older officer may not find it stressful at all. The young officer perceives that justice has not been done and the offender has gotten away with something. The more experienced officer will look at the same set of facts and simply know that the offender is unlikely to change his pattern of behavior and will be apprehended again. Same event, very different reactions. A young officer may find the idea of a new boss stressful while the experienced officer knows that nothing is forever and the new boss, like everything else in the police department, is only temporary.

I recall one incident, years ago, when my chief was walking down the hall with his hands in his pockets, looking at his shoes. As

I walked past him in the hallway and said, "Good morning, chief," he didn't respond or even look up. I could have done several things with this, depending on my perception. I could have spun up thinking that he would have said good morning unless I was in trouble. This would have led me to think I might be disciplined later that day, which would, in turn, lead to worry about what impact the discipline will have on my income, my family, and my career. Or, I could have simply thought that he didn't hear me or that he must have been having a bad day. Either way, how I reacted and the stress that the reaction caused me to feel, if any, was based more on my perception than on the actual event itself.

COMPONENTS OF STRESS

Stress is systemic. That means that all internal systems are impacted. Stress can cause headaches, ulcers, high blood pressure, emotional disorders, and relationship troubles. The impacts of stress can also be broken down into physical, emotional, and cognitive components.

Stress has a physical impact. Your physiology changes under stress, thanks to an evolutionary adaptation for survival known as the "fight or flight" response. Your body is preparing to either confront the threat head on (fight) or get yourself as far away from it as possible (flight), and you cannot change that. It is an instinctive response. You won't stop and think, "Ok, this is something stressful, so let's kick in all of those important old-time survival mechanisms." Your body will respond automatically. Your pupils will dilate for better vision; your breathing rate will increase to get more oxygen to the blood; your heart rate will increase to pump the freshly oxygenated blood more quickly to the muscles; your circulatory patterns will change so more of the blood goes to the larger muscles of the body and less to the surface capillaries; and your digestive action will slow considerably or halt completely. These are not conscious changes; they simply happen. They are necessary and beneficial in the short term and will give you a burst of strength, but they are not good for the body long term and will cause serious problems if allowed to persist without a break. Competitive weight lifters will sometimes try to fire up these changes within the body because it increases their strength and the amount of weight they can lift. Compare this to running your car on nitrous oxide. The car will go faster while burning nitrous oxide, but before long you will end up rebuilding your engine because the increased power is more demanding and harder on the engine.

We train in specific ways because of this response. For example, firearms training has gone from shooting bulls-eye targets to human silhouettes, and often there is a degree of physical exertion involved in the shooting to imitate a physiological stress response. So, your body is preparing to fight or to run, and the problem is that, most of the time, neither of these responses is appropriate. When you are summoned to the chief's office, you can't tell him you're not coming, nor can you punch him out when you get there. Either of those responses is counterproductive.

Stress has an emotional impact as well. The basic passive emotion displayed under stress is fear, and the basic active emotion is anger. Which do you think cops might express more often? Undoubtedly, anger. The basic emotions that are ok within in the police culture are anger and laughter. Anger covers most situations, and we make sick jokes about the rest. Emotions like fear, sadness, shame, guilt, and embarrassment are not "ok" among cops. So under stress, when any other emotion might have been more appropriate, police officers are most likely to show anger or laugh about it. Neither of these emotions displays any vulnerability. Anger will tend to distance people from us and push them away, whereas laughter will tend to distance us from the event.

As one officer said, "The only emotion that you can show effectively is anger. That's acceptable; all others are weakness. So you live on anger and you live on jokes. You adopt a gallows humor, and that keeps you going." In explaining how he handled the stress of the job, another cop said, "You'd drink over it, you could have sex over it, you could party over it, you could buy toys, you could work a lot. You could do almost anything except face your feelings."

When cops talk about how a suspect or "perp" made them angry and caused them to do what they did, what they are really saying is that they gave that person control over their lives. The officer allowed another person to have such an impact on their emotions that they were forced to respond as they did. Is that really a good idea? Do you want to let someone you don't even like control your emotions? Or your actions? If you were to ask me who impacts my emotions and thereby influences my behaviors, I would tell you that my wife has an impact on my emotions, close friends impact my emotions, and even my kids impact my emotions to a degree. All of them have the ability to influence my behaviors through the impact they have on my emotions. I am consciously giving them a lot of power in my life, but I would not give that same power to a stranger, or even worse, to someone I don't even like. Yet far too often, police officers allow suspects, judges, attorneys, and even complaining citizens to have an undeserved power over their lives. When you allow that suspect to make you angry, you act in ways that are often contrary to *your best interests*. You might find yourself yelling at friends, shouting at your spouse or kids, or even placing your career in jeopardy by "giving the jerk what he deserves." Don't let someone who doesn't matter control your life in any way.

Stress has a cognitive component as well. When you are functioning under a great deal of stress, you are likely to find yourself preoccupied and unable to concentrate. It will feel like the cause of your worry is just spinning around in your brain. You aren't trying to solve the problem, you are simply ruminating over it. The parts of your brain that are devoted to problem solving are shut down, and the only parts still working are those parts that focus on immediate survival—the fight or flight described earlier. It seems that all of the higher level function is shut down. You won't be able to think about how to balance your checkbook, your next vacation, or even what to name your next child. Your brain isn't working that way right now.

STRESS AND LAW ENFORCEMENT

Law enforcement stress is not a one-time experience; it is part of the daily routine. And while we are all impacted by the things we do, the things we are exposed to, and the way people respond to us, this is exceptionally true for police officers because so much of what we deal with happens in an emotionally charged atmosphere. When a parent calls because they have lost a child, the emotions are high; they are scared to death. Even those calls we consider a waste of time can involve emotions that are high, such as a complainant calling because his neighbor has parked in front of the complainant's house again; it is legal to park there, but it really annoys the complainant, and so he calls the police to complain. This type of work can change people.

If stressors are not dealt with as they occur, they will accumulate—it will be one thing on top of another, on top of another, on top of another. We tell ourselves, "I don't have time to deal with this now, I'll handle it later." The problem with that for police officers is that, far too often, "later" doesn't come until the crash. We try piling one thing on top of another and use excuses like, "It's no big deal," or, "I can't show weakness," to justify avoiding dealing with stress. Yet each of these "excuses" is merely a lie we tell ourselves. Trying to carry this mounting pile of stress is like carrying a load on your shoulders every day and, every day, adding 5 pounds to that load. If you don't stop and lighten the load at some point, no matter how strong you are, it will become too much and your knees are going to buckle. We all have limits to how much we can handle. As cops we are usually able to carry more of a load than most people, but we still have limits. Everyone has a limit.

Cumulative stress can result in a progressive loss of idealism, energy, and purpose. If you've been a cop for a while, ask yourself: what happened to the person I was when I started this job? Ask yourself how you might have changed and what caused those changes. Do you still find the job rewarding, or are you now one of those cops who comes to work every day and hates it? Far too often we find that if we let the stress accumulate, we sacrifice our quality of life. We don't enjoy who we have become, and we don't find any satisfaction in our job. When the job is less satisfying, we put less energy into it, and it becomes even less satisfying. You can see where this vicious cycle is going. Since many people find a great deal of personal satisfaction, and even a great deal of their identity, in their job, the cops who let the stress continue to accumulate are now finding little satisfaction in who they are and in the other areas of their lives. When we let the work stress accumulate, it flows over and impacts relationships, on duty as well as off duty.

STRESS AND THE COP "PERSONALITY"

Let's look at what kind of people want to become cops and what happens from there once they are exposed to the stresses of the job. Most of the people who want to be cops are people who want to make a difference. They want to make the world a better place, yet many are fairly unaware about the real problems and injustices in this world. As new officers become more and more conscious of the extent of pain and suffering in the world, they are changed by this awareness. It shakes the new officer to the core of their being. One officer said,

> "For me it was a total transition, from total innocence and being totally naive. You can't know this job! I don't give a damn what anybody says, you can't know this job until you've done it, 'til you've lived it! Anybody that says they can is as naive as I was. I mean, I didn't know from nothing, I was real square. I was probably more of a victim of what my job did to me as a human being than some other coppers.
>
> I never in a million years would have guessed there was so much sadness, so much bitterness, so much anger, so much ugliness. I had no idea how people live, the degradation. The way children are being brought up all over the city in filthy conditions, in cruel conditions, and in ignorant conditions is just unbelievable. I never knew that it was as bad as it is and that there were that many people living like that. It was tough to find out the extent of the human condition."

Joseph Wambaugh's 1975 book, *The Choirboys*,[1] is based on his experience as a Los Angeles cop and tells of a group of fictional yet stereotypical and realistic police officers and how they interact with each other and with the rest of the community, as Wambaugh notes that police departments are just a collection of identities. While his police characters had names like "Spermwhale Walen," "Father Willie Wright," and "Whaddayamean Dean," they represent these common police stereotypes:

- the cynic—[These social problems are] "much, much greater than we can repair. We're just here to pick up the pieces and that's a hard lesson." "I found out the hard way that cops aren't the ones that are going to fix the system, it has gotta be somebody else."
- the drunk—"You're required to be very cool and calculating when you dispense your emotions. You can't do it impulsively. I would have a calculated response to any occurrence." "The things that you don't talk about are your

---

[1] Wambaugh, J. (1975). *The choirboys*. New York: Random House Publishing Group.

real inner and emotional feelings. You can share the same bottle of whiskey and the same woman and the same apartment or a lot of things and be really close. But when you get really sad, you go do that by yourself. That's a private thing that's done by yourself and you don't share that."

- the new kid—"When I first came on I almost abandoned my family with the love of the job, the excitement, the excessive drinking, the job was much more important than my family."
- and the old timer—"Now, I get a drunk down call and I don't wonder what drove him to drink anymore, I don't particularly care and I have absolutely no compassion for him whatsoever. I just wish that he'd get off my street and out of sight because he's disgusting."

Police officers all over the country look at these stereotypes and see their friends, their partners, and their coworkers. Some are humorous and likeable, whereas others are not people we would warm to. Yet they are all cops and, to some degree, you can find them in every police department in the country.

Police officers often adopt a type "D" personality. These types of personalities are negative and tend to see the worst possible outcome. Of course this seems to be a natural part of police work, preparing for the worst possible outcome. However, when it becomes more than *what you do* and becomes *who you are*, then you have become a type "D" personality. Research has proven that this personality type has an adverse impact on health. Type "D" personality types were found by several different studies to have died at a significantly higher rate following cardiac procedures than other personality types. The whole idea of preparing for the worst is important, but always *expecting* it to the exclusion of all other possibilities can be harmful to your health.

STRESS AND EXPECTATIONS

While the veteran officer may have grown so hardened and jaded from years on the job that they expect the worst and see only the negatives, most officers don't start out that way. We all come into policing with a set of expectations about the work and what our role will be within the organization. We often bring a great deal of enthusiasm and idealism to the job. We become police officers thinking we are going to change the world but, over time, find it very stressful when we're not making the difference we thought we were going to make. One of the most difficult things for me to learn as a young police officer was that not everyone who needs help wants it. I believed my job was to help all in need, and it was difficult for me to understand that some people liked living the way they did, even though I thought they should live differently. Live better.

We come into police work expecting to make an immediate impact and be an immediate success. The problem is that law enforcement is a complex occupation, and it takes time to learn all of the nuances of this career. You come into the job with some basic skills but for the first several years you are learning. You are learning how things really work, and when you go to your first robbery, you learn and your skills improve. This is true for almost every "first" in your career. As you handle more and more of one type of call, you get better and better at handling that type of call. It can be stressful to be in that "first time" situation and not know the things that you think you should know, or to find that you are not the expert you thought you were. But be patient. You will learn in time, and there is no substitute or short cut for time.

We come into police work with expectations of simple solutions. Rookies may believe they can solve people's problems but will find that, in too many cases, the response is merely putting a band-aid on the problem. When we respond to a domestic assault and make an arrest, the marriage does not necessarily improve. In fact, we may find we're only there for crisis management and return to the same home for domestics on a fairly regular basis. Each time we return, things are the same. The couple is fighting about the same issues, and the situation ends with the same results—no improvement.

STRESS AND THE POLICE CULTURE

It is impossible to look at police stress without looking at the culture in which we work. The police culture is an incredibly closed culture. Very few people really know what it is like to be a cop other than those who have been one. Cops tend to close ranks and draw in closer to each other rather than to open up to "outsiders." So when you are looking for support to deal with the stress you encounter on a day-to-day basis, your tendency will be to look inwards, towards the group of people you work with. However, often they are unable to provide the type of support you are looking for, maybe because they are experiencing the same sort of stressors you are going through at work. Stressors of a more personal nature and their emotional impacts are especially difficult for police officers to discuss. Coworkers might not have the words to use, or they may be afraid that if they open up to your emotional difficulties they may be forced to deal with their own. So, while the tendency is to look to your peers for help in managing stress, you may be better served by looking outside your law enforcement network.

STRESS AND THE POLICE AGENCY

There are a number of internal stressors within any police agency. We see punitive transfers, undeserved promotions, internal affairs complaints, discipline issues, policies we don't agree with, favoritism, and rumors or gossip. These are most often things within the agency that we cannot control. We can't stop the punitive transfers, the internal affairs complaints, or the policies we don't support. But we can stop spreading rumors or being involved in the departmental gossip. Some officers have said that the most stressful part of their work involves the rumors that seem to float through the department like wildfire. It might feel good to be one up on another cop for a few minutes by spreading gossip, but realize that if you are involved in that, it won't be long before there are some great rumors floating around about you. When the shoe is on the other foot, it doesn't feel so good. The best practice is to simply not get involved with rumors.

Another stressor in law enforcement is the lack of criteria for measuring accomplishments. You never know if you are a good cop or not because standards for career success are different in each agency and can even vary within an agency. For example, some agencies will tell you that you are a good cop if you write 20 moving violations each day, while others want you to focus on felony arrests or drunk driving arrests. Yet none of these external criteria are suitable for truly measuring accomplishment and deriving true job satisfaction. If you adopt the agency's definition of success, you may be setting yourself up for failure. The agency has established criteria that are dependent on external variables you cannot control. There will be times when you simply can't find 20 moving violations in a day, or you may not be able to find a drunk driver or make a felony arrest on every shift. In those cases you will not have met anyone's criteria for success and, consequently, you might find it difficult to be thought of as a good cop by others or to think of yourself as a good police officer. It is important to find satisfaction in your work and to feel good about what you do, but you will not get that satisfaction if you base your personal standards for success on external standards you have no control over. Instead, look at what you can control. You can control what you do, you can control how hard you work, and you can control the effort you put into your job. So, rather than basing your definition of success on others, base it on yourself. Set attainable goals and know that you can always determine how hard you work, even if you can't control the results. At the end of the day you need to be able to look at yourself and say, "I worked hard today."

Police officers frequently perceive that they have inadequate institutional support. They feel as though their administrators, after years of driving a desk, have become disconnected and no longer understand what it is like on the street. While this might be true, it might also not be true. Patrol officers and administrators have entirely different functions. The police officer is there to perform the law enforcement duties while the administrator is there to provide support and to make sure the officer has what he or she needs to do the job. Each is operating in an adversarial role, simply with different adversaries. The officer works in stressful situations dealing with citizens while the administrator works in stressful situations dealing with city management personnel, politicians, and other community stakeholders. Each has their own battles to fight to get the job done, and far too often each group overlooks or minimizes the other's battles.

Understand that, most of the time, each group—front line and management—is doing the best they can, given the limitations they are working under. Far too often we judge by stereotypes. One chief that I know spent more than a week's pay out of his own pocket to make sure that his officers got the help they needed after a particularly troublesome critical incident. He spent the money without fanfare, and his officers never knew, and never will know, what he did. He didn't tell them, and he didn't brag about what he had done. He just quietly did what he needed to do to protect his officers.

A related stressor is the perceived inefficient use of resources in every police department. It always seemed to me that whatever unit I was assigned to was constantly short of personnel. When I worked in the Narcotics Unit, fellow officers would complain that we didn't have enough people in that unit and that, because such a large part of crime was related to narcotics, the unit should be much larger. It seemed a waste of personnel to put cops in the schools when we needed them in narcotics. Yet if I had worked in the schools, it would have seemed a waste of personnel to have a mounted unit. And if I worked in the mounted unit, it might have seemed a waste of time to put police officers in the narcotics unit. You can see how this works. The resources appear to be used inefficiently because they are not being applied directly to support what I am doing.

STRESS AND ASSIGNMENTS

Sometimes it is necessary to rotate responsibilities, to move people from current assignments into other, less stressful ones. One high-stress assignment is the investigation of child pornography, which can take a heavy psychological toll on the investigators tasked with searching computers for such images day after day. It can impact their emotional state as well as their home and family life. However, far too often, investigators are left in these positions too long, well after the assignment has become harmful to them. The reason given for such abuse has been that there is significant time and expense devoted to getting an officer trained for these types of investigations, and agencies are reluctant to move people out as long as they remain functional at work, disregarding the price the individual is paying in other areas of their life by doing this work.

Another high-stress assignment is narcotics investigations. It generally takes several years for an officer to develop informants and the required familiarity with search warrants to be a productive member of the unit. Once this expertise is developed, agencies often prefer to keep these investigators in place.

The responsibility for a transfer may rest with the agency, but the responsibility to ask for one is yours. The responsibility to monitor your stress levels is yours. Too often police officers will not acknowledge this stress and will do everything they can to "control" it. This can lead to disaster because by the time they do acknowledge it, there may be significant secondary damage. Their marriage may have ended, they may have become dependent on alcohol or drugs, they may have lost their job, and they may have even ended up in jail.

When you realize that you are working in a stressful environment, it is common to want to make changes so that you are not experiencing such stress, and you should seek change if the stress is getting to you. However, understand that the change must be realistic. If you find that working as a patrol officer on an afternoon shift is stressful and consider transferring to an overnight shift, you should realize that the job is still the same and, in most cases, may be even more stressful because of the new environment. The change must be stage appropriate. A change that might work for a very senior officer might make things worse for a newer or younger officer. For example, if a senior officer is experiencing a great deal of stress from patrol work, a desk assignment might be an appropriate change to relieve the stress. However, if a newer or younger officer is transferred from a patrol assignment to desk duty, the stress is likely to increase with the transfer.

GETTING SUED

Civil suits can be incredibly stressful. It is a very official statement that someone thinks you did something wrong. Often the litigation will assert that you did a lot of things wrong and your errors were intentional or negligent. There will be assertions that make you look like a terrible person, and you may feel a great deal of concern. Some of the questions you have might be, "Will this be in the media?" or "Will the whole town hear this?" Your concern might be that people will believe what they hear or what they read. You may fear that somehow you will be found at fault, or even that your agency will "settle" the lawsuit, expressing their lack of faith in you.

First of all, realize that while you cannot control what the media does with information, the people who really know you will not be influenced by the "spin" put on by the media regarding the events. The best way to deal with civil suits from an emotional perspective is to simply remember that they are not always so much about what you did as they are about money. Some people think they can get free money from your agency simply by suing or threatening to sue. Don't take on this emotional baggage. If you are comfortable with what you did, don't let others tell you it was wrong.

WHAT YOU *CAN* DO TO CONTROL OR MANAGE STRESS

Accept the givens. You cannot control prosecutors, judges, or juries. There will always be things in the criminal justice system that you cannot control. If you assume responsibility for outcomes within the system, you are assuming responsibility for something you cannot control. Do not self-impose this responsibility or allow others to impose it on you. Don't interpret results self-referentially. It's not about you. Your responsibility is to make an arrest, write a good report, and testify in a professional manner. If a judge or a jury decides the person is not guilty, it's not your responsibility or your fault.

Focus on success. Far too often we focus on the negatives in police work and overlook those times we *did* make a difference. While the negatives might be big and the successes small, there are still successes. It might be something like the time you stopped to talk with a boy playing basketball, and when you left he felt very special. One of the difficulties in focusing on successes is that, too often where we have made a difference, we no longer see the people we have helped. They don't get arrested anymore. They don't have police contacts. Watch for the small successes. They are important.

While we can minimize the stress of police work, we cannot eliminate it. Law enforcement is simply a stressful occupation; nothing will change that. Since that is a given, it is important to minimize the impact of stress on your life. Remember at the beginning of this chapter we defined stress as systemic? That's true, so you need a systemic response to stress. Simply dealing with one aspect of stress will be insufficient. If you deal with the physical aspects of stress by working out at the gym but then go home and take the emotional impact out on your family, your life will not get better. Similarly, if you only express your emotions and repress the physical aspects of stress and then have a heart attack, that isn't healthy stress management either. So a comprehensive stress management plan is just that—*comprehensive*. It addresses all facets of stress to include physical stress management, cognitive stress management, emotional stress management, and spiritual stress management or what I call management of the soul.

Physical stress management is important. Stress puts a lot of demands on your body, and it is important that your body be prepared to take the pressure. You wouldn't dream of shooting a firearm with a weak barrel because of the danger from the internal pressure. Your body is like that barrel; you need to stay in shape and watch your diet. Consult your physician before beginning any new form of workout. Make sure that your body is ready. If you have a heart attack the first time you work out, it won't reduce your stress. Secondly, consult a certified fitness professional and work with them to develop a plan that fits with your age, body type, time, and interests. If you are 45 and try to use the same workout program that was successful for you when you were 20, you are likely to get hurt or get too frustrated and quit. Your body is different now, and your workout needs to be different, too. If you are particularly out of shape you will need to be patient. You didn't get out of shape overnight, and you won't get back into shape overnight either. Your department may have a fitness professional on staff with whom you can consult free of charge, or your agency may have an arrangement with a gym so you can get a discounted rate. In any case, get some help with this, and don't wait until tomorrow to get started.

The next phase of stress management is cognitive. In short, when you leave work, take your brain with you. Far too often we get stuck thinking about work-related stress when we are not working. I don't know of any agencies that will pay overtime for you to worry about work on your days off. Take care of yourself and, while it may sometimes be very difficult, try to leave work at work. Just telling yourself, "Don't think about work, don't think about work, don't think about work," won't work. It puts work at the forefront of your thoughts. Instead, focus your attention on something pleasant, something having to do with your life away from work. That is assuming you have a life away from work. If you don't, get one as soon as possible. Everyone needs a hobby. Don't make yours police work. Take up some sort of pastime that has nothing to do with law enforcement. Get away from your job, and get away from your work identity. This is a chance for you to just be who you are and enjoy it. One of the ways to get your mind off work is to simply relax. I know that sounds easier than it is, but if you practice progressive relaxation, you will find that you can move into that relaxed state much quicker. When you get used to relaxing, it will become second nature.

There is an emotional toll to police work. You are dealing with people's problems every day, and in the midst of that you are often trying to help those who don't want your help or who are lying to you. Your emotions will be impacted. You might find yourself angry, bitter, or just simply wanting to be left alone. This kind of an emotional impact can cause isolation, keeping those who are most able to help you at a distance. It will prevent those who care about you from being able to reach out and touch you in a way to promote healing. Too often police officers will say, "I'll deal with this later" (remember this from earlier?). Yet by the time they get to it, there may be seven or eight more things piled on top of it. Deal with the emotional toll of police work every day. Don't let it build. For example, if you are so stressed about some of the things at work that you don't put the necessary energy into your marriage or into parenting, you might find yourself facing a divorce or a child who has grown up and doesn't really know you. You can handle the little things in small chunks much more easily than you can the "big stuff," so take care of those little things while they're little.

The last domain is called "spiritual," but it is about more than just "religion." It's about keeping you someone you can be comfortable being. The spiritual domain is that part of us that knows and understands right from wrong, good from evil, and the important from the unimportant. When this part of you gets into trouble, that's when you will find yourself dissatisfied with your job, the prosecutors, the courts, and pretty much everyone else in your world. You might find yourself taking shortcuts to get the job done, justifying this by saying something like, "Criminals don't follow the rules, why should we?" Well, quite simply, that's the difference between us and them. We understand right from wrong, and good from evil, and we need to define ourselves by doing the right thing in the right way. Too often when our spirit gets into trouble we begin to think that the end justifies the means. We think that we need to stop crime by whatever means necessary, even if it involves breaking the law ourselves to do it. But once we cross that line, it is very difficult to come back. Those officers who have a strong spiritual life tend to do better in this career than those who do not.

Finally, we frequently forget or take for granted what is important in our lives. When I ask officers what is most important in their lives, they will often tell me it's their family. Yet when I ask how they spend their time away from the department, they have often filled it up with part-time jobs, police league activities such as bowling or softball, and other leisure pursuits that rarely, if ever, include family members. Recall the response given by one officer at the end of Chapter 6. What was really most important in that officer's life? The people he worked with and his job certainly seemed more important than the family as he indicated originally. We tend to put our energy into those things that are most important to us. Be honest with yourself. If your job or the people you work with are the most important thing in your life, admit it. If they aren't, look at where you are putting your energy. It's a simple trap that a lot of cops fall into. They come to depend on the extra money from part-time work to pay bills because they have overextended themselves. They are making payments on a new truck, a boat, a four-wheeler, or a hunting cabin—maybe all of these—and can't afford not to work extra jobs. When you stop and think what is really most important in your life, I don't think it will be toys. They are a convenience and a trap. If you can afford them, that's nice. Otherwise, stay focused on what is really most important. Remember: money doesn't buy happiness. Look at lottery winners. A lot of them are worse off 5 years after they win millions of dollars than they were before they won the lottery. Put first things first.

Quick Stress Management Tips:

1. Take time for yourself. Remember you are the center of your world, and others in that world count on you.
2. Relax actively. Watching television is not relaxing, it is simply numbing, no matter how big the screen is.
3. Allow yourself to have a truly intimate relationship. Let someone get inside where they could hurt you worse than anyone else in the world and trust them not to.
4. Take time to get away from work. Don't let what you do become an identity. Remember, it's a great job but a lousy identity.

Chapter 8

SURVIVING THE INEVITABLE TRAUMA

"It's an invisible bullet. It goes in and nobody knows they're hit. It eats up your emotional system, your psyche."

—Bill Genet
President/Founder of POPPA[1]

Trauma. The word comes from the Greek and means "wound." Trauma can certainly apply to a severe physical injury, but for the purpose of this discussion, we will be referring primarily to an emotional wound.

Trauma is one of those things people don't like to think will happen to them—it happens to someone else. But if you are a police officer, you *will* deal with trauma at some point in your career. The only questions are when and how. As an officer, you will be exposed to other people's trauma almost daily but also to your own periodically. It is not possible to have a child die in your arms and not feel something, whether it's anger, fear, sadness, guilt, or any combination of these feelings and others. You will be affected by your work. Sometimes you won't want to admit that you are impacted or how strongly you are affected, but you *will* feel trauma when these things happen to you.

TRAUMA DEFINED

Trauma has been defined in many ways. Some consider only incidents with a severe injury or violent death to be traumatic; others describe any life-changing event as traumatic. The first definition might involve something like an uncontrollable, violent event that affects you or others, with the degree of violence and the number of people impacted as deciding factors in the severity of the trauma. This definition, however, is too limiting. A number of things with no physical danger affect us strongly. An officer falsely accused of raping a woman during a traffic stop found it to be very traumatic but

---

[1] Police Organization Providing Peer Assistance, http://www.poppanewyork.org/

without any immediate physical danger. The second definition, on the other hand, is too broad; a number of life-changing events are positive. Having a first child is a life-changing event, but it needn't be considered traumatic.

A good working definition of *trauma* seems to be ***any event in which police officers believe justice has not been served for them or someone else***. This includes such life-changing events as the first time you lose in court after you have sworn to tell the truth, the whole truth, and nothing but the truth, and a defendant or witness gets on the stand, takes the same oath, and then lies. Or when you find the world is not quite as nice a place as you thought it was or should be. It also includes the accident scene where a child has died and you tell yourself, "It just wasn't fair; he was so young." Or when you discover small children living in filth in a crack house.

Pause for a moment and recall some of the life-changing events you have experienced as a police officer, and you are likely to find those most troublesome are the ones that have been the most unfair. If you haven't yet experienced any, reflect on those you anticipate might affect you most strongly, or recall some stories you have heard from other officers and ask yourself how you might respond.

Police officers do not necessarily define trauma in the same way others do. Because first responders are exposed to violence, injustice, and death more often than others, we risk normalizing trauma. Sometimes an officer will find themselves referring to a "routine child abuse" or a "normal rape." It is important to remember that child abuse is never routine and rape is never normal.

Your definition of a critical incident may change over your life. For example, the first time you see a dead body, even under normal circumstances, might be something that bothers you, but after having seen a number of them, it takes more than just that experience to make it traumatic.

TYPES OF TRAUMA

As a police officer, you will experience a wide variety of traumatic experiences over the course of your career. Some of the first might be the shattered disillusionment you experience when you find the world is very unlike the world you grew up in and very different from your expectations. Early trauma may simply include a realization that everyone who needs help does not necessarily want it. Or, you may be exposed to severe trauma immediately, like the officer who responded to a homicide/suicide on her first day at work. As your career progresses, you are likely to get your share of the fatal accidents, the gruesome homicides or suicides, and other bizarre death scenes. Critical incidents can include such things as:

- Violent death of a co-worker in the line of duty
- Taking a life in the line of duty
- Shooting someone in the line of duty
- Suicide of a coworker
- Violent or traumatic injury to a coworker
- Responding to or handling infant mortality
- Responding to or handling multiple fatalities

Several factors make our exposure to critical incidents more debilitating. First, if we know the victim, we are more likely to be more severely impacted by the event. Second, anytime we identify with the victim in some way, we will experience more trauma. If you find yourself saying, "There but for the grace of God go I," you are likely to be more severely impacted by the event. These are two ways in which we find the event crossing from our professional lives into our personal lives. Once the event crosses that line, it is much more difficult to deal with.

PERSONAL TRAUMA

When trauma comes home it becomes more difficult to deal with because you aren't the only one affected now. This trauma comes into your life away from the police department and affects those you love most. It usually happens in one of two ways. The first and most common way is when you are unable to "be there" in relationships at home. Maybe you don't have the energy to go to your son or daughter's basketball game, or you don't want to be around lots of people, so you stay home. Your family can tell something is wrong. You're not fooling them.

The second way trauma comes home is when you are involved in something very public, such as a call in which an armed subject fires on you and your partner and you are forced to take the subject's life. Such an event will attract a lot of media coverage, and your name and perhaps your photo will be in the local newspapers and on television. Everyone in your neighborhood knows who you are, and they know who your spouse and children are. Your spouse will undoubtedly be asked about the shooting. Your children may not only be asked but may get flack about the incident, depending on popular sentiment.

The effects of the trauma on your family are called *secondary victimization*. It means they are affected by the effects of the initial trauma—your primary victimization. Your family will need you to not only work through your own trauma but to help them deal with theirs, too.

RESPONSE TO TRAUMA

Often the response to a traumatic event is based on individual variables. Some of the factors impacting our response are how we saw our parents deal with traumatic events (if we did), how this event fits with the way we see the world and our role in the world, the duration of the incident (the longer the incident, the stronger the impact), the degree of violence involved (to the victim or others), and the circumstances surrounding the experience (did we do what we needed to do, were we prepared to do it, was is according to policy, etc.).

For police officers, the other thing about dealing with trauma is that we are not restricted in the number of traumas we can be exposed to—there is no "one to a customer" limit. Police officers can be exposed to multiple traumas, even on the same day. This exposure becomes even more problematic for cops because we keep telling ourselves, "I'll deal with this later," except that often, "later" doesn't come, or it only comes when we are no longer functional or we are forced to deal with that and probably lots more traumas that have happened afterwards.

When we are exposed to repeated trauma, we tend to deal with it based less on the immediate situation and more on our experience in past situations. For example, one officer involved in a shooting had a terrible time afterwards. He lost almost everything—his wife, his home, and his children. Finally, after about 3 years, he had begun to rebuild his life. He was engaged to a wonderful woman and was beginning to have hope for a good future when he was confronted with another use of deadly force situation. In that instance, he waited as long as possible before using deadly force. As he was waiting and backing away from a mentally ill suspect armed with a knife, that officer was praying, "Please God, don't make me do this again! Please God, don't make me do this again!" His prayers were not so much about the current situation as about the future he believed would be caused by another shooting. From past experience, this officer "knew" that if he used deadly force again he was going to lose everything he had started to rebuild. Although his reaction was not "logical," it was very "experiential." This was what happened to him the first time, and he feared it would be the same again. However, this time the officer got help soon after the shooting, before things started to go downhill, and everything turned out well.

How Trauma Hits You on the Inside

The personal response to processing trauma has three stages, the first of which is the *impact* stage. Initial reactions at this stage may include shock, numbness, and disbelief. Many get through this stage functioning on auto pilot. You have a job to do, and you continue to do it. During this impact stage, you do not process any of the emotional affects caused by the experienced because they may be too overwhelming. Consider this: have you ever delivered a death notification only to have the person respond with a resounding "NO"? They weren't calling you a liar; it is just that the news you had brought was too powerful for them to accept at that time.

One officer who responded to an "accident with injuries" call found the victim to be his wife of 3 weeks. She died at the scene in his arms. When asked what he did next, he said he started to process the scene; it was a fatal accident, no different from any of the others he had been sent to. However, the extremely personal nature of the event made it *very* different from any other call he'd ever taken. He was denying the emotional impact of the trauma—he couldn't even consider them because he was a cop and had a job to do. Sometimes we deny the emotional impact because we want to, indeed we *need* to, stay with what we know. In this case, the officer knew how to process the scene of a fatal car accident. He did not know how to process his wife's sudden death or how to be a grieving husband.

In other less severe cases, we cannot take time to deal with the emotional impact because the suspect may get away or crucial evidence may be lost if it is not collected immediately. Sometimes we can keep the emotional aspects out of our conscious mind for a long time. At other times we may barely finish the required work before losing control. For example, it is not uncommon for police officers to show physical responses after shootings. More than one officer reports feeling physically sick and even vomiting immediately after the use of deadly force.

As you start to deal with the emotional effect of the trauma, you go through a number of emotions. You are likely to feel anger at the injustice of this particular trauma. It doesn't seem fair. It's unfair that this happened to the victim, and it's unfair that it happened to you. Somehow this should have been prevented. You may find yourself questioning what you did or didn't do on this call, searching for alternate, more acceptable outcomes. This flood of emotions may also include a sense of powerlessness because you can't change what happened, and you can't protect those who suffered or died. This feeling of powerlessness is particularly threatening to police officers because if you can't make a difference or don't believe you can make a difference, why are you out there doing what you're doing?

The second stage of trauma is *recoil*, when the trauma is a major focus in your life. It becomes something you just can't shake. Maybe you can't sleep because an image keeps popping into your head. Maybe you just don't have an appetite. At this point the trouble you are having working through the traumatic experience may affect your relationships because it assumes primary importance. If your emotions are raw, even the most loving of touches can be painful. You might find yourself pushing away those closest to you.

During recoil, you may have difficulty focusing on other things. The experience you have just endured may fill your mind, not in a productive problem-solving way but as a constant, stagnant preoccupation. The thoughts might just be rattling around, not working toward any kind of resolution, only taking up space and energy. This preoccupation can actually be harmful because it can keep you from focusing on real problem-solving strategies.

The final stage in working through a traumatic experience is *reorganization*. At this point the experience becomes just something else you have gone through. It may still affect how you see the world, your trust level in others, or your willingness to risk in relationships, but by this time the actual pain has dissipated.

If this trauma were physical, the impact stage would be that time when you know you've been injured but it doesn't hurt yet. You may look at the injury and say to yourself, "Damn, this is going to hurt." But you don't yet feel it. As you move into the recoil stage you begin to experience the pain, and that injury is all you can focus on. If you've suffered a gunshot wound to your arm, that arm is all you think about. It's not a time you could plan an evening out with friends. Finally you hit the reorganization stage. At this time the wound becomes a scar. You still remember the pain but you no longer feel it.

Wounds that don't heal properly are a risk for police officers. When you are whacked hard enough and deny the problems, it's like trying to walk with a broken leg. The situation will only get worse. You may tell yourself, "I'll deal with this later." But the problem with "later" is that by the time you get there, other problems and issues things have been piled on top of the original injury. These wounds don't go away. They stay where they are and fester. They may have healed on the surface and look okay but are actually infected below the surface. Then there is no recourse but to reopen the wound and scrub it out. This isn't an easy process. It's painful and time consuming.

Post-Traumatic Stress Response

The post-trauma stress response generally brings about a series of symptoms including a re-experiencing of the traumatic event and an avoidance of things that might remind you of the event. During these times it may feel as though your world has gone out of control.

Re-experiencing the event may involve intrusive memories or images, nightmares, or flashbacks that keep coming, day after day, and don't seem to diminish over time. The nightmares may become a terror or trauma in themselves. Cops may self-medicate to get to sleep, with alcohol being the drug of choice. Don't fall into that trap.

After a traumatic incident officers frequently attempt to control symptoms by controlling their exposure to situations that remind them of the traumatic event. However, it is not just the event itself that brings stress—a number of things that used to be meaningless, or even held positive associations, can take on a negative meaning after trauma. People, places, or things can remind you of the traumatic event. You may be reminded of a shooting whenever you put your duty belt on. Or seeing other people who were at the event with you may remind you of it, and you avoid them because you don't like that memory. It may even be that officers in general remind you of the event, and so you begin to avoid other officers. No matter what you do to get away from these reminders, you can't get away from yourself. You can't run from the event because it is etched into your mind forever. You can't make it go away; you can only work to make it heal.

There may come a point when you don't recognize what is traumatic because you are exposed to trauma so frequently that it becomes the norm. Remember, police officers tend to normalize trauma. They don't give it the importance it deserves and don't take care of themselves in the ways they need to. This normalization also affects their relationships because they don't pick up the signs that a relationship may not be what they need or think it should be. Consider the officer who is so used to trauma that anything less than a death or serious injury is nothing. When he got home one day his wife was somewhat hysterical because the baby had fallen off the couch. The officer's response, "How high did she bounce?" wasn't what his wife needed to hear. For her this was traumatic—for him it was nothing worth mentioning.

Survivor Guilt and a Search for Control

Survivor guilt is one of the ways that trauma hangs on, and it is often illogical. It may make no sense for you to feel guilty, but you do. Much of the time survivor guilt involves a search for control and a way to believe that such control can prevent a traumatic event from ever happening to us again. This need to control might involve such phrases as "if only" or "I should have." Don't get sucked into this kind of thinking. It is based on false logic.

For police officers, survivor guilt is about some event that was so terrible they can't bear the thought of going through it again and the crushing anguish they feel for surviving when others did not. Consider the example of the officer who was making a routine traffic stop and had called for backup. After his partner arrived at the scene, things went south real fast, and the driver ended up pulling a gun on the officers. The first officer was able to disarm the driver but not before the driver squeezed off a round, which struck and killed the partner who came to provide backup. In the aftermath of the shooting, the officer was so overwhelmed by survivor guilt that his quest for control over the situation—to never lose a partner to a traffic-stop shooting again—led him to the unrealistic solution that he would no longer make traffic stops or, that if he did make a stop, he wouldn't call for backup. This "solution" protected the officer from facing the reality that this traumatic event truly was out of his control, as well as the more devastating realization that if he couldn't control it, it might happen again.

But an officer who says, "If only I hadn't made that traffic stop or called for backup, my friend and partner might still be alive," is setting himself up for failure. You can't be a cop without making traffic stops or calling for backup when there is substantial risk. In fact, this officer was so deeply traumatized by that incident that he was unable to perform traffic stops anymore, which ultimately led to his dismissal from policing. He was never able to absolve himself of the guilt or accept the fact that when an officer calls for backup on a traffic stop and his partner responds, and that partner is killed after arriving, it isn't the officer's fault or his partner's fault. It is entirely the fault of the person who pulled the trigger and shot the officer.

Keep in mind that although this need for control is a significant factor in classic survivor guilt where someone has died, it is also evident in response to other traumatic events.

BEFORE THE TRAUMA: PLAN AHEAD

Since exposure to trauma is inevitable, take time to develop a plan *before* it sinks its teeth into you. When you are in the middle of a traumatic response, you won't have the ability to develop a plan. Your objectivity may be gone, and you may not think clearly.

The first step in developing a trauma plan is to identify a resource who will be immediately available. This is an important selection and may be among the most important of your career. This is the person who is likely to help you through an experience or experiences that have destroyed many police careers. Make the selection carefully.

One of the most important considerations in selecting someone to talk to is whether or not communication with that person is legally protected. The concept of legal privilege boils down to a legal confidentiality, meaning the communication is not subject to subpoena and cannot be used in any court proceedings. There are several different kinds of legal privilege: medical privilege, clergy privilege, marital privilege, and attorney/client privilege. You may reach out to someone in an employee assistance program, one of your health care providers, or some other therapist you have been referred to. But you should insist on protected communication!

For example, if your agency hires someone for you to talk to after a critical incident, you need to know where that person's obligations lie. Are they there solely for you, to listen to you, and to offer counseling to you? Or will they be submitting a report about you after your session or providing any type of evaluation of you to your agency? If it is the latter, you are strongly advised to walk away and find someone else. Be aware that some departments have a policy that requires an assessment be made of an officer's fitness for duty following a critical incident, and that's fine. But that's a separate deal, and it has to do with the agency protecting its interests. What you are trying to accomplish here is to find someone you can talk to whose priority is protecting your interests. You need to ask them, "Who is the client here?" and "What are the limits of confidentiality?" The answer you should hope to hear is something along these lines: "You are my client, and our sessions are completely confidential. The only feedback your agency will get from me is an invoice." So if you don't get the answers you want, look elsewhere.

When looking for privileged communication, your first thought might be your physician, but consider the challenge concerning that person's availability. What will it be like to contact your physician at 3 a.m.? Or even 3 p.m. for that matter? When trauma strikes and you need someone to talk to, you don't want to make an appointment two weeks from now. So if your physician is not available on very short notice, 24 hours a day, consider looking elsewhere.

Medical privilege also applies to communications with most licensed mental health professionals. Again, check availability. Your agency may have a contract with a mental health provider for critical incident response. If you are going to select a mental health provider, make sure they understand police work. Do not select based only on title; interview the person first. You need to know if that provider is comfortable working through the types of critical incidents police officers are involved in and that your personalities mesh. You won't want to be trying to discuss your incident with someone you don't like.

If you are going to use your police chaplain, ministers, or other clergy, again, make sure they understand the types of critical incidents that police officers are involved with and that they are comfortable working with you on these. If you decide not to use any of these, consider looking for peer support personnel in your agency or nearby agencies. Often there is legislation protecting these communications (check your local laws). Peer support personnel can be exceptionally helpful because many times they have experienced something similar to what you are going through and, for that reason, can be of help. Otherwise, realize that if you are simply going to talk to a friend, anything you tell them may be subpoenaed in a criminal or civil action because that type of communication is generally not legally protected.

Sometimes your attorney will advise you to not talk with anyone about what happened. However, if you have been involved in a traumatic event that is generating legal consequences, you are likely to need some emotional help as you process this situation. Don't risk your emotional survival out of fear of legal consequences. Select someone you can trust where the communication is privileged and work through the emotional impact of the traumatic event. Don't ask your psychologist for legal advice, and don't let your attorney give you advice about your emotional wellbeing.

After you have selected someone you can talk to when a traumatic event happens, think about the rest of your plan and what you will do after the event. You will want to mentally rehearse these steps (discussed shortly) before the need to use them arises. Think through them from time to time so they become reflexive because in the chaos following a critical event, your mental, emotional, and physical capacities might be so tapped out that you need to rely on an automated response.

AFTER THE TRAUMA

After a critical incident you are likely to find yourself buried in a pile of feelings that are powerful, intrusive, and even contradictory. This is not unusual. There are a lot of different things going on for you. You are likely to feel as though you are alone in all of this because no one can possibly feel the way you do. There is a grain of truth there because no one feels exactly as you do even if they were involved in the same incident. Each of us is a unique individual with a unique set of life experiences, perceptions, and involvement. Therefore, we all respond differently. But that doesn't mean that you shouldn't reach out to people you trust and share what you're feeling with them. In fact, one of the most important things in overcoming trauma is social support.

Take the time to share the experience with your spouse or your friends. They will not necessarily need to know exactly what happened but will, more importantly, want to know, "How are you doing?" Let them be there for you, to remind you that you are important and they care about you. Be honest about your feelings and understand that repressing or ignoring them doesn't make them go away. They will come out later in different ways: outbursts of temper, depression, or isolation. Take care of yourself through this experience and allow those who care about you to help.

You may feel a mixture of sadness and fear. The sadness about the event you have experienced is wrapped around the past but the fear is future oriented. We can't be afraid of the past because it has already happened. The only thing to fear is the future—what will the experience bring? How will I be viewed by my peers, my supervisors, my friends, and my family? Sometimes we even worry about how this event might be portrayed in the media. You may feel vulnerable because of the mix of feelings and your inability to "control" them. That's normal. These feelings aren't necessarily controllable, and we often just need time to work through them.

As you continue processing the trauma, you may find yourself wondering if it's all worth it. You might ask yourself why you keep working the job and putting yourself through these kinds of experiences, over and over, when all they do is mix up your life. You may also start wondering if this is really the way that you want to live your life, asking yourself, "Is this all there is to it?" or telling yourself that you're not satisfied with your life as it is. Many cops find significant changes to their marriages after a critical incident. The marriage may become stronger because the officer realizes the importance of that relationship, or it may end because of a realization that it's an empty union.

Immediately after the Trauma: Your Plan

After the trauma, get away from the scene as soon as reasonably possible. Certainly you can't leave a crime scene unprotected, but as soon as someone else gets there to take over, leave. Don't stick around to chat or to process the crime scene. Not only does that increase the potential for you to contaminate the scene by your continued presence but it's not emotionally healthy for you to be there. After a shooting, one officer was confronted by the deceased's mother who proceeded to spend an inordinate amount of time telling the officer what a "good boy" her son had been. The officer did not need to be subjected to this. He needed separation from the scene.

After you're away from the scene, call home. You don't need to go into a lot of detail about what happened; just let your spouse, your parents, your roommate—whoever is at "home"—know that you're all right and that you will give them the rest of the information when you get home. You don't want your family to find out about this event on television or to get a call from a well-meaning but uninformed person with a scanner. If, for some reason, you can't call home, make sure that another officer will notify your family where you are and what has happened. It is often a good idea for the officer to transport your family to whatever hospital you might be in rather than to have them drive themselves there. Then, once the home front has been handled, call the individual you have previously selected as your "go to" for post-trauma communication and set a place to meet with them.

If you have been involved in a shooting, you may be required to give a sample of your blood, breath, or urine and may be read a *Miranda* warning by members of your own department. Know that this is not personal but department policy and may be judicially required as part of a custodial situation. It is likely to feel awkward to be treated as a criminal by members of your own department, but you can get through this. It is in your best interests to have the most thorough investigation possible if you didn't do anything wrong. That investigation will reduce allegations of a cover up and will help convince others that your actions were appropriate. You may ask a friend you trust or a peer support person (if your department has them) to accompany you through this process.

Give an initial statement to investigators so that they can begin their investigation, but try not to write your detailed report until the next day or sometime after you've had a chance to relax, catch your breath, and gather your thoughts. The reason for this is that traumatic events often cause a perceptual distortion. Time may seem to either slow to almost a complete stop or move amazingly fast. Sound is often muffled, and shots fired may sound like small firecrackers off in the distance. You may experience tunnel vision and be unaware of things outside that tunnel because you are so intently focused on the event that you miss what is happening around you peripherally. It is also common to not remember everything that happened during a traumatic event. In such cases you may try to mentally fill in the blanks, guessing as to what might have happened, but this information is often wrong, which means that when you do remember the details, you will need to change your report so it is accurate. Thus you can see why it is better to wait for the detailed report until you have a better sense of what happened than to rush things and guess.

Immediately after the event, before you are allowed to go home, there may be an initial *defusing*. This is typically an unstructured educational process where you get a chance to discuss with a peer support officer or a mental health professional some of the things that happened and how you feel about them. Find out if this communication is protected from later subpoena before disclosing facts of the case. In the event there is little or no legal protection, focus on the emotions rather than the facts of the event. You will also be given information about some of the more common trauma responses so that you understand this is a normal process and you are not going nuts.

When you have finished the work you need to do at the department, do not go home to an empty house. If you live alone, stay with a friend. You don't need to be sitting home alone playing the "what if" game, rethinking everything that happened and how you dealt with it.

Avoid the use of alcohol or stimulants during the time after the traumatic event. While alcohol has long been a way for police officers to self-medicate, it brings its own problems. Too many officers have gotten drunk right after a critical incident, thinking it will ease some of the stress and take their mind off the ugly events of the day, only to find that the alcohol made things even worse. One officer talks about how he went drinking after a critical incident to help him forget the trauma but it only added to his troubles because he was involved in an accident while driving home and was arrested for DWI. Not only did he have the original event to deal with but now he faces additional legal and departmental ramifications of the arrest. His situation went from bad to worse. Another problem with using alcohol to self-medicate is that it can become habit forming or addictive. Both of these, as discussed more in depth in another chapter, bring their own set of problems. Don't use alcohol to help deal with trauma because you may very well crash more than you thought you might.

When you get home, be prepared to sit quietly and discuss with your spouse what happened. The incident is likely to impact his or her life in many ways. Friends will be asking about the experience, he or she will be dealing with you while you are dealing with the event, and he or she will have their own traumas regarding your incident. Your spouse is likely to have two questions for you: "Are you ok?" and "Are we ok?" These questions could take several forms but however they are asked, you need to be prepared to answer them, honestly.

Also be prepared to talk to your children. Describe the event in an age-appropriate manner, but don't tell them things they don't need to know or things they cannot understand. Answer their questions simply and honestly.

Screen your phone calls. You are likely to have achieved a status some describe as "instant celebrity." You may get phone calls from people you don't know well but who seek a vicarious thrill from your trauma and think they can get you to tell them about the event. Don't accommodate them. Talk to the people you want to talk to and avoid the others. If you get calls from friends and don't answer, they will be comfortable leaving a message simply expressing their concern. Take care of yourself in this area.

Also avoid contact with the media. In most cases they are not your friend and do not have your best interest in mind. Their job is to sell air time or newspapers, which might come at your expense. You may give an interview but should understand that you have no control about what they chose to air or print. Some of the less scrupulous reporters may show up at your home and try to trick you into an interview, or they may urge you to "tell your side." Avoid these traps and let someone uninvolved in the trauma handle media releases.

As you have avoided talking to the media, avoid watching television reports or reading newspaper articles of the event. You know what happened. You don't need to hear their distortions. They are looking for news and may sensationalize the event just to sell air time. This can cause officers to second guess what they have done and lead to more problems in the long run. This means don't look for responses on the internet either. If you get sucked into reading blogs you will only be getting the very biased opinions of people who, most of the time, have their own axe to grind. They aren't writing to express any statements of fact, because most of the time they know nothing about you or the event. Don't give them your time or energy.

Critical Incident Stress Debriefings

Many departments will hold a critical incident stress debriefing (CISD) after a traumatic incident, usually 24-72 hours after the event. This is an opportunity for you to process the emotional impact of the event in a structured and supportive environment facilitated by trained peers. A critical incident debriefing is strictly confidential, and in some states that confidentiality is protected by law. While there is controversy surrounding the effectiveness of the CISD, current research supports involvement in the debriefing. Again, there is debate about whether such debriefings should be voluntary or mandatory. My experience indicates that, far too often, those who would benefit most from the support offered during the debriefing are the ones who do not attend for fear of looking weak. My professional belief is that attendance at these debriefings should be mandatory to maximize their effectiveness. The CISD is a time to process the emotional impact of the event. No one should be criticized for how they feel; free expression of feelings is essential to the healing process. During the CISD there should be no notes or recordings, and there should be no formal record of what happened during the session. It is also important to note that a CISD is not the appropriate forum to conduct an operational critique of the event. Such an assessment should be done separately.

While this debriefing is a chance for you to process the event with others who were there, it also gives you a chance to fill in the blanks so that you understand more completely what happened. Consider this scenario: One officer who had been involved in a shootout was very angry with his partner afterward because his partner had abandoned him during the crisis. However, in the debriefing it came out that his partner had, in fact, been standing three feet away throughout the entire incident. The officer's tunnel vision had prevented him from being aware of his partner's involvement, or even his presence, in the traumatic episode. For the first officer, his partner's "absence" was a very real part of his experience and needed to be addressed, which happened at the debriefing. Participate in a debriefing if you can because they help mitigate the effects of trauma.

A Word about Critical Incident Policies

It is important for officers to know what to expect following a critical incident. Every agency should have a critical incident policy, and many do. This is a unique policy and should be written to protect the officer as well as the agency. Some considerations in writing a critical incident policy include the following:

1. It must define a critical incident.
2. It must be flexible enough to provide for variations in response to the critical incident.
3. It must address criminal/crime scene concerns.
4. It must provide a mechanism to deal with the emotional impact of the event.
5. It must provide for legal representation of the officer if necessary.

Once written, it is important that the policy be followed in all critical incidents. Selective application of this policy will only add to the uncertainty and confusion felt by the officer and may open the agency up to liability. If the policy is followed sometimes, but not others, each officer will wonder why the policy is being followed or not followed in their particular case.

Legal Fallout

As you are forced to deal with the legal issues that may follow a shooting, remember that most often a civil suit is not about whether you did things right or wrong. It's about money. The arguments will be that your actions were not appropriate and that there's a price tag on that error, but the focus is most often on the money to be won and not about you. Remembering that will help you get through the court battle.

One officer was caught between his union and his chief after being involved in a shooting. It was the first time the union had decided to bring in an attorney to represent the officer before the officer spoke to the investigating detectives. In this case when the officer was advised of his rights per *Miranda*, he thought he should take advantage of the legal counsel being provided by the union and said that he would wait for his attorney. When his chief heard what the officer said, the chief's response was, "If he wants to act like a suspect, treat him like one. Book him." The officer's attorney was able to get him out of the police station before the officer was booked, took the officer to a motel, checked him into a room, and told the officer to wait there until the attorney contacted him. The officer was instructed not to call anyone or to speak with anyone before then. The officer was left alone at the motel for 24 hours with no contact from anyone. During that time he wasn't even thinking about losing his job—what weighed most heavily on his mind was being locked up behind bars. He remembered his chief's last words: "If he wants to act like a suspect, treat him like one." This officer was most worried about how his family was going to survive while he was in jail.

Knowing When to Seek Professional Help

As time passes, you may continue to experience after-effects from the traumatic experience. For example, you may have nightmares after a shooting, which is not uncommon. Such nightmares often involve a sense of powerlessness, such as dreaming that the bullets are falling out the end of the barrel of your weapon, or that the trigger doesn't work, or that you just keep shooting and shooting but the bullets have no effect. These nightmares are likely to pass fairly quickly, but if they don't go away within a couple of weeks, seek professional help. Other symptoms might include sleep disturbances, difficulty focusing, avoidance of anything that might bring back memories of the event, and intrusive thoughts where you can't stop thinking about the incident or it just keeps popping into consciousness. Again, if any of these symptoms persist for more than two weeks (at the longest), seek professional help.

Sometimes traumatic events stay with us and feel as though they are a current event rather than something that happened in the past. If you find that things just seem to be sticking with you and you can't seem to shake images of the incident, consider looking for a therapist who does Eye Movement Desensitization and Reprocessing (EMDR) therapy. EMDR is a treatment for the residual effects of trauma and has been found to be extremely effective. To find a qualified therapist in your area, go online and search "EMDR" to find a listing of local EMDR trained therapists.

THE BOTTOM LINE: DON'T RUSH THE HEALING

Healing from a critical incident is not an event, it is a process. Plan time to allow yourself to heal. There will always be people telling you to "just move on with your life." However, it's not their life. It's yours. You will process things at your own speed, not at other people's speed, and that's okay. Give yourself permission to accept that you are going at the right speed for you.

We often try to rush the process and don't give ourselves the necessary time to heal properly because we want our world back to normal as soon as possible. The problem with this is that what used to be normal doesn't work anymore. You've been changed by your experience, whether you want to admit it or not, and whether you like it or not. We don't choose to be changed, but we are.

Exposure to critical events changes us in two ways. The first is through new learning. We learn things about life, death, human nature, and injustice that we had no idea of prior to the event. We might have had some intellectual knowledge or understanding of these types of events and knew, cognitively, that they might happen, but that's not the same as the experiential knowledge we gain by living through it. When our knowledge of something is only an abstract concept in our minds, it is merely a possibility. But when we live through it, it becomes a reality. We not only know it in our heads but now we feel it with every fiber of our being. When we experience a critical incident, we experience it in a thousand different ways. We experience the sights, the smells, the textures, the tastes—the entire context of the event. And we experience it not only with our own emotions but with those of others as well. This kind of experiential knowledge is the type of knowledge we base our lives upon.

Think about this: How many officers know that every shift brings with it the possibility of a deadly force incident? Everyone does (or should). After all, there's a reason you go to work wearing a bullet-proof vest and carrying a gun, Taser, night stick, pepper spray, and various other "tools of the trade" on your duty belt. Yet how many officers neglect to keep their weapons clean? Or maintain a high level of weapons proficiency? If you really believed that your next shift would have you in a deadly force situation, and that you might not be coming home afterward, you might live today very differently.

The second way that we are changed by exposure to trauma is through classical Pavlovian conditioning. You may recall from a psychology course how Pavlov taught (or more accurately, conditioned) dogs to salivate when he rang a bell by pairing the ringing of the bell with the presentation of food to the dogs. The presentation of food elicited the desired response, the salivation. When the ringing of the bell had become paired with the presentation of the food, the ringing of the bell would, by itself, could cause the dogs to salivate. In other words, the dogs' response had become conditioned. So, Pavlov took something that was neutral for the dogs (the ringing of the bell) and gave it meaning. As a police officer there are lots of things in your community that have a specific meaning for you that they do not have for anyone else. For example, if you are sent to a small grocery store on a robbery call and discover that the young woman working there has been stabbed repeatedly for less than $20, that store now has a meaning for you that it has for no one else. This experience is likely to begin as a wound (trauma) that will hopefully heal until only a scar is left. If you have been a police officer for any length of time, you will find that you accumulate more scars every year. There is no way to avoid it. If you are new to the profession, you cannot yet imagine how many scars you can accumulate during your career.

A FINAL WORD

There is no guarantee that you won't be exposed to a number of traumatic events throughout your time on the job, but you don't have to let them destroy you. Take care of yourself as you experience trauma. Don't let something like this end your career, your marriage, or your life.

Chapter 9

SURVIVING BURNOUT

"You can only be everything to everybody for so long before something has to snap."

— One officer describing his frustration

Initially police work is challenging, it is fun, and it is exciting. There is always an adrenalin dump in responding to a domestic or a fight call, a chance for a new and thrilling experience, and a chance to make a difference. However, as cops progress in their careers, they sometimes feel as though they are putting their health and even their lives on the line for people who really don't appreciate it. Cops also sometimes feel like, despite all of their efforts and intentions, what they do doesn't even make a difference. In fact, I think there comes a time in every police career when a cop wonders, "What in the hell am I doing here?" You'll ask yourself if it's worth it and if you're making a difference, at the same time feeling like it *isn't* worth it and you *aren't* making a difference. That's when you start to fizzle. Each time you go on these calls and later see that you may not have made any difference whatsoever, you may find you have less and less to give. This diminished capacity to give stems from an accumulation of long-term stressors and is the essence of burnout.

There are many assumptions about burnout. Everyone assumes that it won't happen to them, it won't happen to someone they know, or maybe even that it's just an excuse to not work. These assumptions are based on each person's unique perspective, their history, personal experiences, feelings, and even the comments from those around them. Yet, for each person, burnout is something unique. Not only does it come from our unique perspective, but takes us to our own individual hell.

BURNOUT DEFINED

Burnout is a catch phrase that seems to be popular right now. People use expressions like, "I'm really fried," or, "I'm just too burned out to keep doing this." Certainly they are expressing dissatisfaction with their lives, but what do they really mean? The meaning may not be the same for everyone. Yet however burnout is defined, all agree that it can suck the life out of those it hits and is something that no one wants to fall victim to.

Burnout is much easier to observe than define. We know it when we see it. It's apparent in disgruntled employees or co-workers but there is no concise definition. Burnout is a complex problem that cannot be addressed through a simplistic formula or solution, such as if you only worked out more often, you won't be burned out. Or if you change your diet you won't be burned out. If only it was that easy. While these solutions may address specific symptoms of burnout, they can't begin to address the depth of the problem.

Burnout has been defined as a progressive loss of idealism, energy, and purpose experienced as a result of work conditions. Burnout may first become apparent through physical symptoms such as ulcers, headaches, backaches, frequent colds, and sexual problems. It causes a basic, fundamental change to the core of who you are. It doesn't mean that you are overweight, in poor physical condition, or anything like that. These may be some of the symptoms, but they are not the problem. The problem is that the way you see the world has changed and everything is affected. You may be burned out because of work-related issues but it affects your marriage, your family life, your social life, and even how you feel about yourself. Burnout can impact every facet of your life.

The phrase "burn out" is used in so many different ways that it is often difficult to tell what it really means. One frequently hears talk about burnout as a state of being or as an experience, as in the expressions, "I'm all stressed out," or, "The stress around here is killing me," but this is not quite accurate. Burnout is really a process, the result of extended over-exposure to a high-stress environment. Stress is the demand on the human organism for an adaptational change (physical monitoring). It is when cops are unable (or unwilling) to make the necessary changes that we "burn out." For most police officers, the common response to work-related stress is to keep pushing as long as possible, without letting up, until they hit a wall and collapse. Subsequently, when they do crash, it is serious.

FACTORS CONTRIBUTING TO BURNOUT

Burnout can be a result of a high stress level maintained for too long. Such levels can only be maintained for so long before the organism (you) can no longer function. Most police officers can handle intense stress for short periods of time—called *burst stress*—and function quite well. In fact, some may even have entered this career because they enjoyed burst stress. To use an analogy, if they were runners, they would be sprinters, doing short intense races and giving everything they have for 100 meters. But what would happen if they tried to maintain that same pace for a marathon? The body would simply collapse from the exertion. Similarly if you ran nitrous oxide in your car's engine for an extended period of time, the engine wouldn't last or would need frequent rebuilding. That's the burnout—you've gone too fast for too long. The demands placed on you have exceeded your ability to respond.

Some of the factors that contribute to burnout are the initial noble aspirations, high initial enthusiasm, and unrealistic expectations; the lack of criteria for measuring accomplishment; low pay; inadequate institutional support; inefficient use of resources; and high public visibility coupled with popular misunderstanding and suspicion.

Noble Aspirations, Initial Enthusiasm, and Unrealistic Expectations

We've talked about the noble aspirations, initial enthusiasm, and unrealistic expectations. I'll bet that if you think back you can remember your first night on the street. Think about how you planned to make a difference. Think of the things you planned to do that night, or that first week, or even that first year. How much of that have you gotten done? How much are you not even concerned about doing anymore? How much isn't even worth doing? I think the basic question here is, "How much have I changed?" because you know the system hasn't changed.

Remember, burnout is a process. A little bit gets chipped away each time you are disappointed or something doesn't go as it is supposed to. While it is unrealistic to expect everything to always work to perfection, it is still disappointing when it doesn't. On the other hand, cops tend to focus on the negatives and articulate negative expectations. The police world is filled with negatives, and cops tend to have negative outlooks. Even so, while cops are preparing for the worst and expecting the worst, part of them is still hoping for a positive outcome. But after they have been let down enough, cops start to build on their disappointments. They stop hoping for positive outcomes, and that contributes to the burnout. When the hopes have been unfulfilled over an extended period of time, the hopes die along with the ability to hope.

Lack of Criteria for Measuring Accomplishment

In police work there is no objective way to measure progress. If you write a thousand citations a year, are you a good police officer? Not necessarily. All that means is that you have written a lot of traffic citations. If they are parking citations, they will not likely have a significant effect on the accident rate. Even if they are good "movers," does it mean you are a good police officer if you are busy enforcing traffic laws when there are burglars operating in your community or there are pedophiles picking up kids off the streets? Of course not. It seems that to be a good police officer we have to be everything to everyone. Simple, right?

We are set with an impossible challenge, and our level of performance is most often evaluated by special interest groups, a community that doesn't understand what we do, or even a supervisor who is not with us all of the time and may not have the same understanding or attitude we have about good police work. Even if these people knew what we were supposed to do, there are no effective criteria for measuring success as a police officer. We can't measure the crimes that didn't happen, the assaults that didn't take place, or the kids that didn't get into trouble because you were there. While people will try to say crime was prevented or lives were saved because of some program, it doesn't relate to the individual—you. So, how do you know you've done a good job? You need to tell yourself that you have, and you need to believe it. If you wait for others to tell you, it may be a long wait.

Unfair Pay

Another factor that contributes to burnout is the low pay that police officers get. Compare the work that you do and the dangers you are exposed to, and ask what might happen if you held out for a multi-million dollar contract over the next 5 years or didn't want to go to work unless you got an endorsement contract with Nike. If your boss is like mine, you'd either be out of a job or confined to a bed at the nearest psychiatric facility. Cops put their lives at risk every day and yet aren't paid nearly what they are worth. It is frustrating to hear crybabies whining about the dangers of professional sports and why they should be paid so much.

Compare your salary to that of your friends who are working in private industry. Again, we often find the salaries are not commensurate with the work police officers do, the responsibilities they have, or the risks they take. Consider this: When most people are running away from gunshots or explosions, cops are running toward them.

Finally, the most frustrating part might be to compare your salary with the income of some of those you arrest. You arrest a pimp or drug dealer and see that he has a six-figure annual income, tax free, while you work 40 hours a week plus off-duty jobs and still struggle to make ends meet. For some, crime *does* pay, and pay well.

Some of the people you try to help regard you with hostility and contempt, and you might be spit on and verbally assaulted by complete strangers, simply because you wear a uniform for which they have no respect. They would not spit on their physician or their attorney. You are told to be "professional" no matter how you are treated, yet you feel as though your pay is not in line with these expectations. This is a double standard. You are expected to be the consummate professional but are neither paid nor treated that way. These incongruities make cops question the system of rewards and values held by the community in which they work.

Inadequate Institutional Support

Inadequate institutional support is often seen as another factor in burnout. Your interests may not be in line with those of the department and, for this reason, go unsupported. You may think that protection of life and property are the most important parts of police work, but when your boss says, "Write more tickets," you may become frustrated. On that rare occasion that you respond to citizen with sarcasm, find the IA complaint sustained, and get a reprimand, you may feel as though there is no one on your side.

You can't be perfect and feel as though you are being penalized for being human. It's ok for everyone else to have a "bad day" but not for you. When these complaints hit the media and your chief or public information officer responds with something like, "No comment," even though you know you've done nothing wrong, you might wonder why someone didn't just have the guts to stand up and say, "This cop didn't do anything wrong. Get off his back!" Yet that never seems to happen. It feels like the politicals are all trying to cover their own backsides at the expense of yours.

Inefficient Use of Resources

Another frequent cause of burnout is the inefficient use of resources. When your priorities are not those of your department it can be very frustrating. When the department buys bicycles and computers and you think they need squad cars and more police officers, the situation can be very discouraging. When you see the patrol function as the basic function of all police work, yet the patrol division is decimated to support "special" programs, it can cause you to ask whether you even have the resources to make possible the things you consider important. This can lead to an attitude of "the hell with it." Your belief that, "if the department doesn't think it's important, why should I bother," is symptomatic of burnout and will spread to the rest of your life if you are not careful.

High Public Visibility and Popular Misconceptions

Two final factors contributing to burnout are the high public visibility of the police coupled with popular misunderstandings and suspicions on the part of the citizens. People often don't trust police officers, and they certainly don't always show officers the respect that is deserved. Have you ever been standing somewhere in uniform and hear a parent say to their child, "See that police officer over there? If you don't behave I'm going to have him take you to jail."

Such comments and threats are frustrating because (1) it isn't our role to haul misbehaving children off to jail, and (2) it paints a very negative image of the police in the mind of the child. But if you were to confront that parent and ask them who they want their child to call when they are lost or otherwise in need help, it could lead to an altercation that will just cause further problems for you.

It becomes even more frustrating when you remember that these are supposed to be the citizens who are on our side. Often people complain about unsafe driving in their neighborhood, but when you stop them and give them a citation for their unsafe driving, they ask why you aren't out looking for real criminals. Or they are hostile and angry toward you for doing the job they asked you to do; they just didn't want it applied to them.

If a police officer makes a mistake, it is not the same as when a plumber or a carpenter, or a teacher or an attorney makes a mistake. Our mistake is big "news." The officer's mistake is made public, and all of the people in the community know about it. Not only does the officer have to deal with that mistake but his or her entire family is subjected to the pain and humiliation of that publicity. It doesn't even need to be a real mistake. Too often police actions are blown out of proportion by an exploitive media seeking to boost circulation or viewer ratings.

TYPES OF BURNOUT

There are two types of burnout. The first is individual burnout, which is evidenced by a deterioration in an officer's personal and interpersonal performance as a direct result of continued involvement in a stressful work environment. The second is organizational burnout in which a critical mass of the individuals within an organization are "burned out" and, because of this, the tasks essential to the organization are not accomplished. Thus, organizational burnout, in which organizational goals go unmet, is a result of the cumulative burnout of the individuals within that organization. Some of the organizational features that can contribute to individual burnout are inconsistent role expectations, role ambiguity, role conflict, rotating shifts, physical conditions at work, and poor or ineffective communication within the organization.

In a burned out organization there are often inconsistent role expectations. The chief may have one set of expectations, for example, expecting officers to provide active community service. Yet the sergeant may expect officers to enforce the laws, regardless of who the violator is. The sergeant may not be receptive when officers check out of service to meet with members of the community regarding specific problems and may show this lack of receptivity by punishing officers in some informal manner.

Role ambiguity is also prevalent in dysfunctional organizations. It is often unclear to the officers what their responsibilities are or what the true priorities of the organization are, making it difficult for the officer to be successful. There is no way to meet the responsibilities of the role when they are unclear and may change frequently.

Studies have shown that rotating shifts are hard on officers. The human body doesn't adjust well to weekly or monthly changes in sleep patterns. In fact, some people never adjust to a pattern of working nights and sleeping days. As this becomes more frustrating for the officers within the department, it can contribute to organizational burnout. Additionally, it is far too common that only lower ranking officers—primarily patrol and sergeant supervisors—rotate shifts. Administrators don't rotate. Yet they give reasons for subordinate officers to rotate such as, "I don't want any of my officers to become too familiar with a given neighborhood or shift," or, "We've always rotated shifts," or, "It makes things fair for everyone." Yet, not only do these reasons pale when health effects are considered, they run counter to research findings and common sense.

First, officers can function far more effectively if they are intimately familiar with the neighborhood and shift they serve. Second, just because things have always been done one way is no reason to continue doing them that way. And finally, when shifts are assigned by seniority it generally puts the younger, most aggressive officers on during the evening, which is often the busiest time of the day, and puts the older officers on during the day shift. It also puts the older officers, whose bodies and circadian rhythms are often less able to adjust to changing sleep patterns, into a more stable routine where they are not trying to shift back and forth between working nights and trying to be awake during the day on their days off. Thus, straight shifts, assigned by seniority, are the fairest way of assigning shifts—rotating shifts are not.

The physical conditions at work are often seen as a reflection of the importance the department or community places on the officer, the role of the officer, and the relationship with the community. If the physical conditions are poor, it seems as though the department or the community places a low priority on the services provided by the police officer. As competition for diminishing funds increases among government services and communities are forced to do more with less money, the risk to police of driving old squad cars, working with outdated equipment, and occupying offices in old buildings needing repair increases. Over time, an officer working in this environment is going to feel as though his or her work is not appreciated, which will contribute to individual burnout and, if the conditions expand and persist, to organizational burnout.

When an organization has burned out, communications are generally rigid, formal, and most often from the top down. There is little solicitation of input from the rank-and-file, and if thoughts, ideas, or opinions are expressed from the bottom, they are often ignored or even punished. Communication in burned out organizations will often take the form of written policies and procedures that incorporate no input from those most affected by the changes, which generates a feeling of being "done to" by the line officers. Management in this type of organization often justifies the one-way, top-down approach by expressing a belief that the officers don't care enough to get involved anyway, so why bother asking for input? Or they state that line officers only want things to benefit them without considering others' needs or ideas.

The management in these dysfunctional organizations may even express the almost paranoid belief that if officers are allowed *any* input, they may do everything they can to subvert the process or even destroy the current administration. This negative communication and attitude leads to a low-trust environment which makes things even worse. As trust continues to erode, participation by both parties decreases, which leads to less trust and less participation, and the cycle continues until the organization is destroyed. An indirect result of organizational burnout is that the agency becomes less and less attractive to enthusiastic new employees. Younger officers might say things like, "Why would I want to work there? It's not a good place to be." This, in turn, impacts public perception, which impacts funding and again, sets in motion a vicious cycle that is destructive to the organization.

THE EFFECTS OF BURNOUT

The consequences of burnout are serious. The following things are likely to occur in varying degrees. First of all, those ideals you brought to the profession are challenged because your job has become frustrating and often unrewarding. I think one of the most difficult lessons for any police officer to learn is that not everyone who needs help wants it. We come into the profession believing we will make a difference for those people we deal with, but we can only make a difference if they allow us to. In many cases the people we deal with don't want things to be different, even when those things are bad or harmful. They just want a band-aid solution to a serious problem.

As this process of burnout evolves, the services we provide to the community become less because we invest less of ourselves. It's tough to keep investing when it seems like nothing is coming back and there is no reward or sense of satisfaction in what you have done. As you become more burned out, you will feel more frustrated, and the more frustrated you feel, the more burned out you will become, the less you will invest, and the more frustrated you will feel. It becomes a vicious cycle that feeds on itself until there is no energy expended and no reward felt.

A parallel risk here is that while this process is happening at work, it may also be happening in the rest of your life. The less you invest in your marriage, the less you get back. The less you invest with your friends, the less you get back. Most importantly, the less you invest in yourself, the less you get back.

You may begin to feel trapped because of the job market, career paths, pensions, and benefits. You may be trapped because there is nowhere else you can go work as a police officer and there is nothing else you can do that will generate anywhere near the same income. It may be that there is a lot of competition in the market and you are unlikely to get hired right away in another department. Additionally, the more burned out you are, the less likely it will seem any different in another department and the less interest they will have in hiring you. You are still dealing with people who are the same wherever you go. You may be locked into a specific career path. You may be stuck in a squad car answering calls because the chief doesn't like you and won't make you an investigator. Or maybe you work in a smaller department where there is simply nowhere to go; the other assignments and promotional spots may be filled by people who are not planning to leave soon because, for them as with you, there is just nowhere else to go.

The more you are burned out, the less likely it is that you will be assigned to a position that will be different enough to matter. Again, this is a spiral that only leads downward. You may be stuck in your department because of a pension, sticking it out and every day saying to yourself, "I've only got 5 more years until I can get the hell out of here." But think of what those 5 years are going to be like—1,250 days just like this one, with no hope for change and no hope for things to get any better.

KNOWING WHEN YOU'RE BURNED OUT

In police work, weariness is inevitable. Cops are constantly exposed to the most negative things this world has to offer and fighting a daily battle against them. You see friends betraying friends, family members stabbing each other in the back, and people actively stealing from or physically assaulting those they "love." These are the battles police officers face daily. With this kind of exposure, how could anyone *not* risk losing their belief in those things that are good, happy, honest, and worth caring about? As officers are subjected to these things more and more, there is a loss of adaptational energy. They no longer have the strength or maybe even the desire to change. It takes work to see the world as a better place, and as people become more and more burned out, there may be little or no energy left to put into recovery or rebounding from these changes.

As you find yourself becoming more and more burned out, you can't just look ahead to a certain point in your career and say, "Once I get there, once things get so bad, then I'll stop," because it doesn't work that way. If there is no intervention, it gets worse until there is "no joy in Mudville." This isn't something that can be measured on a point to point scale. It is subjective, like the difference between "good enough" and "not good enough," or "tall enough" and "not tall enough." There is no exact cut off where you can say, "I'm burned out" or "I'm not burned out." It's like asking, "How deep does the water need to be to swim?" There are obvious points where it is not deep enough (6 inches) and there are obvious points where it is (12 feet). But at exactly what point does it become deep enough to swim? It will be a different answer for each swimmer. This is the same question you might ask as, "Exactly when am I burned out?" Well, there is no exact answer. It is a subjective experience and, again, different for everyone.

GETTING BEYOND BURNOUT

Burnout doesn't just go away on its own. It is a progressive state or way of seeing the world. As police officers realize they are beginning to burn out, it is essential to deal with it. The total package must be examined in order to create an appropriate solution. Just because one solution may work for one person doesn't mean that it will work for all, or even most, people. If the solution for one person is something physical, like running, that wouldn't work for someone who has a bad back and can't run. It may work even less for someone who can't even force himself to walk to the store, much less run for the "pleasure" of it. In creating a solution, it is essential to look at the options that are available to us physically, cognitively, emotionally, spiritually, and within our social frame of reference.

Some of the things that can be done to make things better are to restructure the work environment so as to relieve some of the emotional pressure, rotate responsibilities (i.e., switch from patrol to investigative duties), accept the givens and work with them, and try to measure success in more realistic ways.

Sometimes changes can be made to restructure our work environment so that cops are not working 15 days in a row with no days off—it might be essential to take at least one day off per week just to get away from the job. Another way of restructuring might be to focus on different areas while working in the same capacity or to work with a partner if you normally work alone. Either of these changes might make things a little easier and reduce some of the burnout you are feeling.

Another important thing that can reduce the effects of burnout is to rotate responsibilities, if possible. I have found that after about a two-year absence from patrol, I always return with renewed enthusiasm. It is fun again. In the interim, the job is new and challenging. This keeps things fresh and will help prevent burnout.

It is also essential to accept the givens. There are simply some things beyond our power to change, no matter how hard we try. You are not going to get a new squad car every year, you are not going to solve every crime, and you are not going to be able to protect every victim. If you accept these as givens, you can more realistically assess your performance and can find satisfaction in the things you do well without beating yourself up over the things you don't do well or can't do because they are outside your control.

And finally, try to measure your success in ways that are manageable. Don't forget to notice the smile of a small child who waves enthusiastically as you drive past in your squad car, or the hand shake of an elderly man you have just made feel better even though his home has been burglarized. Cops tend to overlook the little treasures of the work and focus on the major disappointments. We set ourselves up for this by forgetting that the small things we do *are* the things that make the differences. In measuring success, set realistic goals. For example, to say, "I am going to work really hard tonight to try to catch the burglars in my district" is very different from, "I am going to catch the burglars in my district." The first is very doable, the second may not be. What happens if the burglars don't strike tonight? If you are measuring your efforts in the first way, you can feel good about what you have done at the end of the night. If you are looking at the second, you are in trouble. You have failed … again.

As you begin to measure success, focus on the process, not the result. Look at how hard you worked, not what you accomplished. A lot of the good arrests are simply a matter of being in the right place at the right time. There is no secret to success other than working hard, and even that is no guarantee for success. Continue to focus on your successes, not your failures. Too often in police work we focus on the negative. The tendency, then, is to focus on your failures. This is depressing and can lead to a sense of worthlessness and hopelessness. Try to avoid this trap by focusing on the things you have done with success.

Keep a time perspective. Remember you are a police officer while you are on duty. Try to avoid taking on the occupation as an identity. Rather, view it as a career, what you do, not who you are. If you can do this, it will be easier to not interpret results on a personal level. When a criminal you have arrested is released, don't take it personally. It's not about you, it's about the system. It means the system may have failed—again, but it doesn't mean you failed. This perspective will slow down the burnout process.

Finally, remember to take time for you and the things you enjoy away from police work. Take time for your non-police friends, your family, and outside recreation. This will help to remind you that you are a person, a unique individual who has much more value than simply as a police officer. Being a cop is a great career but a lousy identity. Just keep balance in your life.

ELIMINATING BURNOUT

Burnout can't be completely eliminated. Again, the things we are exposed to will cause change in anyone. It would be naïve to believe we could go through all of that and not be affected. Almost all police officers will experience transient symptoms of burnout. Yet the important thing is to ensure these are only transient symptoms, not an ongoing thing. When transient symptoms occur more and more frequently, those symptoms become more and more definitive of who we are rather than just something experienced temporarily in the moment.

Chapter 10

SURVIVING MENTAL ILLNESS

With contributions by Carrie Kralicek, MSN, ARNP, PMHN-BC [1]

Mental illness can strike any individual or family at any time, and cops are no exception. If you or any member of your family is afflicted with any type of mental illness, there are some things you need to know. However, we must emphasize up front that this chapter is, by no means, exhaustive and should *not* be used as a diagnostic tool. If you or a family member is suffering from a mental illness of any sort, or if you're unsure, seek professional assistance as soon as possible.

This chapter is intended to familiarize you with symptoms of some mental illnesses. There are many different types of mental illness, some debilitating and some very treatable. Just because someone is diagnosed with a mental illness, it does not mean they can no longer be a productive member of society. Some of the most famous people in history have reportedly been diagnosed with mental illness. Abraham Lincoln, considered by many to be the greatest president in U.S. history, suffered from severe depression, sometimes even entertaining suicidal thoughts. Winston Churchill also reportedly suffered from severe depression and may have been considered to have bipolar disorder. Margot Kidder, an actress perhaps best known for her role as Lois Lane four *Superman* movies, has been diagnosed with schizophrenia as well as bipolar disorder. Musician Billy Joel has been diagnosed with depression and has even attempted suicide by drinking furniture polish. Actress Carrie

---

[1] Carrie Kralicek, MSN, ARNP, PMHN-BC, is a psychiatric nurse practitioner who has worked in the juvenile justice system and as a jail nurse. As the spouse of a former police officer who suffered a near-fatal debilitating injury in the line of duty, she advocates on behalf of public servants through proposed legislation and motivational speaking. She has spoken for Concerns of Police Survivors, the United States Park Service Rangers, the FBI, and numerous others. She has also spoken for the legislature and in academic settings regarding "traumas of law enforcement" and "the aftermath of a critical incident." Carrie is a veteran of the United States Air Force and a published author.

Fisher, the original Princess Leia, has been diagnosed with manic-depressive disorder. And the list could go on and on. These people have all been diagnosed with a mental illness yet have led very productive lives. This chapter will help give you some insights into what you might do if this happens to you or someone close to you.

There are a number of ways that police families are impacted by mental illness. First, the illness may affect the officer. When the officer is impacted, there is a great deal of uncertainty thrown into the family. The officer may continue to work, may be unable to work, or may have their duties limited and everything is up in the air. Mental illness can also strike the officer's spouse, which also disrupts home life, again throwing instability into their world. When mental illness strikes one of the children there is still significant impact to the family. Such an illness changes family dynamics in many ways, regardless of which family member it strikes.

MENTAL ILLNESS DEFINED

Mental illness is often described as consisting of abnormal or maladaptive behaviors or as a violation of norms or deviation from socially acceptable behavior. This abnormal behavior could range from benign conduct, such as a guy wearing a tin foil helmet to keep the FBI from stealing his thoughts, to something far more serious, such as criminal activity. Most states provide a statutory definition of mental illness, which serves two purposes: it defines the law for civil commitments, and it defines the illness for the purpose of providing state assistance. In Minnesota, for example, the concept of mental illness is defined in Minnesota Statutes 245.462 subdivision 13 as:

Subd. 13.Person who is mentally ill.

(a) A "person who is mentally ill" means any person who has an organic disorder of the brain or a substantial psychiatric disorder of thought, mood, perception, orientation, or memory which grossly impairs judgment, behavior, capacity to recognize reality, or to reason or understand, which is manifested by instances of grossly disturbed behavior or faulty perceptions and poses a substantial likelihood of physical harm to self or others as demonstrated by:

(1) a failure to obtain necessary food, clothing, shelter, or medical care as a result of the impairment;

(2) an inability for reasons other than indigence to obtain necessary food, clothing, shelter, or medical care as a result of the impairment and it is more probable than not that the person will suffer substantial harm, significant psychiatric deterioration or debilitation, or serious illness, unless appropriate treatment and services are provided;

(3) a recent attempt or threat to physically harm self or others; or

(4) recent and volitional conduct involving significant damage to substantial property.

(b) A person is not mentally ill under this section if the impairment is solely due to:

(1) epilepsy;

(2) developmental disability;

(3) brief periods of intoxication caused by alcohol, drugs, or other mind-altering substances; or

(4) dependence upon or addiction to any alcohol, drugs, or other mind-altering substances.

PREVALENCE OF MENTAL ILLNESS

According to the National Alliance on Mental Illness (NAMI), a staggering number of people suffer from one or more forms of mental illness.[2] One in four adults, or approximately 57.7 million Americans, will experience a mental health disorder in a given year. One in 17 people suffer from a serious mental illness such as schizophrenia, major depression, or bipolar disorder. And about one in 10 children live with a serious mental or emotional disorder. Specific estimates are that about:

- 2.4 million Americans (1.1% of adults in the U.S.) suffer from schizophrenia.
- 5.7 million Americans (2.6% of adults) suffer from bipolar disorder.
- 14.8 million Americans (6.7% of adults) suffer from major depressive disorder—the leading cause of disability for

---

[2] National Alliance on Mental Illness. (2013). *Mental illness: Facts and numbers.* Retrieved from http://www.nami.org/factsheets/mentalillness_factsheet.pdf

people ages 15-44 in the United States, according the 2004
World Health Report.

- 40 million Americans (18.7% of adults) experience anxiety
  disorders, including panic disorder, obsessive-compulsive
  disorder (OCD), post-traumatic stress disorder (PTSD),
  generalized anxiety disorder, and phobias.
- 48% of Americans age 15-54 have had at least one mental or
  addictive disorder.

Given the commonality of mental illness, it is unreasonable to
believe that no cop or cops' families will be impacted by this
condition. Cops and their family members are not immune to mental
illness, yet it is frequently misunderstood and difficult to deal with.

THE STIGMA OF MENTAL ILLNESS

One of the first concerns when you or a loved one are diagnosed with
a mental illness is dealing with the stigma. Mental illness is shrouded
in widespread misconceptions—that it is somehow indicative of a
character flaw in the person afflicted with it and that whoever gets it
should be ashamed that they allowed themselves to succumb to the
condition. This stigma pressures those suffering from mental illness
to keep it hidden and to not seek necessary treatment, which is unfair
and life threatening. Of course, society does not treat those with heart
disease or diabetes with such disgrace, yet mental illness is no
different. However, people often fear what they do not understand,
and mental illness is greatly misunderstood.
    People far too often believe that when someone is afflicted with
a mental illness it is because of something they have done. This is
completely false. There is no way to "catch" mental illness. Police
officers may experience post traumatic symptoms as a result of
exposure to work related trauma, but that's not the same as
"catching" mental illness. Origins of mental illness can vary from
heredity to unknown causes. In no case has the person with the
illness asked for it or deserved it. Furthermore, mental illness doesn't
show up on an MRI or an x-ray. It isn't something we can see, feel,
or touch. We diagnose the mental illness based on the reported
symptoms or the observed behaviors. Too often there is a
misunderstanding and a belief that the impacted individual can and

should simply make the condition go away. For example, that a person in the throes of a major depressive disorder should simply "snap out of it," that they can get over the illness if they simply try harder. So the first thing is to accept that there is a stigma to mental illness and that such a stigma is inappropriate. Don't internalize that stigma, whether the illness has struck you or a family member. Remember that it is an illness, not a choice.

TYPES OF MENTAL ILLNESS

There are a variety of mental illnesses. Not all of them involve psychosis, or a loss of contact with reality. In fact, many people suffering from mental illness can describe quite clearly the exact nature of their illness. Yet the stereotype of mental illness is that of a person who suffers from hallucinations and is violent, which is simply not true. Many people suffering from a mental illness lead very normal and productive lives. Each individual and each illness will vary in the way that it impacts the officer, home, and family.

A basic distinction exists between neurosis and psychosis. The neurosis is a mental illness where the individual loses no contact with reality but, none the less, suffers from a mental illness. Obsessive compulsive disorder (OCD) often fits into this category. The individual experiences obsessive thoughts, often regarding germs or health issues, and engages in compulsive behaviors to reduce the anxiety created by those obsessive thoughts. In the movie *As Good as It Gets*, Jack Nicholson portrays a man suffering from OCD. He is so concerned with germs and the transmission of disease that when he goes to a restaurant he takes his own plastic eating utensils. Frequently people with OCD can explain the irrationality of their obsessions and compulsions but can't control them.

An example of a psychosis, on the other hand, is illustrated by the police officer who suffered a traumatic brain injury and was found in a large church, screaming at God and unresponsive to the other police officers summoned to the scene. This officer was not in contact with reality and needed to be tazed several times before he was subdued and could be taken to the hospital. Often people who are suffering from a psychotic illness must be hospitalized, at least until they can be stabilized with the proper medication.

Just like any other illness there are diagnosable symptoms of mental illness. It is important to have a sense of what those symptoms might be so that the illness can be dealt with as soon as possible. Following are some of the more common mental illnesses and a general description of the symptoms.

Panic Attack

A panic attack can be one of the most disturbing, debilitating, and abrupt experiences of a mental illness. The symptoms of a panic attack include a racing or pounding heartbeat, chest pains, dizziness, lightheadedness, nausea, difficulty breathing, tingling or numbness in the hands, perceptual distortions, and feelings of powerlessness. These symptoms can mimic those of a heart attack. If you or a loved one is experiencing these symptoms, don't just write it off as a panic attack. It might be a heart attack. Even if you or they have had panic attacks in the past, it does not mean that you are immune to a heart attack. You could have both. Seek medical attention immediately. If your physician diagnoses this as a panic attack, work with it, but don't make any assumptions. Make sure it's not a heart attack.

Depression

One of the most common mental illnesses is a major depressive disorder (MDD). When you stop and think about it, a lot of the stuff that cops deal with is depressing. Cops don't get called when good things happen or to share in happy times. They are called when tragedy strikes. They work in a world of depression and sadness. When it gets to a point where this negativity and sadness becomes the lens through which a cop sees the world, when they are no longer capable of seeing any likelihood of the world ever changing or having any goodness, that's when depression strikes.

This illness is debilitating in that you may find you have little or no energy. Even things that should be "fun" can seem to be just too much work. It may feel like life is just not worth living. Not all depressed people are suicidal but suicide is a common response to untreated depression. In addition to being suicidal, symptoms of MDD can include disrupted concentration, fatigue, psychomotor problems, feelings of guilt or worthlessness, changes in appetite and weight loss/gain, and sleep disturbances. Of these, sleep disturbances, concentration problems, and fatigue are the most common residual symptoms.[3] Other common symptoms of depression that are not part of the formal diagnostic criteria for MDD include painful physical symptoms, excessive daytime sleepiness/hypersomnia with problems of arousal and alertness, anxiety, vasomotor symptoms, and sexual dysfunction.

Depression can often be treated with medication, and you or your loved one can live a very normal and even happy life. Medications should be taken as prescribed, even after the individual begins to feel "better." It can take being on medication for a year or longer for the symptoms to resolve. Antidepressant medications come in a number of shapes and sizes but all work to accomplish the same thing—to alleviate the symptoms of depression. These medications can give an individual more energy and can help eliminate confused thinking or ruminations. They are not the kind of medications that people take to get "high." There are side effects, but euphoria is not one of them.

These antidepressant medications will not have an adverse impact on your job.[4] There are no side effects to antidepressant use that will make you unfit for police work. It is true, however, that the side effects of a mental illness, if left untreated, may have a detrimental impact on being fit for duty. It is important to remember that these medications, as with all psychotropic medications, do not cure mental illness, they merely provide symptom relief. It is also important to remember that these medications can take up to three weeks to take effect because many need to build to a clinical level in the blood stream before they eliminate symptoms.

Antidepressant medications are often difficult to regulate, and their effectiveness is very dependent on individual biochemistry. A dosage that works fine for one individual may leave another person either grossly over-medicated or may be insufficient to make any difference in symptom severity. The medication can also stop working at any time. Just because a particular antidepressant has worked for an extended period of time does not mean that it will continue to work. Therefore, it is essential that these medications be monitored regularly by a trained physician. Many family practice

---

[3] Stahl, S.M. (2008). *Stahl's essential psychopharmacology: Neuroscientific basis and practical applications* (3rd ed.). New York, NY: Cambridge University Press.
[4] Conroy, D., & Wilson, D. (August 2002). Tips for police managers about antidepressant medications. *Minnesota Police and Peace Officers Association Journal, 75*(4), 36-37.

physicians are not accustomed to prescribing these medications, so it might be better to consult with a psychiatrist in this matter.

Schizophrenia

Schizophrenia is a complex mental illness that strikes approximately 1% of the U.S. population. It most often appears between the ages of 15 and 45, with men seeming to get it earlier and more severely. Schizophrenia impacts everything—it alters the way the person thinks and the way they perceive themselves, others, and their entire world. The exact cause of schizophrenia is unknown but it is believed that both heredity and environment play a role in the development of this illness.

The symptoms of schizophrenia are unique to each individual but most often involve disturbances in language, thought, perception, and motor behavior. The disturbance in language may simply involve using the wrong words in sentences or it may involve sentences that make no sense whatsoever. This difficulty may involve a misconnection between thoughts and words for the person with schizophrenia or it may be indicative of a disturbed thought process. In either case it makes the individual extremely difficult to communicate with.

The disturbance in thought may include skewed ideas of reference or the idea that the individual with schizophrenia is the cause of either random or unrelated events. We might joke that a favorite sports team lost because we didn't wear our special socks to the game or because we were or were not in attendance, but unless we are either a player or a coach, our attendance or lack thereof makes little difference. For us it's a joke, but for an individual with skewed ideas of reference, this could be their reality. They might believe that a catastrophic event has happened because of something they did or didn't do.

Disturbances of perception are often related to the disturbed thought process and language difficulties. The individual is having trouble making appropriate connections with the outside world. Such difficulties in connection can be extremely frustrating and can lead a person with schizophrenia to retreat to an inner world. They will shut out the external and live within themselves. Another symptom can be ritualistic mannerisms that may involve such activities as picking, pulling out hair or eyebrows, or just about any personal ritual.

Post-traumatic Stress Disorder

Post-traumatic stress disorder (PTSD) is a serious illness that is generated by exposure to a traumatic event. According to some estimates, up to one-third of all police officers suffer from PTSD at some point in their careers. While these numbers may be difficult to prove, it is important to look at this illness since exposure to traumatic events is such a routine part of police work. Keep in mind that post-traumatic stress is normal; post-traumatic stress *disorder* is not. One is a normal response to a stressful event while the other is life disruptive, long term, and generally much more serious. It is important to note that PTSD is definitely treatable. If even one officer suffers from this condition unnecessarily, it is one too many. And while this is a definite job hazard, it does not need to be a definite conclusion or job ender.

PTSD has been researched most thoroughly in Viet Nam vets, and the research has continued with military personnel serving in other combat zones. We have seen it as a trauma response with intrusive and denial phases. During the intrusive phase the individual is likely to appear very emotional, and the impact of the trauma is obvious. During the denial phases the individual may seem to be functioning normally and, in fact, may even seem to be unemotional. PTSD may involve psychotic episodes including flashbacks, which are a "re-experiencing" of the event. This is different from simply remembering the event; this is an actual reliving of the event with all of the associated sensory responses—the person hears screams or explosions, smells sulfur or gunpowder, tastes bile or ash. They physically relive the trauma.

PTSD may also become apparent long after the trauma occurs. It may be triggered by exposure to a particular stimulus or just the passing of time. Symptoms can appear months, even years after exposure to the traumatic events. Some symptoms, such as hyper vigilance or a numbing of responsiveness to the outside world, may be difficult to spot in police officers because the hyper vigilance can be normal, as well as the distancing from non-police acquaintances.

For a more in-depth discussion of PTSD refer to the chapter on Surviving Trauma.

Adjustment Disorder

An adjustment disorder involves the development of emotional or behavioral symptoms in response to an identifiable stressor(s) occurring within 3 months of the onset of the stressor(s). Common precipitating stressors are marital problems, divorce, moving to a new environment, and financial problems. An estimated 2% to 8% of the general population suffers from this disorder, with women diagnosed twice often as men, and single females being most at risk. As many as half of all individuals with specific medical problems or stressors have been diagnosed with adjustment disorders, and 10% to 30% of mental health outpatients referred for mental health consultations have been diagnosed with adjustment disorders.[5] These symptoms are such as to cause marked distress in the individual in excess of what might normally be expected from the event. This is different from PTSD because the triggering event is a "stressor" which may or may not be a traumatic event. Another major difference is that this diagnosis is temporary; the symptoms must begin within 3 months of the stressor and disappear within 6 months after onset.

PTSD and acute stress disorder better characterize the nature of the stressor and are accompanied by a definitive constellation of affective and autonomic symptoms, whereas the stressor in adjustment disorder can be of any severity with possible symptoms ranging from few to many. If the response to a stressor does not meet the threshold of PTSD, then the diagnosis of adjustment disorder is appropriate.[6]

Generalized Anxiety Disorder

Generalized anxiety disorder (GAD) is just that, a generalized, nonspecific anxiety. The anxiety is difficult to control, is subjectively distressing, and impairs functional areas of one's life such that the

---

[5] Sadock, B.J., & Sadock, V.A. (2007). *Kaplan and Sadock's synopsis of psychiatry: Behavioral sciences/clinical psychiatry* (10th ed.). Philadelphia, PA: Lippincott Williams & Wilkins.

[6] Sadock, B.J., & Sadock, V.A. (2007). *Kaplan and Sadock's synopsis of psychiatry: Behavioral sciences/clinical psychiatry* (10th ed.). Philadelphia, PA: Lippincott Williams & Wilkins.

person is never fully able to relax. This disorder may involve sleep disturbances but the hallmark symptoms of GAD are excessive worry and nonspecific physical tension that is present for most days during a period of at least 6 months. The person experiencing the anxiety may not understand the cause but the symptoms are very real. People have described this as "wanting to crawl out of my skin" or "just feeling all wound up inside." It might be that the individual is worried about things that they have no control over or things that seem trivial. But whatever it is, it's not trivial to them.

This disorder is one that most often coexists with another mental disorder, usually a social phobia, specific phobia, panic disorder, or a depressive disorder. In fact, an estimated 50% to 90% of those with GAD have another mental disorder. It affects more women than men, by a ratio of 2:1, and it is differentiated from panic disorder by the absence of spontaneous panic attacks.[7]

GAD can interfere with every aspect of a person's life. It impacts social activities as well as time spent alone. Often people with GAD are uncomfortable in social settings because they are worried about "doing the right thing" or "leaving a positive impression." They are not comfortable alone either because in the quiet time, with a lack of distractions, there is more opportunity to worry.

Bipolar Disorder

Bipolar disorder, commonly referred to as manic-depressive, is a relatively rare illness that affects between 0.4% and 1.6% of the population[8] but is particularly dangerous because of the high suicide rate associated with it. Data indicate completed suicide occurs in 10% to 15% of individuals diagnosed with bipolar I disorder.[9] It involves a cycling of mood from elation to depression. The depression will be as described previously in this chapter. The manic phase, or the elative phase, is often characterized by a number of symptoms including unusual irritability, a decreased need for sleep,

[7] Sadock, B.J., & Sadock, V.A. (2007). *Kaplan and Sadock's synopsis of psychiatry: Behavioral sciences/clinical psychiatry* (10th ed.). Philadelphia, PA: Lippincott Williams & Wilkins.
[8] Goodwin, G.M. (November 2012). Bipolar disorder. *Medicine*, 40(11), 596-598.
[9] American Psychiatric Association (2000). *Diagnostic and statistical manual of mental disorders* (4th ed.) – Text revision (DSM-IV-TR). Washington, DC: Author.

grandiose ideas or delusions, excessive talkativeness, racing thoughts or feelings of being pressured, increased sexual interest, significantly increased energy, impulsive decisions, poor judgment, and inappropriate social behavior. Hypomania ("below mania") is exhibited by elevated, expansive, or irritable mood and is less severe and shorter in duration than mania. Often those experiencing a hypomanic episode just seem to be going faster. They become irritable when others don't seem to "keep up" with them during this phase. It is not uncommon for people to engage in increased sexual behavior during a hypomanic episode. Such activity can take place with one partner or multiple partners and may involve the additional risk of unsafe sex. Another problem is that once the hypomania subsides, remorse over the poor choices made can increase the sense of worthlessness that accompanies the depression.

One woman I knew would make major purchases while experiencing the hypomanic phase. She bought multiple houses, new cars, and other expensive items, none of which were warranted. She had a good home with her husband and family, and there were no plans to go into the home rental business. The family had two fairly new cars that were both in excellent condition. These purchases were simply symptomatic of her hypomania. Until her husband began to understand the illness and symptoms, these episodes had a terrible impact on her marriage. Once he understood and she was able to get help for her illness, the symptoms diminished and things at home improved.

Eating Disorders

Eating disorders are among the most difficult emotional disorders to understand. For those of us who enjoy food and eating, it makes no sense to either eat so little as to starve yourself or to eat excessive quantities of food and then purge. Eating disorders are a complex set of associated but different disorders in which people are so focused on food and weight that they can focus on little else. The eating disorders fall into two types: anorexia nervosa and bulimia nervosa. These disorders affect women much more often than men.

Do not underestimate the severity of these disorders. They can be life threatening, even fatal. The person struggles with body image and often feels as though they can never get thin enough. If you ask a person struggling with an eating disorder to tell you their ideal weight they may give you a number but their distorted body image is likely to still appear too fat or not thin enough.

Anorexia nervosa is an illness where the individual is obsessed with food and can never seem to get thin enough to be happy. Signs and symptoms of anorexia nervosa include a refusal to eat or not eating enough, a denial of hunger, excessive exercise, an intense fear of gaining weight, preoccupation with food, social withdrawal, flat mood, thin appearance, menstrual irregularities, constipation, abdominal pain, irregular heart rhythms, low blood pressure, and dehydration.

Bulimia nervosa also involves a morbid fear of becoming fat based on body image and size, is more common than anorexia nervosa, and exists in two types: (1) the purging type that involves the misuse of laxatives or diuretics along with self-induced vomiting, and (2) the non-purging type that involves compensatory behaviors such as fasting or excessive exercise without the use of laxatives, diuretics, or self-induced vomiting. A binge-eating episode may occur to the point where the person is extremely uncomfortable, which often leads to feelings of guilt and purging. Other symptoms may include damaged teeth and gums, swollen salivary glands in the cheeks, and sores in the mouth and throat. Complications of bulimia nervosa affect many body systems including the gastrointestinal, cardiac, and neurological systems, as well as the skin and eyes.

ADD/ADHD

These letters stand for the terms Attention Deficit Disorder (ADD) and Attention Deficit Hyperactive Disorder (ADHD). These disorders are most often discovered in children and, while the two terms are somewhat different, they are frequently used interchangeably in the nonmedical community. Attention deficit disorder is an illness that has been with us for a long time and impacts an estimated 3% to 5% of all children, being about three times more common among boys than girls. It is one of the main reasons that children are referred to pediatricians, pediatric neurologists, child psychiatrists or psychologists, or other child specialists in ADHD. This is not an easy diagnosis to make and is best left to a specialist.

The exact causes of ADHD are unknown. However, many researchers and practitioners believe that genetic elements play a role in this disorder because a child with ADHD is four times more likely to have a relative with ADHD. Other factors identified as having an impact are child rearing practices and the presence of family conflict. While these factors have not been directly linked to the illness, they do have an impact on treatment.

Symptoms of ADHD include inattention, hyperactivity, and impulsivity and generally develop over a period of several months. Generally the most visible symptoms are the impulsivity and hyperactivity, with the inattention being less obvious. So the child with ADHD is likely to have difficulty sitting still or staying focused on problems for any length of time. You might notice that your child (typically a boy child) seems to get into a lot of trouble for little things because of a lack of impulse control. It might be that he answers questions or responds to statements before the speaker has completed the sentence. It might be that he seems to fidget a lot and doesn't seem to listen to instructions.

Having an ADHD child can be extremely frustrating for parents, who often tend to blame themselves or each other for their child's condition. For cops, who are generally very controlling people, having an ADHD child is exceptionally frustrating because "nothing seems to work." We expect our kids to listen and do as they are told. But with ADHD we find that we have a child who keeps getting into trouble, doesn't listen, and can't control himself. Police parents struggle immensely with these issues.

Another concern is that the symptoms of ADHD don't always go away. Up to 60% of child patients retain their symptoms as they grow into adults. Many adults were never diagnosed as having ADHD but will display such symptoms. So, if we describe the stereotypical work of a police officer—always on the go, getting involved in sudden activities, generally no long-term focus (at least for a street officer), a great variety of tasks, and excitement—we find an almost perfect refuge for adults with ADHD symptoms.

There are two methods of treating ADHD: psychotherapy and medication. In both cases it is best to consult with a specialist. Therapy with an adult who has ADHD may be different than that for someone suffering from a major depressive disorder. One officer I worked with would come in about once a month to get help dealing with his ADHD and trying to put a degree of structure back into his life. He accepted that he had ADHD, and that was his way of going through life controlling his symptoms. If you decide that medication is an avenue you want to explore, I suggest you consult an ADHD specialist because these medications are difficult to prescribe accurately and to regulate.

DUAL DIAGNOSIS

Mental illness is not a one size fits all. By that I mean that each individual will experience their illness in unique ways and it is not possible to lock in categories. Sometimes clients will come in and tell me, "I have a major depressive disorder." When I ask how they know that, they will tell me that they looked up the diagnosis on the Internet. This is a mistake. A diagnosis is a collection of symptoms and, again, at the risk of being redundant, is unique to each individual. So just because you neighbor had symptoms A, B, and C and was given a specific diagnosis, that doesn't mean it will lead to the same diagnostic conclusion for you or your family member. And, just as the diagnosis isn't a "one size fits all," neither will the treatment be. If you or a family member is suffering from mental illness, get your own help. Don't rely on the internet or your neighbor.

Mental illness is also not limited to one at a time. People can suffer from depression and an eating disorder, or depression and PTSD, or PTSD and panic attacks. They can also suffer from chemical addiction as well as a mental illness. For example, an individual with PTSD might also be addicted to pain medications, sleeping medications, or alcohol. Many mental illnesses are confounded with alcohol or drug addiction, and co-occurring disorders require the alcohol or drug use to be treated as well. Also be mindful that the longer you wait to seek help, the more likely there are to be complicating factors. For example, an alcohol addiction would be easier to work through before there are the complications of job loss, legal problems, and marital problems.

As the diagnosis becomes more complex, treatment becomes more difficult. Again, in these cases it is essential to get help from someone who specializes in mental health including psychiatrists, psychiatric nurse practitioners, psychologists, social workers, and counselors. Often these professionals will specialize in one or a select few categories of illness. Remember, you would not want your family practice physician to do brain surgery. Don't let a general practitioner work where specialists can be more effective.

THERAPY AND COUNSELOR SELECTION

Counseling can be a very effective way of working through mental illness. If you are not feeling "right," you need to get help. Don't let the stigma of getting help force you to live with an illness that is impacting all facets of your life. If you are going to select a counselor, there are a few things you need to consider:

1. Make sure the counselor is a trained/licensed professional.
2. Make sure the counselor understands police work and how it impacts individuals and family members.
3. Make sure the counselor will be available as needed.
4. Make sure your personalities mesh in such a way that the counselor will be effective in working with you.

Counseling is nothing to be ashamed of or afraid of. A good counselor can work with you or your family member to move toward a healthier life. Don't wait until it is too late to get help. Don't wait until you are divorced (perhaps several times), your kids don't speak with you, or your career is ruined beyond repair. And know that just because you see a counselor doesn't mean your career is over. In fact, it may help your career because you're likely to be more able to focus on your work.

If you are concerned about using your health insurance or that your insurance won't cover the counseling, look for a counselor who uses a sliding fee scale, meaning they base their fee on your income. The more you make, the higher your fee; similarly, the less you earn, the less you pay. One counselor I know charges police clients one hour's overtime, which is usually "time and a half." So if the officer makes $20.00 per hour the fee for the counseling is $30.00 per hour. If you look, you can find a counselor you can work with effectively. Anything else is just an excuse.

PSYCHOTHERAPEUTIC MEDICATIONS

Psychotherapeutic medications can provide symptom relief for those suffering from many different types of mental illness. However, it is important to recognize that providing symptom relief is not equivalent to providing a cure for the illness. Antidepressant medications can lift the symptoms of depression by giving the person more energy, helping them to sleep, and perhaps making them more comfortable in social settings. However, as soon as the medications are stopped, the symptoms are likely to reappear.

Psychotherapeutic medications are difficult to regulate and do not produce the same effect in everyone. For example, in children who are hyperactive, chemicals that function as stimulants in most adults will often have a calming effect, which is just the opposite of what one might expect. In other situations, the same medication will impact different people differently. What might be a very effective medication for one person may have little or no effect on another. What might work well for one person might cause someone else to become violently ill. These drugs are frequently used in combination with one another to increase the effect of one drug or to reduce side effects of another.

Among the most commonly prescribed medications are the antidepressants, including Celexa, Cymbalta, Desyrel, Effexor, Pazil, Prozac, Serzone, Wellbutrin, and Zoloft. Antidepressant medications don't make people "high," and there is little risk of abuse with these medications. They simply alleviate the symptoms of depression and help the person feel "normal" again. These chemicals work by controlling the level of serotonin in the brain, and each drug differs in the exact way it works. That is one of the reasons that some of these medications work for some people and not for others. Changing the level of serotonin can also impact digestion, pain, sleep, and other systems. Frequently these drugs are used in combination with another drug to control symptoms or common side effects of antidepressants, such as nausea, insomnia, anxiety, diarrhea or constipation, loss of interest or ability in sex, and weight gain. Some of these side effects may disappear after a few weeks of treatment but others may persist and even worsen.

Antidepressant medications can take up to three weeks to take effect because they need to reach a certain level in the blood stream before being effective. Physicians will commonly prescribe an amount of the drug below the therapeutic level to see how the patient tolerates the side effects. This trial might last two weeks and if side effects are tolerable, the dosage is increased to a clinical level. Such a test-run, however, will mean that it will require even longer for the drugs to take effect.

People get impatient with the slow results, often claiming that "it doesn't seem to be working," and to make matters worse, the unpleasant side effects often happen almost immediately. So an individual who isn't properly counseled on how long the medication will take to show any benefits, or how the negative side effects may be only temporary if countered with another medication, may believe that the drugs aren't working correctly and are making them sicker instead of better, leading them to quit taking the medication. Not a good plan.

Anti-anxiety medications are used to control generalized anxiety, phobias, and panic attacks. Frequently prescribed medications are benzodiazepines which include such drugs as Librium, Valium, and Xanax. The side effects of this class of drugs include drowsiness, lack of energy, dizziness or lightheadedness, slow reflexes, impaired thinking and judgment, forgetfulness, confusion, nausea, and blurred vision. While the benzodiazepines are prescribed to have a sedating effect, some people react very differently and may experience increased anxiety, agitations and even mania, impulsive behavior, and hallucinations. Most of these anti-anxiety medications take effect fairly quickly, usually within hours and often in less than an hour, and seem to be prescribed to be taken on an "as needed" basis, the effects commonly lasting anywhere between 4 and 6 hours. The upside here is that the drugs take effect quickly; the downside is that the effects don't last a full day.

One of the risks with this kind of drug is the strong potential for tolerance and dependence. This means that if you take these medications for any length of time, you may come to feel as though you "need" them, and because you are developing a tolerance to the medication, you will need to take more of the drug to get the same effect. There is also a strong potential for abuse with these medications. They can make you high. You might feel as though you don't have a care in the world, even though your world might be collapsing around you. Taking these medications with alcohol will increase central nervous system depression, and mixing alcohol and benzodiazepines will produce unpredictable results. Anyone taking benzodiazepines should refrain from the use of any alcoholic beverages. While you might think that since alcohol is relaxing and benzodiazepines are relaxing, combining them should make you very relaxed, this is not the case. It's like a crap shoot. You can't predict the outcome.

There is a strong potential that an individual who has been taking benzodiazepines for an extended period will experience withdrawal symptoms. The longer they have been taking the drug and the higher the dosage, the more likely they are to experience withdrawal symptoms and the more likely those symptoms will be severe. Withdrawal symptoms can include anxiety, shakiness, headaches, dizziness, sleeplessness, loss of appetite, fever, seizures, and even psychosis. A major concern with the withdrawal symptoms is that they can easily be confused with a return of the anxiety. While the withdrawal symptoms may be temporary, they won't feel that way to the person experiencing them.

Benzodiazepines may not be an ideal medication for police officers who are experiencing significant anxiety. If you are suffering from anxiety, discuss these medications, their possible side effects, and the potential career impact they may have. Given the listed possible side effects, benzodiazepines may interfere with your ability to function as a police officer.

An alternative to the benzodiazepines is buspirone, brand name BuSpar. This is one of the newer antianxiety drugs that acts by releasing serotonin in the brain like some antidepressants do. Common side effects of buspirone include nausea, headaches, upset stomach, constipation or diarrhea, dry mouth, and drowsiness. The downside is that it can take up to five weeks for the drug to show an effect, but the upside is that it is not as sedating or as addictive. There are also minimal withdrawal effects with buspirone, so it might be a safer alternative for cops.

The anti-manic medications are prescribed to reduce mania. If left untreated, mania may worsen to psychosis. As indicated earlier, symptoms of mania include lack of sleep, impulsive actions, and racing thoughts, none of which are conducive to police work. Lithium is one of the generally prescribed anti-manic drugs and can usually diminish severe manic symptoms in 5 to 14 days. There are, however, risks with lithium, and regular blood tests are important to determine lithium levels in the body. There is an inverse relationship between lithium and sodium so, for example, if you work out hard, in the heat, while taking lithium, you may find your lithium levels high because you have sweated out sodium. Lithium also can burn out the thyroid gland if someone has been taking it for many years. While lithium can be effective, there are also risks of lithium toxicity, which can be fatal.

Another medication found to be effective in treating the manic phase of bipolar disorder is carbamazepine, which is an anticonvulsant and recently received FDA approval. This drug is hypothesized to act by blocking voltage-sensitive sodium channels. Problems with carbamazepine are that it is sedating, can cause fetal toxicity, and is generally considered a second-line mood stabilizer because of these side effects.[10]

CONCLUSION

In summary, if you or a family member might be experiencing a mental illness, it is nothing to be ashamed of. It is an illness just like any physical illness. Consult a specialist to obtain help with this problem and work closely with that mental health professional or team of mental health professionals.

---

[10] Sadock, B.J., & Sadock, V.A. (2007). *Kaplan and Sadock's synopsis of psychiatry: Behavioral sciences/clinical psychiatry* (10th ed.). Philadelphia, PA: Lippincott Williams & Wilkins.

Chapter 11

SURVIVING ADDICTION

This chapter is not intended to be a comprehensive treatise on addiction but rather an overview, designed to give cops and those who love them a basic understanding of addiction and to present a starting place in looking for further resources. While police officers may act like or even think that they are strong enough to handle anything the world throws at them, the reality is that too many cops look to addictive substances or behaviors to help them cope. Addiction is a very real risk, and police officers are not immune. Pay close attention to your behaviors in this area because addictions are like black holes you can fall into and never come out of.

ADDICTION DEFINED

Addiction is an attachment to something that is unhealthy and is broadly defined as "continued use with consequences." This definition can apply to alcohol, gambling, sex, prescription and nonprescription drugs, or even fitness. For example, a runner who continues to run long distances even in the face of health concerns or social issues might be considered addicted to running.

The American Psychiatric Association, in its *Diagnostic and Statistical Manual of Mental Disorders* (DSM-IV-TR), states, "The essential feature of Substance Dependence is a cluster of cognitive, behavioral, and physiological symptoms indicating that the individual continues use of the substance despite significant substance-related problems," and goes on further to identify the following criterion for substance dependence:

1. Tolerance – a significantly increasing need for the substance in order to get the same effects.
2. Withdrawal – physical or psychological change upon a decline of the substance in the blood stream or nervous system of the individual where the person is likely to take more of the substance to alleviate unpleasant symptoms.
3. A persistent stated desire to reduce or control the substance use.

4. The individual spends a great deal of energy surrounding the obtaining, using, or recovering from the use of the substance.
5. Important vocational, social, or recreational activities may be forgone in favor of the substance use.
6. Isolation from family and friends or a change in social patterns to focus on friends who abuse the same substance.[1]

Craving is listed as an important feature but is not necessarily experienced by all. While the DSM-IV-TR lists these as substance abuse criterion, we can see the same pattern with other dependence. With a gambling addiction the person might tell themselves things like, "I'll quit when I get my money back," or, "I will only go to the casino once this week." Or the gambling addict might even find themselves scheduling social events for their friends at the casino. With sexual addiction we often see the addicted officer taking more and more risks to have sexual encounters, including unprotected sex practices with strangers or with multiple partners, and spending more and more time being sexually active with less and less time spent with family or friends.

The DSM-5 has made some changes in the diagnostic criteria for substance abuse. The category is now labeled Substance Abuse Disorder and then the substance is listed. This change might make a difference in how the assessment is labeled, but it shouldn't make any substantive difference from your perspective as a cop, so don't let it throw you. If you think you have a problem with alcohol or any other substance, get help.

ADDICTION VERSUS DEPENDENCE AND ABUSE

People sometimes interchange the words abuse, dependence, and addiction, but there are clinical differences between them. Dependence is milder than addiction and often seen in connection with situations or life stages. When a person is dependent on a substance, they can usually stop use on their own. When someone is addicted, they usually need help to stop and there are usually significant negative impacts on their life prior to quitting.

---

[1] American Psychiatric Association (2000). *Diagnostic and statistical manual of mental disorders* (4th ed.) – Text revision (DSM-IV-TR). Washington, DC: Author, pp.192-194.

Addiction differs from abuse in the interaction with the organism. Abuse can be harmful for an individual but when the use or behavior is discontinued there are no withdrawal consequences, whereas with addiction there can be severe withdrawal consequences. Abuse can often be situational; for example, someone who gets drunk at a wedding and is hung over the next day but who suffers no real negative long-term impact on their life from that drinking episode can be said to have abused alcohol. With alcohol and drugs there are clearly physical symptoms and even physical dangers from an abrupt cessation of use of the addicting chemical. With sexual and gambling addiction the physical dangers of withdrawal are not as clearly established.

Another described difference between abuse and addiction is that with addiction, the relationship with the addictive material is sometimes described as having become a primary relationship. For example, police careers, marriages, and even lives have been lost because the addicted individual put the addiction before all other relationships. It happens with some regularity that cops are fired because of consistent consequences from alcohol use. Yet when faced with the demand to either stop drinking or lose their job, the officers chose to continue their alcohol use. This addiction is often more powerful than the other forces in their lives.

MULTIPLE ADDICTIONS

Addictions are not necessarily limited to one area or one category, and it is not uncommon for someone to become addicted to more than one substance or compulsive behavior at the same time. The original term used to describe this condition was "dual addictions," but this misnomer was replaced by the more accurate term "co-occurring addictions" following criticism that multiple addiction may involve more than just two addictions at the same time. Studies have shown that the more trauma a person has experienced, the greater the chance they are addicted to more than one thing. For example, research has found that 42% of those addicted to sexual behaviors are also chemically dependent, 38% of sex addicts have an eating disorder, 26% suffer from compulsive spending, and 5% have a co-occurring gambling addiction.[2]

If we base an addiction risk on the level of trauma exposure, cops are going to be in an extremely high-risk category. Look around you and take note of how many of your fellow officers are having some real quality-of-life issues because of addictions. Look at the divorce rate, the suicide rate, and the "general dissatisfaction with life" rate. If we assume that the level of trauma exposure impacts addiction risk, it is essential to be constantly aware of how our behavior patterns or chemical use are impacting our lives.

Multiple addictions are not uncommon, nor are sequential addictions, which can be seen as substitutes for dealing with other issues or concerns. For example, an alcoholic might stop using alcohol but instead begin running with addictive properties or eating to extreme. One officer I am aware of turned to a series of addictions to hide his response to trauma; they were his way of self-medicating to dull the pain. After a line-of-duty death in his agency, this officer turned first to alcohol. After going through treatment for alcoholism, he turned to gambling. After treatment for gambling addiction, the officer turned to a sexual addiction. All of these behaviors were mistakenly treated as addictions, with the officer simply shifting from one addiction to another. But in his case, the addictions were the symptoms of, rather than the root cause of, the problem. In his case, the trauma was the real issue, even though the addictions caused behavioral problems and got him into trouble with his marriage and his job.

INDIVIDUAL DIFFERENCES IN ADDICTION

Each of us is impacted differently by the same substances or situations. In some cases a person is impacted by alcohol in one way while another may find it has a completely different effect. Just as we know there are strong differences in the way that medical prescriptions impact people, there are physiological differences in the way alcohol and other drugs impact people. Some pain medications will have little or no effect on some people but for

---

[2] International Institute for Trauma and Addiction Professionals (2011). *FAQs about sexual addiction.* Retrieved from http://www.sexhelp.com/sex-education/what-is-sex-addiction-faqs

others can become debilitating. I've spoken with people who feel no effect from a pain killer such as Vicodin while I am strongly impacted. I took it once after a root canal and needed to focus just to walk. It was a very unpleasant sensation. For others this drug creates an incredibly pleasant sensation.

CHEMICAL ADDICTION

Becoming dependent on chemicals, such as alcohol or pain medications, is often what first comes to mind when we think of *addiction*. Alcohol, prescription meds, streets drugs, and steroids are common chemicals to which officers develop addictions.

Alcohol

Our culture has historically made alcohol consumption an element of many social engagements, as well as accepting its use as a way to get through traumatic events, to deal with administrative frustrations, and to cope with painful divorces or loss. How often have you heard the phrase, "It's Miller time," referring to the use of alcohol? Or heard people express the opinion that after a hard day at work you deserve to have a drink? If I were to organize a softball tournament involving teams from different police departments, in any area of the country, but said there would be no beer or other alcoholic beverages allowed, the tournament would most likely be poorly attended, if attended at all. Similarly, if I scheduled a fishing contest with no alcohol allowed, the number of cops fishing would drop significantly. Sometimes it seems police social events are simply an excuse to drink. Alcohol is such a part of the police culture it might be summed up in quoting author James Crumley, when he said, "Son, never trust a man who doesn't drink…."

In law enforcement, "choir practice" refers to a gathering of cops, generally after a shift, in which the discussion of daily frustrations or traumatic events is accompanied by alcohol. When a police department or an individual officer experiences a significant loss, whether through divorce or death, a common response is to turn to alcohol to bring about forgetfulness. One cop said that drinking was the only way he could stop thinking about a dead child.

There is pressure on new officers to be accepted as "one of the guys" by going to "choir practice." The younger and newer the officer, the more pronounced the risk because, as they work for acceptance, and often without realizing it, the alcohol use becomes a habit and, with that habit, the risk of addiction increases.

Officers working specialized assignments are often exposed to frequent alcohol use. A vice cop who goes into a bar and orders water or a soft drink might find it more difficult to blend in or to gain the trust of some of the people in the bar. So it's easy to take a drink. Then it can, if you aren't careful, be easy to take a second, and a third, and a fourth, and so on, until you are drinking much more than you intended. One vice officer reported that he drank very little when he first joined the unit, maybe one or two beers *a year*. However, after several years in that assignment, he was drinking a baseline of a 12-pack of beer *each day*. And although this officer reports that he had drinking rules for himself, such as he never drank when he wasn't working, those "policies" only meant that he found himself working more and more.

Prescription Medications Including Steroids

Prescription medications can come from several sources. They can come from a physician or from several physicians. One officer I knew was obtaining pain medications from four different doctors, getting the prescriptions filled at four different pharmacies, and taking all of these drugs at the same time. He said that it started because he was in pain and it expanded to multiple sources because no one seemed to understand his pain.

It's easy to get addicted to prescription medications. Sometimes it starts with a physical injury where we are prescribed these meds to reduce pain, to make any kind of activity bearable, or to help with sleep. But our bodies don't know that these drugs can be addictive; they just know that they work. Soon you might be relying on the medications to get up in the morning, to get through the day, and to go to sleep at night. You find you are starting to schedule your life around when you take your medications, which can lead to real trouble. Consider the real-life case of a former officer who went to see his physician for migraine headaches and was prescribed a pain medication. This officer became addicted to the medication and watched his life slip away through a cloud of narcotics. He admitted to breaking into at least ten homes to obtain drugs but doesn't remember all of them because of the effects the narcotics had on his brain. He was arrested and charged in two different counties for burglary. Many who knew him described him as a hard working cop, recognized for life-saving activities, yet they also talked of how they watched him slide downhill over a two-year period. His addiction led him from a life of law to a life of crime and ended his career.

Street Drugs

The use of street drugs by police officers presents several unique problems. First and most obviously, they are *illegal* drugs, meaning that an individual who has sworn to uphold the law is now breaking it. It means that, for a cop, the mere possession of these drugs can constitute a crime and the end of their career. For most people the possession of an illegal drug is likely to lead to probation, especially for first possession and personal use. For a police officer, however, it is not just a question of illegal chemical possession but a bigger issue regarding integrity. Once the integrity of the officer comes into question, there will be a career impact. It is a bigger moral leap for police officers to use illegal drugs because these are chemicals that are not sanctioned by the law enforcement community. In fact, they are associated with things cops fundamentally oppose—increased crime and violence. While cops may talk openly to each other about "getting drunk last night" or today's hangover, they don't talk about the crack cocaine they just smoked or the meth they used this morning. These drugs are not part of the police culture. So, when an officer is addicted to or even abusing street drugs, they are stepping outside the culture that often defines them.

Most police officers understand the lack of quality control in street drugs. There is no such thing as "standard" strength street cocaine or heroin. And still, despite those risks, some officers use these drugs, offering excuses or justifications such as, "I got hooked doing undercover work." Yet how many police officers have successfully worked in narcotics units without becoming addicted to or even using illegal drugs?

A lot of cops don't trust street dealers enough to buy illegal drugs from them. If a police officer buys street drugs from a street dealer, there is huge potential for the officer's career to be ruined. Once the cop buys the illegal drugs, that dealer can own him. The

officer can be blackmailed and controlled by the dealer, which can
have obvious negative impacts on the cop's career.

Anabolic Steroids

Reported use of anabolic steroids among law enforcement personnel
is nothing new. A segment titled "Beefing up the Force," which aired
in 1989 on the television program *60 Minutes*, featured three police
officers who admitted not only to using steroids but that the drug use
had led to aggression which got them into serious trouble.[3] In 1991,
the *FBI Law Enforcement Bulletin* published an article stating,
"Anabolic steroid abuse by police officers is a serious problem that
merits greater awareness by departments across the country." [4] And
in 2007, the U.S. Drug Enforcement Administration (DEA) led
Operation Raw Deal, an international steroid investigation that
uncovered several links to current or former law enforcement
officers.[5] While the exact number of cops using anabolic steroids is
certainly unknown, one police psychologist conservatively estimates
that five percent of his patients are either current or former steroid
users.[6]

The use of illegal steroids might be quasi accepted by some in
the police community because it is seen as a way to make the officer
stronger and thus, by way of rationalization, better able to fight
crime. But the psychological side effects, such as intense anger, can
easily more than negate any tactical physical advantage. One of the
strongest weapons a police officer has is his mind. Anabolic steroid
use can, over time, cause mania, psychosis, and personality change.
As with street drugs, the same integrity issues come into play with
steroids. These drugs are being purchased by a cop from a criminal.

---

[3] Humphrey, K.R., Decker, K.P., Goldberg, L., Pope, H.G. Jr., Gutman, J., & Green,
G. (June 2008). Anabolic steroid use and abuse by police officers: Policy &
prevention. *The Police Chief*, 75(6). Retrieved from
http://www.policechiefmagazine.org/magazine/index.cfm?fuseaction=print_display
&article_id=1512&issue_id=62008
[4] Swanson, C., Gaines, L., & Gore, B. (August 1991). Abuse of anabolic steroids.
FBI Law Enforcement Bulletin, 60(8), 19.
[5] Humphrey et al., op.cit.
[6] Lallanilla, M. (May 24, 2005). Big guns: When cops use steroids. *ABC News*
online. Retrieved from http://abcnews.go.com/Health/US/story?id=775659&page=1

Their very possession is a crime, and the side effects of illegal steroid use often lead to other crimes or charges of misconduct.

One story making news as this book goes to press is the trial of a Texas police officer who was charged with possession and sale of illegal drugs to fellow cops as well as using the police database to tip off his steroid dealer. It's unlikely that this officer started his career with the intent of dealing drugs to other officers and sacrificing his integrity by tipping off the dealer, but that's what happened. Steroid use often comes from wanting to get just a "little stronger" or a "little bigger." It comes from trying to take shortcuts, and in this case, it cost an officer his career and may send him to prison.

GAMBLING ADDICTION

Cops gamble every time they go to work or every time they answer a call for service. There's that part of us that looks for the excitement, the adrenalin rush. Cops are not made to lead boring, routine lives. They enjoy their job with the knowledge that anything, literally anything, could happen today. Some people call cops (including many cops) adrenalin junkies. Our job can often become a big gamble with us trying to beat out the bad guys, competing with the criminals to see who is going to win. We do everything we can to shave the odds in our favor. We use all of the specialized gear, the specialized training, and the specialized knowledge we can get our hands on. But often we still find ourselves looking for the excitement in the challenge.

Well, it's something similar with gambling. There's always the big score, the chance to make it big, to win everything. Gambling is legal, and many contend that it hurts no one. Gambling is well accepted in our culture with strong historical roots. Remember the old western movies where the cowboys (and ladies) sat in the saloons gambling? Even then we would see some poor soul gamble away the family farm or the money he brought to town to get supplies. Sometimes we even saw people get shot over gambling disagreements. Throughout history gambling has been difficult.

As we move into modern times we see more and more opportunities to gamble, legally. There seem to be casinos within a reasonable drive from most places, and if you can't readily get there, you can often buy a pull tab or lottery ticket quite easily, or try online gambling. You can lose your money without ever leaving the comfort of your home. One of the requirements for addiction is exposure. If there is no exposure to a substance or an experience, there can be no addiction. Exposure to gambling seems to be all around us and increasing all the time.

It's not logical to gamble because the odds of winning are never with the individual. In many cases the "house" wins if there is a draw, payouts on table games have a built-in house advantage, and slot machines only pay out a certain percentage of what they take in. Consider American roulette, in which there are 38 possible numbers or pockets on the wheel on which to place a bet but the best payout a winner can get is 35 to 1. So a gambler wanting to ensure a win will place a bet (let's say $1 for simplicity's sake) on every space, spending $38 in the process, but only one of those numbers will be the winner, paying out $36 (the original $1 bet plus $35). Even though the player "won," the house still kept some of the money. Stretch this pattern of betting out over the long term and, no matter how many times a player "wins," the house still comes out ahead. Similarly, if a slot machine is paying out at 95% it means that for every $100 put in, only $95 will come out. It might be, in either of these cases, you put your dollar on a number or into the slot machine and on the very first try you win. However, in this game of probability, odds are you'll lose. And statistically you will continue to lose over the long term if you keep playing.

Addicts don't stop after the first time. They play until they can't play anymore. Addictions have been defined as a "primary relationship," and the gambling addict puts everything they own at risk. I once drove past a billboard with a picture of a man holding open an empty wallet and the caption read something like, "Compulsive gamblers lose everything in their wallet." Not only was the obvious gone—his cash and credit cards—but so were any photos of the gambler's spouse and children. He had lost it all.

SEXUAL ADDICTION

Sexual addiction is described as more than just loving sex. Main symptoms include a loss of control over sexual activities; unsuccessful attempts to eliminate unwanted sexual behavior; multiple sexual partners or extramarital affairs; compulsive masturbation, as often as 10 to 20 times a day; anonymous sexual partners; anxiety about the secrecy of being discovered; and a consistent pattern of negative consequences.

The question always asked is, "Is sex addiction real or just an excuse for bad behavior?" Dr. David J. Ley, a clinical psychologist who specializes in treating sexuality issues, asks the same question about one of his patients on the *Psychology Today* web site: "Was [this male officer] a sex addict? Or was he a powerful, high-testosterone male, with an identity issue, who was put in a role where a sexual buffet was laid out in front of him, and he didn't have any reason or internal resources to use to resist diving in?" [7]

Sexual addiction is not listed in the American Psychiatric Association DSM as an addiction. Yet, if we go back to the definitions we have used for addiction, there is an element of continued use with consequences. So, in this case, the addict continues to be sexually active despite adverse consequences. These consequences can be anything from physical exhaustion, venereal disease, divorce, loss of job, or even death. Sexual addiction also involves "secrets" or hidden use. Just as alcoholics sometimes drink in secret to hide the level of their use, sex addicts are often secretive about the identity or number of their sexual partners.

One officer came to me to see if I could save his job. When I asked what happened, he told me that he was being investigated for having sex with a woman from a retail outlet while he was on duty. It was her lunch break, they met in an empty fire station, and had sex. When his department discovered what had happened, he was immediately placed on administrative leave while the matter was investigated. He told his wife he was being investigated for excessive use of force because he was ashamed to tell her what really happened. This officer lost his job and his career but, after coming clean with his wife, was able to save his marriage.

Sexual *addiction* is a difficult concept to deal with when, according to many evolutionary biologists and sociologists, males are supposed to want all of the sex they can get. So how can wanting more and more of it be an addiction? In our culture, males who have been sexually active are often envied by their friends while women who are sexually active are shunned or ridiculed. Yet it is a solid line between sexually active and sexually addicted. Look at the people

---

[7] Ley, D.J. (2011). "Sex addict? Or kid in a candy store?" *Psychology Today* online, Retrieved from http://www.psychologytoday.com/blog/women-who-stray/201103/sex-addict-or-kid-in-candy-store

who have faced serious consequences for inappropriate sexual behavior. One of the most famous was the scandal involving then-President Bill Clinton and Monica Lewinski. Representative Anthony Weiner stepped down from Congress after admitting to "sexting." Tiger Woods checked into a rehabilitation center after admitting a number of extramarital affairs. Some have said that John Edwards lost his bid for the presidency of the United States because of his extramarital affairs. These sexual activities are not logical, they are based on an addiction. The National Council on Sexual Addiction Compulsivity estimates that 6% to 8% of the U.S. population, or between 18 and 24 million people, are sex addicts.[8] They further estimate that each week 25 million Americans spend between one and ten hours visiting cyber-sex sites, and another 4.7 million spend in excess of 11 hours per week.

Police officers are often sought out as sexual partners. One officer reports that on his first night as a solo officer, he was approached around midnight by an attractive woman wearing very revealing clothing. She asked him to meet her later in a school parking lot, and when he arrived, not only was the woman there but she had brought a friend. Before he could say anything, the two women had dropped to their knees and performed oral sex on him, no questions asked. There are many terms for women who want to have sex with cops; groupie and badge bunny are two of them. Remember, another of the key components of addiction is exposure, and police officers are frequently exposed to sexual opportunities.

Stefanie Carnes, a certified sex addiction therapist and author of *Mending a Shattered Heart: A Guide For Partners of Sex Addicts,* states, "People use sex to escape and medicate," as the experience delivers a high dose of dopamine to the brain's "pleasure center" and produces the same chemical reaction that someone who gambles or eats compulsively receives.[9] Just as alcohol or drugs can be used to temporarily escape the impact of trauma, so too can sex. However, when the sexual activity becomes an addiction, it complicates treatment for the traumatic event, just as chemical dependency or a gambling addiction can complicate treatment for the original trauma.

[8] Kulbarsh, P. (2010). Sexual addiction. *Officer.com*. Retrieved from http://www.officer.com/article/10232760/sexual-addiction
[9] Frank, J. (2011). Woes of famous, powerful shine light on sex addiction. *Reuters* online. Retrieved from http://www.reuters.com/article/2011/06/16/us-addiction-sex-idUSTRE75F6ET20110616

GETTING HELP FOR ADDICTION

One of the common symptoms of any addiction is shame. When the addiction becomes more important than job, career, family, and relationships, and everything is lost, people are ashamed of what they have done. The first thing to know about getting help is that these addictions are very treatable and there are a number of ways to get help. In some cases insurance benefits can be used to pay for treatment, and in others they cannot. If you are concerned about the cost of treatment, check with your insurance company and check with an addiction specialist. Often they can help design a treatment plan that works within a budget.

Addicts are often resistant to treatment, and getting them to accept professional help is often a difficult task. Those who love them keep hearing things like, "I can control it," or, "It's not as big a problem as you make it out to be." One increasingly common strategy being used to get an addict to treatment is called an *intervention*, a technique that has been popularized through the media. The problem is that, like many things the media popularizes, we don't get the real story. It is important to remember that an intervention is not simply a confrontation with the addict that happens on the spur of the moment. An effective intervention may require several weeks of planning, is likely to involve a number of people close to the addict, and should include a trained professional. An intervention is often a last step in an attempt to force the addict to treatment. Sometimes even after an intervention is agreed on, the people involved might decide that they are not ready to follow through with it or that the addict is not likely to respond to it. In considering an intervention, consult with a professional interventionist first because these are usually only a one-shot thing. Usually, multiple interventions are neither recommended nor likely to succeed, so it's important to get it right the first (and only) time.

One of the oldest addiction treatment plans is Alcoholics Anonymous. This model began as an off shoot of a religious group called the Oxford Group, which practices self-inventory, admitting wrongs, making amends, prayer, meditation, and carrying the message to others. Roland H. and Edwin T. began to practice this lifestyle as a way of controlling their alcoholism, which they had been told was untreatable, and both had success with the method. They introduced a friend of theirs (Bill W.) to the process, and after several others became involved, Alcoholics Anonymous (AA) was

born. One of the individuals associated with Bill W. was Dr. Bob.
June 10, 1935, was the date of Dr. Bob's last drink and is considered
to be the founding date of AA.[10] Since then the AA model has been
incorporated into treatment programs run by professionals across the
country and used successfully by millions of alcoholics to deal with
their alcohol addiction. Today's AA uses the following 12-step
model to help addicts get treatment:

THE TWELVE STEPS OF ALCOHOLICS ANONYMOUS

1. We admitted we were powerless over alcohol—that our lives had
    become unmanageable.
2. Came to believe that a Power greater than ourselves could
    restore us to sanity.
3. Made a decision to turn our will and our lives over to the care of
    God *as we understood Him.*
4. Made a searching and fearless moral inventory of ourselves.
5. Admitted to God, to ourselves, and to another human being the
    exact nature of our wrongs.
6. Were entirely ready to have God remove all these defects of
    character.
7. Humbly asked Him to remove our shortcomings.
8. Made a list of all persons we had harmed, and became willing to
    make amends to them all.
9. Made direct amends to such people wherever possible, except
    when to do so would injure them or others.
10. Continued to take personal inventory and when we were wrong
    promptly admitted it.
11. Sought through prayer and meditation to improve our conscious
    contact with God, *as we understood Him,* praying only for
    knowledge of His will for us and the power to carry that out.
12. Having had a spiritual awakening as the result of these Steps, we
    tried to carry this message to alcoholics, and to practice these
    principles in all our affairs.[11]

---

[10] Alcoholics Anonymous World Services. (2013). *Alcoholics anonymous: Over 70
years of growth.* Retrieved from http://www.aa.org/aatimeline/
[11] Alcoholics Anonymous World Services. (2002). *The twelve steps of alcoholics
anonymous.* Retrieved from http://www.aa.org/en_pdfs/smf-121_en.pdf

The AA model of a self-help program run by addicts to deal with their own addiction has been so successful in treating alcoholism that there have been 12-step programs developed for many other addictions, including drug addiction, sexual addiction, gambling addiction, and other problems. The 12-step model is used for programs like Emotions Anonymous and Overeaters Anonymous. Other recovery programs have been developed based on the 12-step model to help family members of those addicted. One of the most prominent is Alanon, a 12-step program based on the idea that addiction is a family disease and that all who are involved with the addicted individual are in need of help. A similar program is Adult Children of Alcoholics (ACOA), again based on the idea that all members of the family are impacted by the addicted person's actions. The focus of ACOA is expanded to include the impact of living with an addict through the developmental process, based on the understanding that the things that kids growing up in an alcoholic home think are normal are *not*, in a healthy, addiction-free family, normal.

One of the premises of AA is that the alcoholic will always be an alcoholic. The goal of AA is to help the addict maintain sobriety through the motto, "One day at a time," to help keep the focus on today's sobriety and prevent the task of sobriety from becoming overwhelming. With this "one day at a time" philosophy, many addicts, through ongoing involvement with a 12-step program, have maintained sobriety for many years.

While the 12-step model is one of the most common, if not *the* most common, treatment modalities, there are others. Some are based on the 12-step model but have given control to the individual rather than a "higher power." Some models attempt to treat addiction as abuse, offering the addict a hope of drinking again. Other models are chemically based programs. Antabuse (disulfiram) was the first medicine approved for the treatment of alcohol abuse and alcohol dependence by the U.S. Food and Drug Administration. It is prescribed for people who want to quit drinking alcohol, and it works by causing any one or combination of negative reactions if the person consumes alcohol while taking antabuse. The more of each substance consumed, the more violent the reaction is likely to be. One of the problems with antabuse is that if a person wants to drink alcohol, they just skip the antabuse for a while.

People may also get help for addictions through established treatment programs run by mental health and medical professionals, whether based in a clinic (outpatient), a treatment facility (inpatient), or even a hospital. Each different modality has pros and cons. The outpatient program in a clinic does not take the individual away from their normal routine—they still go to work as usual and go home each night. During the nonworking hours the addict attends treatment. This treatment modality can be effective if the individual really wants to change their behaviors and does not have a long-term history of addiction. However, too often, outpatient programs are forced upon addicts as a consequence of their behaviors. For example, an alcoholic may be sent to outpatient treatment after being arrested for drunk driving in hopes of receiving a lighter sentence or as part of the sentence, but there is no real motivation on the drunk driver's part to change their ways. Only if there is a real commitment to change on the part of the addict will an outpatient programs be helpful.

Inpatient programs at a treatment facility can range from a few weeks to six months or longer, depending on the addict's history. Here the focus is on making major changes in the lifestyle of the addict and getting a history of sobriety prior to discharge. These programs are often recommended only after a series of outpatient programs have proven ineffective or if the addiction history is severe. Hospital treatment programs generally range from a few days, for the sole purpose of detoxification, to a month or more, to provide comprehensive treatment. When the chemical use has been severe, there are often withdrawal symptoms that can be physically dangerous and which require monitoring by a medical professional. In some cases other drugs are used to help the addict detoxify.

Far too often the treatment modality selected is based not on what the individual needs but rather on what the insurance company will pay for. Obviously, outpatient treatment is the cheapest and likely the most frequently recommended plan for addicts. Costs for outpatient treatment are generally around $10,000, while the costs for inpatient treatment can range from $20,000 to $32,000 depending on what services are needed. Another issue in selecting a treatment modality is that medical insurance often does not cover treatment for certain addictions, such as gambling or sexual addiction, and inpatient costs can make such treatment prohibitive for an individual. Consequently, addicts sometimes have very limited avenues by which to seek professional help.

CLOSING THOUGHTS

Addiction is considered to be insidious, chronic, and fatal. There are few things that can destroy as many lives as an addiction can. If you or someone you love is suffering from an addiction, try to get help early. Don't make or listen to excuses; just draw firm lines and stick to them. Far too many cops have lost money, property, jobs, careers, and loved ones because of addictions. Take care of those you love, and allow those who love you to care for you. Get help. Addictions are treatable.

Chapter 12

SURVIVING LEGAL BATTLES

With contributions by Robert Fowler, JD [1]

Cops are a part of the legal system and, as such, will inevitably be involved with that system. Most of the time when we think of police involvement in legal matters it's in the capacity of an arresting officer or a witness in a courtroom drama. Yet there is another aspect, another way that cops fight legal battles. Sometimes cops are the defendants in civil and criminal cases.

It is prudent to be aware of situations that have a higher chance of leading to lawsuits. For example, while many officers go through their entire careers without being required to use deadly force, this is one aspect of police work that will almost always generate a civil suit. Other situations or actions that commonly generate civil suits include use of force, squad car accidents, and unlawful entry. It might be that the person thought the entry unlawful, or maybe you executed a search warrant and it just happened to be the wrong house. Mistakes happen. Try to keep them to a minimum but accept the fact that this is a litigious society.

Be careful how you use the resources you have. Abuse of authority and misappropriation of agency resources are one-way tickets to legal trouble. One former police officer in Minnesota sued,

---

[1] Robert Fowler, JD, is the owner of Fowler Law Firm, which serves as General Counsel for the Minnesota Fraternal Order of Police (FOP) and the Minnesota Public Employees Association. Since 2000, Robert has dedicated his law practice to serving law enforcement in the areas of critical incidents, criminal defense of officers, and civil and administrative cases, as well as serving as a union attorney. His firm administers the MN FOP's legal defense plan, serving law enforcement officers throughout Minnesota. He has taught numerous Continuing Legal Education seminars on critical incidents and legal issues facing law enforcement.

Robert Fowler is a graduate of the Massachusetts Institute of Technology and earned his law degree at the University of Minnesota. Born in Sioux City, Iowa, he has lived in the St. Paul (Minnesota) metro area since 1996. In his spare time, he enjoys grape growing and is an award-winning home winemaker.

successfully, a number of cities in that state after discovering that police officers in those jurisdictions had checked on her driver's license inappropriately and with excessive frequency. The lawsuit alleged that more than 100 police officers had viewed her driver's license information, on more than 400 separate occasions, without legitimate purpose. The plaintiff in this case has reportedly collected more than $1 million in settlements.

There are federal regulations that came into play here, and this lawsuit ended up costing officers and their agencies a substantial amount of money. While most agencies did pay for their officers' actions, at least one agency decided that the alleged behavior was outside the scope of the officers' employment and chose not to protect their officers in any way. In this case the officers were responsible for their own defense and settlement. This is an example of where a state has rules regarding data practices, and the federal government has rules regarding violation of the state regulations. Federal regulations here made the improper access of this data a violation punishable by a $2,500 fine for each infraction. So if you were an officer who inappropriately ran this driver's license ten times, you could be subject to a $25,000 fine. Be careful.

BEFORE YOU ARE EVER SUED

If you expect to get through a 30-year law enforcement career without being sued, you are being naive. You need to be prepared for this situation ahead of time because most cops do get sued at some point in their career. Don't wait until you are served or notified that you are the defendant in a civil suit before you begin to prepare. Just plan that it *will* happen to you; it is only a question of when, how, and in what case. Some of the things to think about ahead of time are whether to enroll in a legal defense plan and who you will turn to for legal representation when you need it.

Choosing a Legal Defense Plan

One way you can prepare for litigation is by considering a legal defense plan. These plans are more than just a prepaid legal program; they are more like an insurance policy. You don't drive your car without insurance because the costs if you have an accident can be too great. Similarly, if you get sued, the costs can be staggering, both financially and professionally. Often these plans are available through the Fraternal Order of Police or your union, or one may even be available for individual purchase. Plan prices vary but are generally available for around $100 to $200 per year.

If you are sued and must provide for your own legal defense, the cost of an attorney can vary from $200 to $350 per hour, or more, depending on what the issue is and how specialized the attorney needs to be. Obviously, the more specialized, the more expensive. However, there is also an old saying that you should never hire a cheap attorney. Generally when you go with the low bid, you get what you pay for. At the end of this chapter is a comparison of four legal defense plans offered in Minnesota, to give you an idea of how such options may differ. Each plan has its strengths and weaknesses. Make sure you understand what you are getting for your money.

Knowing When You Need a Lawyer and Where to Get One

If you think you might get sued, check with an attorney, and sooner is better than later. It is always easier to prevent mistakes than to try to correct them once they are done. And if you think that you don't need to worry about finding a lawyer because your department will protect you, think again. While it is generally true that your agency will be required to "defend and indemnify" [2] you in a work-related lawsuit, your agency may take the position that you were acting outside the scope of your authority and, therefore, they do not believe they have any responsibility to defend or indemnify. At that point you will want to get your own attorney. Fast. But you may have already said or done things your attorney would have advised against, things that will be damaging to your best interests. Nevertheless, a consultation with your own attorney is always a good idea. Remember, your attorney is representing only *your* best interests, whereas your employer's attorney is not necessarily representing only you.

---

[2] In simple terms, *defend* means the agency will provide you with an attorney acting on your behalf, and *indemnify* means they will cover any damages.

If you consult with your own attorney and they tell you that the agency will need to defend and indemnify you and that there is no real need for you to have your own lawyer, you haven't lost much at that point. At a minimum, your own attorney can get it confirmed in writing that your employer will indemnify you. However, if you don't consult with an attorney who will act strictly on your behalf, you may have things to regret. So remember, the sooner the better.

GETTING SERVED

If you are going to be sued you will be notified at some point. Receiving this notice of litigation is commonly called "getting served." You should be aware, however, that a lot of time may pass between the event which sets off the lawsuit and the actual filing of a lawsuit. Civil statute of limitation laws vary by state, with some allowing a plaintiff up to six years after the event to file the actual notice of intent to sue. Because of this lag time, it's not unheard of that some officers are caught off guard when they get served for an event that took place years prior.

Getting served might happen at work or at home, but you can be served anywhere. Often the service is performed by a civil process server and not necessarily by anyone you know. Sometimes people spend a lot of time and effort trying to avoid being served. Don't waste your energy. The process server can leave the notice with any adult in your household, including adult (even teenage) children. The notice can even be left with a housekeeper because they are in your home with your permission.

You might be served through your agency, and the notice may be left with your supervisor or in the chief's office. In fact, agency attorneys may have been aware of the pending litigation for some time but just didn't tell you because they thought it unnecessary until you were either served or they needed something from you.

PUTTING YOUR PRE-LAWSUIT PLAN INTO ACTION

Once you've been served, immediately check your resources. If you belong to a legal defense plan or have some sort of prepaid legal resource, contact them immediately. If you need to find your own attorney, don't just open the yellow pages and pick one at random. You want to hire a good, competent attorney. *My Cousin Vinny* might have been a great movie but would be a lousy real-life experience. You have too much at risk to let it ride on an unknown or inexperienced attorney. Think about the attorneys you have met while in court; perhaps one of them has impressed you. Or ask other cops who they have used and how they fared. Make this a priority decision because, while you want to get an attorney sooner rather than later, you don't want just any attorney. You might need a specialist depending on the nature of the litigation. Think of it this way: I have a great family practice physician but if I needed brain surgery I would go to a specialist, someone who does this all the time. Your brother-in-law may be a great corporate attorney, knocking down 6 or 7 figures every year, but he is not necessarily a trial attorney. Hire the specialist for law enforcement.

Once you've been notified that you're being sued, you need to notify your department. Chances are they already know, but they may not and they need to. As mentioned, your agency will generally be required to defend and indemnify you. There may be a specific statute in your state that covers this. For example, in Minnesota there is MN. Stat. CH 466, called the Minnesota Tort Claims Act, which defines situations in which the employer must indemnify.

It is likely that your agency is also named in the suit because, most of the time, lawsuits are about money, and the agency has more of it than you do, as well as an insurance policy which may cover them. They are also likely to be named because they are considered to be responsible for the actions of their employees, and you are deemed an "agent" of your employer. Through the concept of *vicarious liability*, your employer is liable for what you have done unless it is determined that you acted outside the scope of your duties. If you have an accident while traveling in excess of 99 miles per hour to take a burglary report, the agency may say that those actions were outside the scope of your duties. The bigger pitfall is where you may have broken state law or clear employer policy. If so, watch out! Based on that determination, your agency may decide they will neither defend nor indemnify you.

So if you, your chief or sheriff, and your city or county are all being sued, who are the attorneys representing? If you believe they cannot represent you *and* represent others listed in the lawsuit, you might try to determine if there is a conflict of interest for the agency attorney(s). If you believe it is so, get your own attorney or at least consult with an attorney not connected with the agency to see if such a conflict exists. Most attorneys will tell you if you are better off letting your agency's attorneys represent you or if you need your own attorney. Trust your instincts on this one. If you really believe there is a conflict, get an attorney but be careful that you aren't acting out of paranoia. Don't just cry wolf.

WHY ME?

Getting sued can be embarrassing. It is a very public statement that someone is accusing you of wrongdoing. Try to remember that the lawsuit is not necessarily about right or wrong, what you did or did not do, but about money. That's right, M-O-N-E-Y. Grab on to your socks here, partner, because there are unscrupulous people out there who might slander you and tarnish your reputation just to get money. They may lie to an attorney to get representation in the lawsuit, or they may find an unprincipled attorney who will take the case simply for the chance to make some money. If you believe you did the right thing, hang on to that belief. Just because you are getting sued doesn't change what happened.

ADMITTING A WRONG

If you really did do something stupid and are willing to admit it, check with your attorney prior to making any statements. Even if you are willing to take complete responsibility for your actions, there are good ways to admit your mistakes and there are poor ways to admit them. You want to admit them in such a way as to minimize the resulting damage. Your attorney will know the best way to go about this and will certainly be more objective about the process than you will. Once you have made your admissions, you cannot change the things you have said or the way you have said them. Don't just blurt something out. Have a plan before you move forward. Your attorney is generally the best person to help you with that plan.

KNOWING WHO TO CONFIDE IN: CONFIDENTIAL VERSUS PRIVILEGED

With all that is going on when you're involved in a legal battle, you may very well want to talk with someone about the situation. If you need to discuss spiritual concerns, talk with your chaplain or pastor. If you need to talk about the emotional aspects and the toll this lawsuit is taking on your sanity, talk with a licensed mental health professional. And if you need to discuss legal concerns, talk with your attorney. It's important to have someone to talk to, but it's just as important to make sure you are not talking to the wrong people. The right or wrong here depends more on legal status than what kind of a person they are.

In deciding who you can talk with, there are some concepts you need to be aware of. Often people confuse confidential for privileged. If someone says that communication is *confidential*, it means that they will not voluntarily disclose the conversation to a third party. This is an ethical concept meaning they will keep your secret, but it is not a legal term and provides you no legal protection. *Privilege* is a legal term and means that the material discussed cannot be disclosed without your permission, even under subpoena. As discussed in the chapter on Surviving Trauma, there are several different kinds of legal privilege, including medical privilege, clergy privilege, and attorney/client privilege. There is generally also spousal or marital privilege, but this privileged communication does not apply to "girlfriends," "boyfriends," or even "fiancés." You must be legally married for the communication to be legally protected. Along these same lines, if you discuss this legal issue with your friends, clearly there is no protection here. You may be putting your friends in a position where they have to either testify about what you told them or face disciplinary action of their own or contempt of court charges.

Be aware, also, that there is no *absolute* privilege. Most states have mandatory reporting statutes which often supersede privilege. Many professionals who maintain privileged communication are required to report such things as child abuse or the abuse of vulnerable adults. They are also required to warn any intended victims of violence. Check the privacy limits of your communication before you disclose anything.

Sometimes officer who have been named in a lawsuit think it's a good idea to seek advice from their supervisors, who have often been on the job longer and may have been through something similar. First of all, no matter how much you like your supervisors, they are *not* the people to discuss potential legal issues with. They may be the ones who end up investigating the incident, acting in an official capacity on behalf of the department, and they will have a conflict of interest if you ask them to be your sounding board on any of this. Second, even if your supervisors are not involved in another capacity, anything you say to them is subject to subpoena because that type of communication is not legally protected and, consequently, they can be forced to testify against you in any legal or administrative proceeding.

Often we think we can discuss the issue frankly with union officials. But be very careful here. Union business may be protected communication but anything that is not specifically designated as such is not going to be protected. If you discuss concerns about litigation or even criminal charges, that discussion may be subject to subpoena as well. The bottom line: Be careful who you talk with. Remember the World War II saying, "Loose lips sink ships."

REPORTS

There are always reports to write but the important thing is to know when to write the reports and what needs to be in those reports, as well as what needs to *not* be in those reports. It is essential that you write comprehensive reports because you may be called to testify from them years later, long after your independent recall of the event has diminished. Also keep in mind, however, that once something is written down, it is as though it was cast in stone. You can't go back and erase it. If you have any concerns at all that there may be some legal issues with what has happened, make sure you consult an attorney prior to writing your reports. Your attorney may advise you to not write the reports at this time, or legal counsel may have specific input into how the reports are written. It may be that there are details that need to be included but that you may not think of, or it may be a simple matter of how you phrase something. If you are in doubt, have your attorney review the reports before you submit them.

LEGAL WARNINGS AND RIGHTS

Two legal warnings frequently given to a police officer who has become embroiled in a legal matter are *Garrity* and *Miranda*. The *Garrity* rule stems from a 1967 case where allegations were made that officers were fixing tickets.[3] The officers were required to give statements under threat of termination, and those statements were later used against them in a criminal case. The United States Supreme Court ruled that this requirement to give self-incriminating statements under threat of termination was an unconstitutional violation of the Fifth Amendment, underscoring the fact that constitutional rights cannot be exacted at a price. Another such example of setting a price for exercising constitutional rights would be a "poll tax," where people are required to pay a fee to vote. These have consistently been determined to be unconstitutional. As a result of the *Garrity* ruling, if you as a police officer are required to give a statement and threatened with termination if you refuse, any statement you make can be used *only* for the administrative purpose for which they were taken and cannot be used in a criminal trial.

Under *Weingarten*, you have the right to have a union representative present during any investigative interview conducted by a supervisor.[4] If you are advised of your rights under *Garrity*, you are required to give the statement at that time. *Weingarten* does not apply if the decision to discipline has already been made and the only purpose of the supervisor/employee meeting is to inform the employee of the decision, or if the purpose of the meeting is merely to educate or counsel the employee.

You must invoke your *Weingarten* rights by a clear request for union representation. Employee rights under *Weingarten* are the sole responsibility of the employee. The supervisor is under no obligation to advise the employee of the *Weingarten* rights. If an employee is the subject of an investigatory interview and asserts their rights under *Weingarten*, they cannot be forced to answer questions from

---

[3] *Garrity v. New Jersey*, 385 U.S. 493 (1967)
[4] *NLRM v. J. Weingarten, Inc.*, 420 U.S. 251 (1975)

the supervisor but must still sit and listen to the supervisor. Once the employee has asserted these rights, the supervisor has three options:

1. The supervisor can immediately end the interview,
2. The supervisor can pause the interview while waiting for the union representative to be present, or
3. They can give the employee the choice of these options.

If the supervisor continues the interview, they have committed an unfair labor practice and, for governmental employers, violated your civil rights.

The *Miranda* warning, as all cops know, is given to suspects in criminal offenses and advises them of their Fifth Amendment right to not be compelled to provide any self-incriminating statements.[5] Specifically, *Miranda* is an advisory that the suspect does not need to answer questions, they have the right to an attorney, and if they cannot afford an attorney, one will be appointed for them. This is a warning that police officers use frequently when questioning an in-custody suspect.

Miranda seems almost to be the opposite of *Garrity*. *Garrity* tells you that you need to answer questions, and *Miranda* says you do not need to answer questions. It is the responsibility of the investigator to advise suspects of their rights under *Miranda* whereas with *Garrity*, it is only the responsibility of the investigator to advise if there is a possibility of discipline. With *Miranda*, the right to an attorney is stated by the investigator. Yet under *Garrity*, through *Weingarten*, there is no requirement for the investigating supervisor to even advise the employee that they have the right to have a union representative present during the questioning.

If you are the subject of a criminal investigation, most investigators will go out of their way to make sure you understand that it is "*Miranda*" and not "*Garrity*" that they are applying. As a "best practice," the investigators will frequently explain in detail the rights to which you are entitled and will make sure you understand before proceeding. It is almost like a reverse *Garrity*, explaining not only that you don't need to talk to them but why you don't need to talk to them.

---

[5] Resulted from *Miranda v. Arizona*, 384 U.S. 436 (1966)

Garrity and *Miranda* warnings are given under different circumstances and for different reasons. It is essential they be kept completely separate so that any information obtained under *Garrity* has no impact in any criminal or "*Miranda*" case. Often these investigations are conducted by different personnel or different units, and frequently they are conducted by different agencies. While the different personnel are conducting parallel investigations regarding the same behavior or series of behaviors, these investigations are not to converge. There can be no sharing of information obtained under the *Garrity* rule with those investigating criminal charges. Information obtained after the individual has been advised of their *Miranda* rights can be shared with *Garrity* investigators, but it is a one-way sharing. Any *Garrity* information shared with criminal investigators may taint the criminal case and seriously hamper any prosecution. Remember they are completely separate, and while you might be required under *Garrity* to provide answers to your supervisor's or an investigator's questions for administrative purposes, including disciplinary actions, don't think that just because you have shared information in one setting you are required to share in the other. This isn't even like comparing apples to oranges because these are completely different situations. In one you are represented by your attorney and in the other you are likely to have a union representative. The only real similarities are that you are at risk in both situations and you need to listen to the people you have selected to advise you.

FACING BOTH CRIMINAL AND CIVIL CONSEQUENCES

Be aware that the same action or series of actions can generate both criminal charges and civil litigation—they are not mutually exclusive. This brings up the concern of what impact a criminal charge will have on a civil suit and vice versa. Because of the different levels of proof required in each type of case, a civil suit is not likely to have as great of an impact on a criminal charge as the criminal charge will have on the civil suit.

In the civil suit the jury can reach a verdict based simply on a "fair preponderance of the evidence," meaning it is more likely than not, or the certainty level is greater than 50%, that the facts of the case support one side of the argument. In a criminal case, however, the prosecutor must prove the defendant's guilt "beyond a reasonable doubt." So in the civil case, the jury can find for the plaintiff even though there may be some doubt as to the way the events happened, or even as to what happened. As long as the weight of the evidence tips the scales, however slight, in favor of the plaintiff, the defendant or respondent will lose. But with a criminal charge, the case must be proved almost completely, to as near 100% certainty as to leave no reasonable doubt that the defendant is guilty of the accusation. So if there is a criminal conviction already in place, having met the much higher standard of proof, the civil suit becomes almost more of a formality or redundancy, using the criminal conviction to prove the civil case. But this doesn't work the other way around. Even if the criminal case has not been proven, there may still be a successful civil suit. This was what happened in the O.J. Simpson trial. He was acquitted of the criminal charge of killing his wife and yet the civil jury found in favor of the plaintiffs. So while both legal battles may stem from the same event, they are not necessarily locked together.

WHAT'S AT RISK?

Besides your reputation, career, and possibly freedom, another question that is frequently asked is whether or not your personal property is at risk. The simple answer is that it might be. There's no way of knowing what kind of decisions any judge or jury is going to make, or whether or not your agency will decide to defend and indemnify you. You might check with your insurance provider to determine exactly what kind of coverage you have. Sometimes individuals have some sort of umbrella policy that covers pretty much everything. Your homeowner's insurance might cover you, but it's impossible to make any kind of a blanket statement here because every situation will be different and there is a wide variation with insurance coverage.

So the next thought about your personal property might be, "How can I protect it?" This becomes extremely complicated and might, again, vary with judge or jury, but it can also vary from state to state. Some officers mistakenly believe that by putting all of their property in their spouse's name, it will be protected because they will then own nothing. Yet if your state is a "community property" state, marital assets are all jointly owned and your plan is unlikely to be successful. If you try to hide assets and get caught, the court is not likely to look at your actions favorably. These assets will not only be included in consideration of any judgment or settlement, but there may be penalties assessed as well. The best way to protect your assets is to not do anything to generate a civil suit, to not do anything outside the scope of your employment, and to get your attorney involved as soon as possible if you think you are at risk of a lawsuit.

WHERE YOUR CASE IS FILED

Sometimes civil suits are filed in state court and other times they are filed in federal court. There are a number of differences between the courts. Each is designed for a different purpose and will cover different issues. For example a civil rights suit will most likely be tried in federal court rather than state court because the issue is covered by federal laws. A negligent behavior suit may be tried in state court if there are no applicable federal regulations. There are not only different laws determining what kind of an allegation is tried in each court, there are significant procedural differences between the courts.

TRIAL VERSUS SETTLEMENT

One frequently asked question is whether it is better to go to trial or to try and reach a settlement. While this might sound like an easy question because it is common, when we feel wrongfully accused of something, for the immediate emotional response to be that your case go to trial so you can prove your innocence, that might not be the best advice in every situation. Every lawsuit is different, every situation is different, and every court is different. You may find it frustrating if your agency pays a settlement on your litigation because you believe it means they think you have done something wrong, but that isn't always the case. Sometimes your case may not be win-able. Your agency may argue that it's cheaper to pay the settlement than risk losing at trial where the court might impose an even larger settlement.

Another reason your agency might settle is because you may have done what you are accused of doing, and it may have been captured on video. In this instance, there is no denying what you did, and the best thing to do is to just get it over with.

Some attorneys argue that it is generally not a good practice to pay settlements because it encourages lawsuits and that even marginal cases get litigated when there is a likelihood of free money to be had. Remember: It's not about right or wrong, good or evil. It's about money. Don't let it become more than that. Remember that the law often boils down to simple economics. So let your attorney advise you on this matter.

MEDIA FALLOUT

Often the same types of events that generate legal concerns also generate media interest. Cops are big news, and cops in trouble are even bigger news. Your legal battles will be public data at some point, and the media will swoop in to make the most of your misfortune.

It can be incredibly frustrating to see your picture in the paper or find that your personal information has been released to the media. There are no hard-and-fast rules about this even though it is unpleasant. If this is a concern, consult with your attorney, look at your employment contract, and check your Peace Officers Bill of Rights. If you are involved in a legal battle, you become a celebrity; the media will want all of the information they can get about you.

It is rarely in your best interest to talk with the media, and it's never in your best interest to talk with the media without first talking to your attorney. It is also important to remember that some agencies have policies which will prevent you from talking with the media. If you do, however, decide to talk with the media, it is usually recommended that you read from a prepared statement rather than just responding "off the cuff." If you are using a prepared statement, you are less likely to say things that are contrary to your best interest. While many reporters are quality people, there are some who will attempt to get you to say something in an effort to sensationalize their story. You don't want to discover you've been talking to one of those reporters when you find the exaggerated version on the front page of tomorrow's newspaper or the lead story on the ten o'clock news. If at all possible, it is best to simply not talk with the media. Let your chief, sheriff, or public information officer do that. It's their job, and if they say something stupid, it's not as likely to have an adverse impact on you. If you are cornered by the media, it is generally a good idea to refer them to your attorney rather than to make comments at that time.

Regardless of whether you talk to the media or not, the story will likely be covered, and when it comes out in the newspaper or on television, you may be painted in the worst possible light. The story may be sensationalized to the point where you don't even recognize the description of the events, or it may even involve outright lies. Often you will see "eyewitness" accounts given in the story. Remember, these versions of the events are frequently exaggerated by the witness to make themself look or feel important and then further slanted by the reporter who wants their story to headline the evening news or make the front page of the paper. Your friends and family are going to see this. Your barber, your grocer, and your mechanic are all going to see this. Everyone in your world is likely to see these uncomplimentary reports.

Your first response will probably be to want to defend yourself and to tell friends and family what really happened. DO NOT DO THAT. Other than with your spouse, any communication you might have with friends or family is *not* protected. You may find that they are suddenly in the middle of the case, being asked questions about what you said and how they might have interpreted your statements. If you feel strongly that you need to say something to friends and family, do so very carefully. Your attorney will advise you to refrain from discussing this with anyone. You might tell your friends and family that you did nothing wrong, but do not discuss the facts of the case with them. With the exception of your spouse, any family or friends can be subpoenaed and required to testify.

When all of this happens you are likely to be angry. Your first thought might be to countersue. Certainly you may explore that with your attorney, but there are pros and cons to countersuing. First of all, what do you have to gain? In many cases the plaintiff in your lawsuit may not have anything worth getting. It doesn't do you a lot of good to win a huge judgment if you can't ever collect. Second, any countersuit means that this whole ordeal will be in the media for a longer time. The whole court process will be extended, and you will need to live with it even longer than you wanted to. Countersuits also have an impact on settlements. If you want the entire legal process to end quickly, a countersuit might be counterproductive. In many cases plaintiffs are less likely to settle for minimal payouts if there is a countersuit pending. So again, ask yourself, "What's in this for me?" and, "Is it really worth it?"

The anger you feel at reading or hearing things that you know are wrong may lead you to want to sue the media for printing or airing false information,[6] but this is not as easy as it sounds. First, you are likely to be considered a "public figure" so the rules regarding defamation of character suits change. Second, you will need to prove that the false information was spread maliciously. Whether or not the media knew the information was false, it may be an entirely different thing to prove that it was communicated maliciously. It is difficult to prove malice, and successful defamation lawsuits brought by police officers against the media are quite rare, but if you think you have a case, consult your attorney.

OTHER FALLOUT: PUNITIVE TRANSFERS AND LICENSING ISSUES

Another fear that goes hand in hand with legal battles is punitive transfers. If you get sued for things you do as a patrol officer, you may find yourself sitting behind a desk somewhere, put there so you don't cause any more problems. Whether these transfers are punitive will most likely depend on the terms of your collective bargaining agreement, although generally assignments are an employer right. If you don't have a collective bargaining agreement and are an "at will" employee, you may find you have little or no recourse.

Legal battles, particularly criminal ones, can often lead to licensing issues. In some states any type of theft conviction can lead to a revocation of a police license. Domestic assault convictions can lead to an inability to carry a firearm and, again, a subsequent loss of a license to practice law enforcement. Most felony convictions will lead to a loss of your license as well as jail time. If you are charged in a criminal case, make sure you understand the relationship between the criminal case, any possible plea bargains, and licensing issues.

---

[6] Libel and slander, collectively known as defamation, are civil wrongs that harm an individual's reputation. Libel is printed defamation; slander is spoken defamation.

THE WAITING GAME

Sometimes it seems as though civil litigation can take forever. This can be exceptionally difficult because it is often something you just want to get over with so you can be vindicated. You might find yourself thinking about this litigation daily, yet feeling powerless to do anything about it. Getting a lawsuit over all of the legal hurdles can take a long time. There are motions to make, and deadlines to review the motions, and appeals to the motions, or appeals to the decisions about the motions. It is simply a time-consuming process. Keep in mind this is not the only case these attorneys and the courts are working on, nor is it even likely to be their most important one. It certainly might be the most important case to you, but it is only one of many for them. Think about it in these terms: When you respond to a call on a garage burglary, it may not be a particularly important call to you. In fact, it may be routine and even quite boring. But what is it like for the guy who has lost several thousand dollars' worth of tools and no longer feels safe in his neighborhood? You are now in his shoes.

You may be wondering, "What's happening while I wait?" The best thing to do here is ask your attorney. While it's important that you know what is happening with your case, it's also important that you don't become a pain in the ass for your attorney. Balance your curiosity and desire to know with a true need to know. Discuss your concerns with your attorney and work out a mutually agreeable strategy to communicate about what's happening. Make sure you are both on the same page. You don't want to feel left out but you also don't want to rack up an incredible attorney fee with constant and unnecessary pestering for updates.

It is not unusual to simply want to get things done and over with but there is another side to the coin. Time is not necessarily your enemy here. It might be that some of these motions for dismissal or summary judgment being filed on your behalf will make a difference and that this whole thing might just go away for you. It might also be that the longer this legal process drags on, the more it becomes old news and the less people are interested in hearing about it. There might also be more of a motive for the plaintiff to settle for far less money. So be careful what you wish for—when you just want to hurry up and get it over with, that might just happen and then you come to find out that rushing through everything wasn't really what you wanted.

BEING A WITNESS AGAINST A FELLOW OFFICER

Even if you aren't named as a respondent or defendant in a case, you may be subpoenaed to testify in a case involving a fellow cop. Being called as a witness against another officer can be one of the most difficult times of your career. You are likely to feel as though you are caught in the middle, with no good outcomes. There can be peer pressure to help cover for the other officer because cops are supposed to stick together, and you might even realize that you could just as easily be in that situation. There is also a lot of pressure to not "air our dirty laundry in public," because, "if we don't take care of each other, no one will." But remember that you are also at risk here. Be honest; don't perjure yourself for the sake of another's career. If it is discovered that you lied to cover for another officer, you may well become a party to the criminal or civil action.

A QUICK FINAL WORD

Although cops are enforcers of the law and in service to the public and, as such, have a higher degree of knowledge and expertise in the subject than the average citizen, it becomes an entirely different matter when that officer is named as a respondent in a civil suit or a defendant in a criminal case. That knowledge doesn't apply when you are the defendant. If you think you've been involved in anything that might result in legal action against you, consult an attorney. If you're involved in a critical incident, such as a shooting, a physical fight with a subject, or a situation in which your arrestee winds up injured or dead, get legal representation. If you are ever advised of your *Miranda* rights, ask for your lawyer and stop talking. There may be times during your career when you need an attorney. Listen to their advice, and remember, that's why you are paying them.

SAMPLE LEGAL DEFENSE PLAN COMPARISON

Comparison of Plans Offered in Minnesota
(last updated April 18, 2013)

	FOP State	FOP National	Team Legal	MPPOA
Cost per year – Individual	$150.00	$240.00	$86.88[a]	$96.00
On Duty Coverage – Criminal	YES	YES	YES	YES
On Duty Coverage – Civil Defense	YES	YES	YES	YES
Full On Duty Coverage – Disciplinary/Administrative	YES	YES	NO[1]	NO[1b]
Full On Duty Coverage – Traffic Citations	YES	NO	NO	NO
Full Off Duty Coverage – Criminal	YES	NO[1c]	NO[2]	NO
Off Duty Coverage – Administrative/Disciplinary	YES	NO	NO	NO
Off Duty Coverage – Traffic Citations	YES	NO	NO	NO
Full Criminal Defense Coverage for Spouse	YES	NO	NO	NO
Discounts on Personal Legal Matters – Whole Family	YES	NO	NO	NO
Free Consultation on Any Personal Legal Matter	YES	NO	NO	NO
Uses "Attorney Lists"	NO[2b]	YES	YES	YES
Attorney You Call Must Take Your Case	YES	NO	NO	NO
Uses One Number for DIRECT 24/7 Attorney Consultation	YES	NO	NO[3]	NO[3]
Coverage Limits for Attorney Fees	NO	YES	YES	NO
Distinguishes between Management Positions	NO	NO	YES	YES
Covers DUTY RELATED Incidents outside MN	NO[4]	YES	YES	YES
Covers NON DUTY RELATED Incidents Outside MN	NO[4]	NO[5]	NO[5]	NO
Coverage Determined By a "Plan Administrator Co."	NO	YES	NO[6]	NO
Administrated Locally	YES	NO	NO[6]	YES

[a] *This price may be outdated. This was the price of the former Team Legal Plan over 1 year ago, Teamsters has changed their plan, see footnote 6 below*

[1]   *Disciplinary and labor matters are covered by membership in Teamsters.*
[1b] *Does cover POST licensure issues.*
[1c] *FOP National has an off duty supplement but is limited to a maximum of $2,500 in legal fees.*
[2]   *Does cover off duty situations related to employment status as police officer, must be acting in the capacity as a LEO, for example ordinary DWI is NOT covered.*
[2b] *State FOP plan does have 5 attorneys servicing the plan.*
[3]   *Uses one central number, 24/7, but the person answering is NOT an attorney.*
[4]   *MN FOP now covers all criminal on & off duty related criminal incidents occurring in Wisconsin, but officer must be employed in MN.*
[5]   *Retirees are eligible for HR 218 coverage nationwide, Teamster plan costs extra.*
[6]   *Teamsters within last year has changed how this plan is administered –it is no longer Team Legal, it is now Teamsters Legal Defense Fund administered by Teamsters nationally, according to the information I reviewed.*

"Full coverage" means NO LIMIT on attorneys' fees. State FOP plan has NO LIMITS on attorney fees.

The State FOP plan does have a limit on out-of-pocket expenses (such as expert witnesses) of $5,000.

Note: The National FOP Legal Plan is almost $90 more expensive for far less coverage compared to the MN FOP State LDP.

Chapter 13

SURVIVING AND THRIVING
IN RETIREMENT

*"I talked about it, but I never really wanted to retire. I like this job
too much, I loved it too much. I was hooked on it, I was hooked on
this job. But now, all of a sudden, I'm saying, 'Boy, I want to go, and
I want to go because I'm older and smarter and a little more tired.'"*
— A 20-year veteran of a major urban police department

Preparing for retirement is something you need to begin working on
long before your actual retirement date. It's more important than
most people think. Retirement could easily span 30 years or more.
Think about it for a minute: if you retire at 50 or 55 years old and
live to be 80 or 85 years old, you will have spent as much or more
time retired than you did working as a cop. We spend a lot of time
preparing for our career and making sure we get started on the right
foot, and we need to spend just as much time preparing for the stage
of life that comes after we retire from that career.

We start our police career with enthusiasm and, for most of us, it
is so exciting we'd rather be at work than almost anywhere else. As
we grow through our career, that attitude changes. I don't mean that
we don't like what we're doing anymore but that we reach a point
where we just know it's time to move on. I don't regret even one day
of the 32-plus years I spent as a police officer, yet somehow I just
knew when it was finally time to retire. I didn't retire angry, bitter, or
living in a bottle of alcohol. I retired happy and looked forward to
every day of my retirement. One of my goals now is to live long
enough to bankrupt my pension plan, enjoying every penny of it.

So begin by asking yourself: Is this—retiring—what you really
want to do? Sometimes people retire because they think they are
supposed to. They have hit retirement age, and it is expected that
they will retire. But people aren't always ready on the same time

table or for the same reasons. Retirement is an individual decision, and you need to decide whether this is the time for *you* to retire. It should not be a decision you make based on other people's expectations or even strictly because of financial considerations. The ideal time for retirement is when you are ready to retire and are really looking forward to it. Not just because you "ought to." Some people still look forward to going to work every day and find a lot of meaning in what they do. They might be working long past the optional retirement age, right up until the mandatory retirement age.

Don't let other considerations keep you from retiring. One officer I know worked far past his optional retirement age until he was forced to retire at age 65. He didn't find much satisfaction in his career but he was determined that his ex-wife was not going to get any of his pension. He was only going to retire when she died. The end result wasn't any different for him, though. She lived a long life and still got half of his pension, and he worked ten years longer than he wanted to and retired bitter and burned out. Another officer waited until his ex-wife died and then retired the day after. These are not sound bases upon which to decide when to retire. While they may impact the financial part of your retirement, don't let things like that keep you at a job you don't like. If you want to retire, do it and find something else to do to meet your financial needs. Along the same lines, don't let a boss you don't like force you into an early retirement that you are not ready for. The officers who do best in retirement are those who are going *to* something rather than getting *away* from something.

That sort of retirement doesn't happen overnight or come as an abrupt awakening when we decide, "Time to retire." It takes planning and preparation to make it work. Otherwise all you will be is a cop who one day stopped working.

PLANNING FOR RETIREMENT *BEFORE* YOU GET THERE

Retirement planning takes work and insight. When you are still very active in your career, pause and take a look at what this job is doing to you. Look at how you are being affected by the things you see and how that sets the stage for retirement planning. If you find that you are moving through your career angry, bitter, and cynical, you're setting your retirement up for failure. Cops with that mindset usually are retiring to get away from the department. They don't necessarily have retirement plans, other than to get away from something they have come to hate. If that is your mindset, things won't go as smoothly as you would like, and you may not enjoy your retirement at all. Begin to plan for your retirement mentally, physically, financially, and socially long before the actual retirement date gets here. There are some questions that we all need to answer as we look toward retirement.

Who Am I? Finding a New Identity

First of all "Who am I if I'm not a cop?" It is likely that this is all you have ever done, work wise, and don't know anything else. It has been my experience, both with others before I retired and personally after I retired, that once you retire you aren't in the "club" anymore. Things won't be the same. You might find that when you walk up to a group of your prior co-workers, the conversation might quiet or change altogether. They might be talking about an active investigation and, whereas at one time they might have asked your advice, now they don't even want you to know about it. You can feel that you are now an outsider.

If you're one of those cops who has worked a full police career as well as several part-time law-enforcement-related jobs to supplement that career, you may find your entire identity wrapped up in your career. This career may be how you spend not only your 40-hour work week (or more), but also your time off (doing off-duty work) and even your time away from the job (socializing with other cops). So when you ask yourself who you are without all of this, it gets down to some of the tougher things that we don't often think about.

We too often limit ourselves to, "I'm a cop." Yet I hope that you are much more than that, even though you haven't thought about it much. You might be a husband or wife, father or mother, uncle or aunt, grandparent, friend, cook, bowler, neighbor, gardener, car enthusiast, musician, church member, and any number of other things. So when you limit the "who am I" to only being a police officer, you are excluding everything else that you are. I don't know of anyone who was really only a cop. It might very well be that you have not thought about yourself in other terms for many years and that's why you are stuck. If you are still early in your career, one of the best ways to prepare for retirement is to remember that you are far more than just a cop and never forget that you are all of these other things. Nourish the other parts of you. Remember that police work is what you do, not who you are. If you can remember that throughout your career it will be easier to move into the retirement you have earned.

What Will I Do with All that Free Time?
Staying Relevant

One of the things you will find when you retire is that you will have more time. I hear from a lot of retired cops things like, "I am so busy now, I don't know how I had time to work." If you have prepared for your retirement you will find that you are busy. You are doing all of the things you didn't have time to do when you were working.

As you look forward to retirement, stop to think how you want to spend your time. Are you planning to spend most of your time enjoying the hobbies you didn't have time for while you were working? Are you going to hunt or fish more now? Are you going to spend more time painting or knitting? These are things you enjoy and certainly need to make time for. If you don't have any hobbies, perhaps it is time, *before* you retire, to start looking for some. Look for things you might enjoy doing and try them out. If you think you might enjoy camping, don't rush out and buy a $100,000 motor home. Rent one for a week or two and see how it works out. If you want to try a new hobby, see if you can rent the equipment you'll need so you can try it and see how you like it before you spend lots of money on a hobby you may not really enjoy. If you invest a lot of money on the unknown activity, you might feel trapped into spending more time at it than you really want to. Start gradually and explore your interests, without committing all of your resources (time and money) to them until you know this is something you are really going to enjoy.

In looking at your retirement hobby, make sure you think long and hard about making it more than a hobby. As an example, one of the things I really enjoy is fishing, particularly salmon fishing on the Great Lakes. So, as I began to prepare for retirement, I thought about purchasing a nice boat for that type of fishing and outfitting it with all of the proper accessories. My reasoning was that I could now combine a hobby with a second career, getting paid to fish and using all of the equipment as a tax deduction.

Then one day as I was walking out on the pier, I saw a charter captain friend of mine washing out the inside of his boat, and he was mad. When I asked what happened, he told me that he had taken four men out fishing that morning and, even though he has a "No Smoking" rule on his boat, all four lit up cigars and proceeded to smoke them. Then they began drinking beer and whisky, to excess. One of the men got sick and threw up all over the boat and downriggers. Another, after hooking what seemed like it might be a record steelhead trout, accidentally touched the fishing line with the cigar he was smoking and immediately lost the fish. That man got so angry he began swearing at the boat captain, screaming about his "cheap equipment," and then proceeded to intentionally snap the downrigger rod over his knee. It was at that moment my retirement plans changed. I know that I don't have the temperament to be a charter boat captain. I know that I might very well have told those four men to get off my boat, even though we were 5 miles from shore, and not cared about the consequences. I still love to fish but have made sure to keep it a hobby. If you are doing something for money, it changes the way the hobby works. There are a lot of different pressures added. Here the pressure was to make sure the clients got fish. If you become a pro golfer, the pressure is to win tournaments, not to simply have fun golfing with your buddies.

So let's say you've got a great hobby lined up for when you retire. After a few years, however, you might find that it's not so much fun to hunt or fish every day, or to knit or even travel all of the time. One of our basic needs is to be relevant, to be important, to make a difference somehow. Just because you are now, or are going to be, retired does not mean you can't be relevant. You won't be relevant as a police officer anymore, but you can still be relevant in lots of other ways. You can be important as a grandparent, as a friend, as a parent, or as a spouse. You can still be important in what you choose to do, how you choose to spend your time. One of the things I've discovered is that now I have more time to go to my grandson's football games. He enjoys having me watch; it makes a difference in his life. I have more time to spend with grandkids than their parents do, especially in the summer. It gives me a chance to build relationships with them, be a role model in their lives, and make a difference.

When you are considering how to spend your time in retirement, you might prepare to spend time doing something that makes a difference in other people's lives. Hobbies are great for a few years, but if we plan to live 30 years post retirement, there needs to be more in life than a hobby. You need to do something that will provide meaning in your life, a reason to get out of bed day after day. One of the things you might consider is some sort of volunteer work. Perhaps you would enjoy delivering meals on wheels and spending time with the elderly or disabled in your community who can't get out. They often hunger for companionship and someone who will just talk or play a board game with them. There are lots of things you can do that will make you feel good in a different way than getting a trophy fish or buck or sinking a 35-foot putt. Those things that will put real meaning in your life most frequently mean providing some sort of service to others. After all, isn't that what gave your life meaning for all those years as a police officer?

Who Will I Hang Out With? Finding Your New Social Circle

As we go through our lives we tend to fill them with other cops. We work together, we play together, and sometimes we even marry each other. When we have families, our families hang out together because we all share a similar world view, work hours, and interests. When you retire you don't become a totally different person and suddenly acquire a totally different social network. However, if you tend to spend a lot of time with other cops and then you retire, your schedule may become very different from theirs. For you, there might be six Saturdays every week and one Sunday, whereas they might have a Saturday on Tuesday but be working on the actual Saturday. You will likely find your schedule becoming less and less in line with theirs.

You might also find that the things you found important before you retired really don't matter anymore. The whole notion of "who's running with who" and "who's committing what crimes where" may hold less fascination now that you are retired. You're going to still care about what is going on around your house, but otherwise it just might not seem so important anymore. A lot of the stuff you talked with your cop friends about is now of far less interest, and you have no new information to provide anyway. If you haven't developed a solid relationship with these cops outside of work and interests that aren't about work, you're likely to spend less and less time with them.

Speaking of interests and people outside of work, that's an excellent idea. Remember the friends you had before you became a cop? Think about reconnecting with them and see if those friendships still work. You may find you share interests outside of police work and the gossip that goes with all of that. You might find you enjoy fishing or shopping or doing other things together. If you can't connect with your pre-cop friends, look at making new friends who are not involved in police work. Join a bowling league (not a police league) to meet new people. If you don't want to bowl, become active in community projects of some sort and meet people there. If all of that fails, think about finding something that interests you and take some community education classes in that area. You will find people there who share your interests and may develop new friendships in that way. Friendships are relationships based on a shared interest or goal. Don't hesitate to begin new activities that interest you; you may find new people who interest you as well.

Who Will Remember Me? Leaving a Legacy

Retirement can be a very fulfilling experience with a variety of people in your life. You will find that your interests vary, as will the people in your life. When you stop and think about how you want to spend your time, often we begin at retirement age to think about leaving a legacy. Your legacy will not be in the police department. When you leave they will already begin to forget who you are. After 20 years no one there, or at least very few, will remember who you are or what you did. But the people you touch in a personal way will not forget you. The time you spend with your children or your grandchildren is the foundation of a legacy. Think about who made that difference in your life. For me it was a friend of my father who took the time to take me hunting and fishing because he didn't have kids of his own. He was someone who helped shape my life. My high school wrestling coach was another. He walked home (about a mile) after wrestling practice each night, and since I lived near him, I walked along. We talked about things I could not have talked with my parents about. He was another strong influence.

Several years ago my grandson was about to fail 5th grade. I told him that if he got only one "C" in the fall and all the rest A's and B's, I would take him for a weekend of ice fishing. I told him we would go, just the two of us, and rent an icehouse for the weekend. About November of the following year, he called and told me that he had gotten 5 A's and 4 B's. We went for our weekend trip that year. I kept the arrangement going, and we went on a trip every year thereafter until he was a senior in high school and his life was too busy. He will always remember those weekends. You can leave a legacy by influencing the lives you touch in a personal way. Now that you are planning to retire, think about whose life you would like to touch and put those special people into your life. Be that special person in their life.

HOW RETIREMENT CHANGES THINGS
AT HOME

If you're married, retirement is often a joint decision. Most cops are married (many more than once), and retirement plans need to include your spouse. Retirement will change your life dramatically, and it will change your spouse's life too. For example, if you are home all day and your spouse is at work, will there be different expectations regarding household responsibilities? I would guess the division of labor will change once you become a stay-home partner. If your spouse is still working, your retirement will also have an impact on your flexibility as a couple. You won't be able to just pick up and go because your spouse will have limited vacation or personal leave time. Your spouse may continue working for several reasons: needed income, health insurance, or perhaps simply because of where they are in their career. While it may be important for your spouse to continue working, it will impact your retirement if you are retired and your spouse is not.

If you have children at home, retirement will also look a little different. Your time can be consumed by their activities. You might find yourself coaching baseball or softball 4 nights a week or spending a lot of your free time watching hockey games. Kids can take a lot of time, and when you are retired, they often want more. One retired officer with young children chaffed at the title "Stay-home dad" and referred to himself, instead, as a "Trophy husband." How will you deal with the abrupt change in status?

BEING FINANCIALLY PREPARED

Retirement brings about financial change. Most police departments offer some sort of retirement package, but the financial part of that can vary from a greater take home salary per month to significantly less. For example, I retired at a 97% average of my five highest years of service pay. While I was working I contributed 8% of my income to my pension. So while I was drawing 92% of my income while on active duty. I actually got a 5% pay raise when I retired.

It doesn't do much good to retire if you need to work at a job that pays less than half of what you were making just to survive. So, how have you prepared financially for retirement? If you have a decent pension, that may be all you need. But if you don't, look at your deferred compensation, savings, or other investments. If your spouse is still working, how does that pay contribute to your monthly total income? In short, the bottom line is to make sure you have enough money set aside or coming in on a regular basis so that you can enjoy your retirement. If not, consider postponing your retirement until you are financially secure.

While this may seem contradictory to my earlier advice to not stay in the job longer than you want to because of financial concerns, it's not, and here's why. You have to look at it terms of individual context. Often we say we're working for the money far beyond that which is necessary to live a good life. In those cases, retirement is not about the money. But consider the guy who has three ex-wives, is still paying child support for four kids, and has a net income of $200 per month. He might need to work a little longer. Then again, maybe not. Enough is enough, and you can retire if you have enough. You don't always need more, but you do need enough.

Sound financial preparation for retirement should not be put off until 1 or 2 years before you retire. It's something you should begin planning for the day you start working. For example, if you save $200 per month for 35 years in an account that earns a conservative

3% interest, you will have approximately $138,550 to begin your retirement with. Of course, if you save more than $200 per month, the end result will be higher. Setting aside $400 per month for the same length of time and at the same interest rate will net roughly $277,105. Again, you have a nice start to retirement. If you are planning to rely on your police pension for retirement income, it is essential to look at the financial state of that pension and those who administer it. Not all pension funds are secure. For example there have been concerns about the Detroit police and fire pensions. As the City of Detroit faces financial difficulties, one of the things on the block is the police and fire pension fund. Other cities are looking at the cost of these funds. If you are planning to retire based on your projected pension only, make sure the fund is sound.

As the amount of money available affects the decision to retire, so too does the amount of debt. For example, one police officer retired with a nice pension—at 93% of an average of his highest 5-year salary. But then he bought a new 5th wheel camper for $42,000. Then he found that he needed a new truck to pull the new camper, so he bought a new diesel pickup truck for about $65,000 with monthly payments of $854 per month. So between the new camper and the new truck, this officer was now spending over $1700 per month in payments that he didn't have when he retired. If you are considering retirement in the next few years, either buy what you think you will want and get it paid for before your income drops off, or wait a few years to see how much money you will actually have to spend on toys. This cop has a beautiful truck and camper and no money to go anywhere with them. He gets to camp in his yard.

BEING PHYSICALLY AND EMOTIONALLY PREPARED

Another retirement area that takes a great deal of prior planning is your health. It's not uncommon for cops to gain weight throughout their career. Take a long look at yourself. Is your weight anywhere near what it was when you began your career? If not, consider doing something to change that. Start working out, watch what you eat, maybe get a personal trainer if you aren't sure what you need to do.

The problem for a lot of cops is that we let it go too far, and by the time we want to begin making changes, they are major changes.

It might be that you are 100 pounds heavier (or more) than you were when you began your career, and the thought of losing that much weight is depressing. But it doesn't get any easier as you get older. The longer you carry that weight, the more damage it does to your joints and circulatory system. It makes you a prime candidate for diabetes and heart disease. Begin getting ready for retirement now by getting back into shape. I know, some of you are thinking, "Round is a shape." But that won't get you into a healthy retirement. Don't be one of those statistics that lives only 18 months into retirement.

It's important to take care of your physical health but it's just as important to take care of your emotional health. Make sure you're emotionally healthy to enjoy retirement. If you retire and are still having nightmares about past traumas, you are short-changing yourself. Deal with the emotional issues of police work before you consider retirement. Don't bring the baggage of this job with you into the retirement you have worked so long and hard to enjoy.

FORCED RETIREMENT

If a cop is forced to retire because of physical or emotional injuries, it is a very different kind of retirement. This officer is not permitted to retire when they choose to; the choice is made for them because of the injury or illness, often coming before the officer is ready to retire. It may be that they haven't made any financial preparation for this forced retirement, they still have young kids in school, or they are still dealing with the impact of the illness or injury that forced them to retire. It's been my experience that once an officer is separated from the department, contact with those still working diminishes.

One young officer I know was forced into retirement as a result of a back injury sustained during an on-duty altercation. He got into a fight, injured his back, and went through five surgeries before finally agreeing to retire, an agreement he made only because his surgeon told him that if he got into another fight or twisted his back in any way, there was a high probability that he would spend the rest of his life in a wheelchair. This officer had two young daughters and did not want to raise them from a chair, so he reluctantly agreed to the retirement. He was not happy about it. He was at a high point in his career, working in a gang investigation unit, and doing exciting things. His job and career were abruptly taken from him.

This sort of retirement often comes at a young age and is not satisfying in the way a normal retirement is. It's hard to look back at a 10- or 15-year career, cut short too soon, and see retirement in the same way an officer leaving after 25 or 30 years would see it. It's hard because you can't look back and see yourself as having had a long and rewarding career. Rather, the most obvious and most recent feature of your police career is the forced and premature retirement.

While, again, retirement is a different experience for everyone, there is usually a significant, negative emotional impact with a forced retirement, often including a combination of frustration, pain, anger, and loss. It is imperative for those who are retiring under these circumstances to deal not only with the emotional impact of the initial injury but also with the secondary emotional impact of the resulting forced retirement. Complicating the situation, in many instances, is that not only is the officer dealing with these complex issues but they frequently are doing so without the support system they relied on during their career.

If the forced retirement is for a physical issue, it is easier to explain to coworkers and for them to understand. If, on the other hand, the forced retirement is due to an emotional issue, it's often more difficult to explain or for other cops to understand. It's easy to understand a bad back or the loss of a limb, or a heart attack. These are injuries or illnesses that clearly incapacitate the person. Emotional injuries, however, are more difficult to quantify or visualize. While you might look at a person with an arm that doesn't work and the injury is obvious, post-traumatic stress disorder is much less apparent. There are no visual scars to verify the injury and so there is always police skepticism about whether or not the injury is real. When that happens, the injured officer who is retiring is often made to feel as though they are malingering and don't really deserve their retirement. Only you and your treatment professional know how bad things really are. Don't let people who don't have any sense of what you are going through tell you what it should be like.

CHANGING CAREERS

You may decide at age 55 or even younger that you're ready to retire from policing and move into an entirely different career. If that's your plan, you'll need to figure out long before your retirement date what you want to do or you may find yourself sitting in a classroom with a bunch of 20-year-olds, preparing for your next career. One cop I know wanted to make cabinets in his retirement. He took a 9-month cabinet making course after he retired and found his new career most rewarding. It was very different from police work. He was building things that he could see and feel and touch, nothing like his police career. The difference he was making was obvious.

Most of the time, we can transition smoothly into another career if we plan ahead. If your second career will be law-enforcement related, plan ahead by looking at the qualifications that will be required for what you want to do and make sure you have those qualifications before you go out looking for that new job. If you decide you want to become a trainer in defensive tactics, you may need some sort of certification to do the training. If you are going to be doing something else related to your law enforcement career, you might consider the importance of building your reputation in that area while you're still actively involved in police work.

My second career began after I had been a cop for about 15 years. I went to college and obtained a bachelor's degree, a master's degree, and, finally, a doctorate, all the while working full-time as a cop. I became a psychologist and began working with police officers from agencies other than my own. My last ten years at the agency were spent as the department psychologist, and my transition into private practice went very smoothly. I was still doing the same thing I was doing before I retired but was working on my own rather than for the agency. Not all skills will transfer so easily, but some law enforcement training skills will translate well into post-retirement positions, such as computer skills or skills needed to conduct financial crimes investigation for corporations.

IN SUMMARY

All in all, retirement is a good thing that most cops look forward to in some distant future. It can be some of the best times of your life, if you are prepared. So, remember these simple rules:

1. Retire when you are ready, not on some artificial timetable or someone else's plan.
2. Retirement planning begins as soon as you are hired. Don't put it off too long.

3. Keep yourself physically and mentally healthy so you can enjoy your retirement.
4. Plan your finances so that you can truly enjoy your retirement.

While retirement may be the end of your police career, it is only the beginning of the rest of your life. Make it all worthwhile—enjoy this next step, whatever you have made it look like.

INDEX

abuse, chemical, 166-167
academy training, 9-11
ADD, 157-159
addiction, 165-181
ADHD, 157-159
adjustment disorder, 154
adjustments, 75-76
adrenaline rush, 83, 94
alcohol, 58-59, 83, 169-170
Alcoholics Anonymous, 177-179
anabolic steroids, 172-173
anger, 67, 72, 78, 96, 99, 116, 198
anorexia nervosa, 156-157
antabuse, 179
anxiety, 148, 154-155, 161-163, 175
application, job, 2
aspirations, 133-134
assignments, 82-83, 170
attention deficit disorder, 157-159
attention deficit hyperactivity
    disorder, 157-159
authority, 15, 34, 183, 185
avoidance, 117, 128

background investigation, 6-7
bipolar disorder, 147, 155-156, 165
bulimia nervosa, 156-157
burnout, 131-144
burst stress, 133

change, 63, 90-91, 210-211
changing careers, 214-215
chemical addiction, 169-173
child care, 72-73
child support, 72-73
children, 50-51, 73-75, 85-92
choosing an agency, 3-5
civil lawsuit, 105-106, 183-202
communication, 48-50, 53, 63, 68,
    119-121, 124, 139, 189-190, 197
competition, 10
confidential communication, 119-120,
    126, 189-190
control, 87-88, 118-119

counseling, 68, 69-70, 160
criminal charges, 190, 191-194
critical incident stress
    debriefing, 59, 126-127
culture, police, 30, 96, 101-102
custody, child, 73-75

danger, 18, 83-85
deadly force, 33, 35, 43, 115, 116,
    183
defusing, 124
denial, 67, 153
dependence, chemical, 165-167
depression, 150-152
divorce, 48, 49, 53, 65-77
drinking, 83, 124, 167, 169-170
drugs, 4, 160-161, 170-173

eating disorder, 156-157
education, 4
enthusiasm, 133-134
exercise, 106-108
expectations, 55-57, 68, 89-90, 100-
    101, 133-134, 137-138, 210
extramarital affair, 56, 57, 67, 69, 174

failure, 36, 49, 102, 119, 142
fairness, 34, 49, 62, 69, 70-71, 112,
    116, 135, 138
family, 50-51, 59, 61, 75, 79-92
fear, 57-58, 67, 96, 111, 121, 122, 157
female recruits, 22-23
field training, 12-21
finances, 52, 71, 72, 211-212
fitness, 107, 120, 165
flashbacks, 117, 153
force, use of, 34, 35, 43, 44, 115, 116,
    129, 130, 183
forced retirement, 213-214
friends, 55-57
frustration, 31, 34, 36, 67, 86, 131,
    135, 136, 137, 138, 140, 152, 158,
    169, 195, 196, 214

gambling addiction, 173-174
Garrity rule, 191-193
gay/lesbian recruits, 24
generalized anxiety disorder, 154-155
goals, 103, 143
gossip, 38-39, 57, 60, 102
guilt, 111, 118-119, 150, 157
guns, 85

health, 100, 106, 120, 123, 124, 131,
    138, 147, 149, 154, 159, 160, 165,
    179, 212-213, 216
hiring process, 1, 5-8
holidays, 73, 75, 79, 80
homosexual recruits, 24
hopelessness, 34, 143

illness, mental, 145-164
image, 30, 36, 38, 40, 84, 156, 157
impact stage, 115-116, 117
inadequate support, 133, 135-136
individual burnout, 137-139
informal rules, 10, 19, 21, 22
initiation, 9-25
injuries, 83, 84, 111, 117, 149, 213
institutional support, 135-136
integrity, 40, 171, 172, 173
interests, 52, 54-55, 56, 91, 97
internship, 19
interview, 5, 7
intervention, 177
intimacy, 48, 49, 52, 57-58
isolation, 108, 122, 166

lawsuits, 105-106, 183-202
legacy, 92, 209-210
legal battles, 105-106, 183-202
legal counsel, 69-70, 190
legal defense plan, 184-185, 201-202
legal rights,191-193
legal warnings, 191-193
liability, 187
licensing, 198
loneliness, 57

marriage, 47-63
meals, 79-80
measuring accomplishment, 102, 134
media, 84, 85, 86, 122, 125, 196-198
medication, 149, 151, 158, 159, 160-
    164, 169, 170-171
mental health, 145-164, 212-213
mental illness, 145-164
minority recruits, 23, 24-25
Miranda warning, 123, 128, 191-193,
    200
miscommunication, 48-51
misconceptions, 136-137
money, 52, 71-72, 81, 105-106, 127,
    173-174, 187, 188, 211-212
multiple addiction, 167-168

neurosis, 149
news stories, 84, 114, 125, 196-198
nightmares, 117, 128

on call, 80-81
organizational burnout, 137-139
orientation, 9-11

pain, 40, 49, 54, 55, 57, 58, 71, 116,
    117, 150, 155, 157, 159, 161, 168,
    169, 170, 214
panic attack, 150
parenting, 50-51, 70, 78, 90-91
pay, 135
peers, 9, 10, 19, 29, 34, 40-41, 102,
    121, 122, 123, 124, 126, 200
pension, 54, 71-72, 211-212
perception, 30-34, 41-45, 55-57, 60,
    86, 94, 95, 146
personality, 73, 89, 98-100, 172
physical conditioning, 2
physical health, 5, 212-213
police culture, 96, 101-102, 169
police role, 27-40, 138, 139
post-traumatic stress disorder, 117-
    118, 153
power, 19, 29, 34, 43, 79, 97, 116,
    128, 150, 178, 179, 199

prescription medication, 169, 170-171
pressure, 27, 29, 35, 40, 93, 95, 107, 142, 148, 156, 170, 200, 207
priorities, 68, 108-109, 136, 138, 139, 187
privileged communication, 120-121, 189-190
property, 71-72, 194
psychosis, 149
psychotherapeutic medication, 160-164
public perception, 29-33, 136-137
punitive transfer,198

recoil, 116, 117
relationships, 23, 37, 41, 57, 70, 72, 75-78, 116, 118, 167, 209
relaxation, 107-108
reorganization, 116, 117
reports, 190-191
reputation, 9
resources, 59-61, 136
respect, 23, 40-43, 52, 53, 62, 63
retirement, 203-216
risk, 3, 12, 13, 20, 42, 43, 45, 48, 54, 58, 83, 112, 116, 117, 119, 121, 135, 139, 140, 141, 154, 156, 159, 161, 162, 163, 165, 166, 168, 170, 174, 193, 194-195, 200
role ambiguity, 88-89, 138, 139
rotating shifts, 37, 55, 73, 74, 79, 80, 137, 138
rumors, 57, 102

safety, 12, 84, 85, 93
salary, 135, 211, 212
schizophrenia, 152
secondary victimization, 114
self-perception, 41-42, 45
settlement,195-196
sexual addition, 174-176
shifts, 39, 55, 74, 79, 80, 137, 138
shooting, 96, 113, 114, 115, 116, 118, 119, 123, 127-128
sleep, 37, 116, 117, 128, 138, 150, 151, 155, 159, 161, 163, 170
social life, 55-57, 75-78, 132

socialization, 19
special assignments, 82
special occasions, 75, 80
spirituality, 54, 55, 107, 108, 142, 178, 189
spouse, 47-63
stereotypes, 22, 23, 24, 30, 58, 61, 85, 92, 99-100, 103, 149, 158
steroids, 170-171, 172-173
street drugs, 171-172
stress, 34, 41, 59, 68, 93-109, 117-118, 124, 126, 131, 132, 133, 137, 148, 153, 154, 214
suicide, 41, 113, 150, 155, 168
support, 59-60, 135-136
survivor guilt, 118-119

therapy, 129, 158, 160
tolerance, 17, 50, 83, 162, 165
training, 4, 5, 9-11, 12-21
transfers, 198
trauma, 40, 59, 111-130, 148, 153
trial, 195-196
trust, 34, 52, 57-58, 67, 76, 89, 116, 121, 122, 123, 136, 139, 171

undercover assignments, 82-83
use of force, 34, 35, 43, 44, 115, 116, 129, 130, 183

values, 29, 30, 34, 40, 45
vicarious liability, 187
victimization, 114
violence, 60, 111, 112, 114
visitation, 73-75

weakness, 96, 98
Weingarten rights, 191, 192
withdrawal, 165
witness, being a, 200
world view, 52-54

What Those "In the Know" Are Saying ...

"This book is **essential** for new and experienced officers alike. Denny has 'been there' and describes the reality of the job from a cop's perspective. He articulates the different sources of police stress in a straightforward way and gives concrete, specific, and very helpful suggestions for coping and emotional survival. Denny's vast **experience and wisdom** provides for an informative book; it is well written, articulate, and a very interesting read."
— Roger Solomon, Ph.D.
Police Psychologist

"Dr. Conroy provides valuable insight into the emotional stress and trauma that police officers experience, often unknowingly, throughout their career. He delves into their responses and **the human impact** it can have on officers, both personally and professionally."
— Janeé Harteau
Minneapolis (Minnesota) Police Chief

"Dr. Conroy has captured the meanings of a police career from stay to finish. This book is **a must read** for all considering a police career and their families."
— James M. Horn
FBI Agent, 1970-1996
Program Manager of the FBI's Critical Incident Program, 1987-1994

"Dr. Conroy's perspective is clearly **from the heart of an experienced cop** with hands-on wisdom."
— Shirley Gibson
Past National President,
Concerns of Police Survivors, Inc.